Dependent, Distracted, Bored

Dependent, Distracted, Bored

Affective Formations in Networked Media

Susanna Paasonen

The MIT Press
Cambridge, Massachusetts
London, England

This book was set in Stone Serif and Stone Sans by Westchester Publishing Services. Printed and bound in the United States of America.

Library of Congress Cataloging-in-Publication Data

Names: Paasonen, Susanna, 1975- author.
Title: Dependent, distracted, bored : affective formations in networked media / Susanna Paasonen.
Description: Cambridge, Massachusetts : The MIT Press, 2021. | Includes bibliographical references and index.
Identifiers: LCCN 2020022998 | ISBN 9780262045674 (hardcover)
Subjects: LCSH: Information technology—Social aspects. | Social media.
Classification: LCC HM851 .P25 2021 | DDC 303.48/33—dc23
LC record available at https://lccn.loc.gov/2020022998

10 9 8 7 6 5 4 3 2 1

To Chip, Ken, and Ricky

Contents

Acknowledgments

This book's genesis dates back to Karlstad, Sweden, where I was briefly visiting late in the year 2011. Returning to my hotel after a very full day of travel and academic sociability, I was running a temperature and, to make things worse, unable to connect to the Wi-Fi. Powerless to resolve the glitch, I quickly found myself intensely frustrated to the point of rage, even while being aware of how disproportionate, and ludicrous, my reaction was. Rather than getting some rest, I then spent the next hour reflecting on the sharpness of affect involved in this involuntary disconnection, typing away. This incident sparked a more lingering interest in the affective speeds, rhythms, and intensities connected to technological failure. The following autumn, and for years to follow, I asked the students in my undergraduate class on Media and Networks in the department of Media Studies, University of Turku, Finland, to write short essays describing how mundane instances of technological failure feel. While I have used the essays for teaching purposes (see chapter 2 for details), I was simultaneously collecting research material (with the explicit permission of the students in question). First and foremost, my warmest thanks and gratitude to all the students who wrote and shared their stories. Without you there would be no book.

In a 2015 article, "As Networks Fail: Affect, Technology, and the Notion of the User," published with *Television & New Media*, I drew on 45 of these essays. By this point, the project had grown into a hypothetical book, expanding from the irritating frustrations of failure to the complex entanglements of distraction, attention, boredom, and interest in networked settings. It was my idea to write up the bulk of this work during my 2015–2016 sabbatical leave while visiting MIT's department of Comparative Media Studies and the Social Media Collective at Microsoft Research New England, with kind invitations from T. L. Taylor and Nancy Baym, respectively, and with support from the Jenny and Antti Wihuri Foundation. This, however, was not to be, as I got distracted by not only one but two—then three—other book projects, all thematically disconnected from and finished before this one. While I continued to give talks on distraction and boredom during the sabbatical leave and beyond, progress on the manuscript for this book was slow as it began to feel both overcooked and underdone, having been on the back burner too long for comfort. The saving grace came in the shape of Michael Petit discussing and thinking about the project with me, as well as editing some of it. So, thank you immensely, Chip. In a perfect world, this book would be coauthored.

I would also like to thank all those who have discussed this project in connection with the diverse talks I have given over the years, those who braved the avalanche of animated GIFs during my distraction talks, and especially those who knowingly invited me over: Johanna Sumiala for the 2015 Mediated Belongings Symposium at the University of Helsinki; André Jansson for the 2015 In the Flow ACSIS (Advanced Cultural Studies Institute in Sweden) conference in Norrköping; Jukka Tiusanen for the FINSSE (Finnish Society for the Study of English) 2015 conference at the University of Vaasa; Niels van Doorn and Helen Rutten for the 2015 Bland, Boring, Banal symposium at the University of Amsterdam; Tero Karppi for the 2016 PLASMA (Performances, Lectures, and Screenings in Media Art) lecture at SUNY Buffalo; Lisa Adkins and Mona Mannevuo for the 2016 *Price* workshop at the University of Turku; Judith Ackermann, Asko Lehmuskallio, and Tristan Thielmann for the 2016 Digital Practices conference at the University of Siegen; Catherine Driscoll and team for the 2016 Crossroads in Cultural Studies conference at the University of Sydney; Michael Liegl and team for the 2017 Loose Connections conference at the University of Hamburg; Zeena Felman, Alessandro Gandini, and Paolo Gerbaudo for the 2017 The Digital Everyday conference at King's College London; Jonas Fritsch and Thomas Markussen for the 2018 Affects, Interfaces, Screens conference at Aarhus University; Martin Cloonan for the 2018 Failure symposium in Turku; Beckie Coleman for the 2019 Mediated Presents workshop at Goldsmiths College; and Raili Marling and Andra Siibak for the Troubling Gender: Theory and Method winter school at the University of Tartu in 2020. These events, and the discussions they made happen, not only kept the book project alive but crucially helped it move forward.

In addition to the 2015 *Television & New Media* article that forms the basis for chapter 2, research for this book has previously appeared as "Fickle Focus: Distraction, Affect and the Production of Value in Social Media" in *First Monday* Vol. 21, no. 10 (2016), a special issue on "Economies of the Internet," edited by Kylie Jarrett and D. E. Wittkower; as "Infrastructures of Intimacy" in *Mediated Intimacies: Connectivities, Relationalities, and Proximities*, edited by Rikke Andreassen, Michael Nebeling Petersen, Katherine Harrison, and Tobias Raun (London: Routledge 2018); and as "Affect, Data, Manipulation and Price in Social Media" in *Distinktion: Journal of Social Theory* Vol. 19, no. 2 (2018), a special issue on "Price," edited by Lisa Adkins and Turo-Kimmo Lehtonen. In addition, a text critiquing nostalgia in media studies inquiry building on this book is forthcoming in a special issue on "Mediating Presents" coedited with Rebecca Coleman for *Media Theory* as "Distracted Present, Golden Past." Many, many thanks to these editors for their feedback and support that helped me frame the project in novel ways. As always, I very much appreciate the labor that anonymous peer reviewers put into thinking through other people's work: this work has been pivotal to how this project has gradually progressed. Thank you especially, reviewers 1, 2, and 3 of the articles and the book manuscript.

Finally, my heartfelt thanks to Caroline Bem, Ken Hillis, and Jenny Sundén for taking the time to read, discuss, and comment on this work. Jenny's emotional and intellectual support when I was writing up the manuscript was invaluable, as was Ricky Barnes's affective labor. I would also like to collectively thank the research team of the Intimacy in Data-Driven Culture consortium funded by the Strategic Research Council at the Academy of Finland (2019–2025) for thinking through themes central to this book with me and for making it possible to take the discussions further. Many thanks also to Caroline Bassett, Beckie Coleman, Andrew Herman, Tero Karppi, Mari Pajala, Laura Saarenmaa, Will Straw, and Jaakko Suominen for support and discussions that helped me find enthusiasm in the more somber registers of affect. Also, thanks to Lauren Berlant for serendipitous words of compositional solidarity—and, of course, Irina Shklovski for all the daily creepies.

1 Introduction: From Loss to Ambiguity

The scene, dear reader, is set for crisis. According to a plethora of cultural diagnoses, networked devices, apps, and social media services are atrophying our attention spans, eroding our capacity to focus and think, addicting us, boring us, and stealing our time, as well as stopping us from truly relating to one another, engaging in critical thought, or contributing to public life in a meaningful way. The prognosis, it is said, is poor: if things are currently bad, they are only getting worse.

These concerns are raised by a broad range of authors, from the journalist Nicholas Carr in the best-selling 2010 *The Shallows: What the Internet Is Doing to Our Brains* to more careful scholarly analyses. Just consider this exhausting, albeit hardly exhaustive listing of diagnoses relevant to this book: Discussions of the accelerating speeds of media, culture, and society have come to abound, not least in connection with online connectivity (e.g., Adam 2003; Gleick 1999; Rosa 2013; Scheuerman 2003; Virilio 1995). The excessive and ever accelerating volume of stimuli rendered available in networked media is seen to result in sensory and cognitive overload, portrayed largely as a paralyzing force rendering extended or deep focus difficult, if not impossible, to achieve and sustain as attention merely floats and shifts from one digital impulse to another in anticipation of novelty (e.g., Andrejevic 2013; Crary 2014; McCullough 2013; Shenk 1997). Such perpetual quest for pleasurable dopamine hits, it is argued, is addictive and contributes to a neurological rewiring of the brain that impairs our ability to think, remember, be, and relate (Stjernfelt and Lauritzen 2019, 43–58). Some identify this as an addictive dynamic leading to a state of "terminal" (Anderson 2009) and "chronic" (Hassan 2012) distraction—or even to "digital dementia" (Spitzer 2012) and loss of cognitive capacity (e.g., Hassan 2014; see also O'Gorman 2015).

Jonathan Crary (2014, 34) sees the corrosion of memory functions resulting in "mass amnesia sustained by the culture of global capitalism" while
Bernard Stiegler (2013, 96) argues that social media and accelerated consumer capitalism are destroying predigital social relations and paving the
way to disorientation and ill-being (see also Stiegler 2009, 2012b; O'Gorman
2011, 462). Byung-Chul Han (2017) conceptualizes this as all-encompassing
neoliberal psychopolitical exploitation and governance whereas yet other
critics consider smart devices, social media, and mobile communications,
rather than forms of production or monetization, as being to blame for
corroding our capacities to deeply focus or process information (Carr 2010)
and for hurting our relationships, family ties, and forms of sociability
(Turkle 2012). Encapsulating and symbolizing these developments, social
media in particular comes across as a toxic, punishing "addiction machine"
(Seymour 2019).

Despite dramatic differences between these diagnoses—for their authors
hardly agree on the overall significance, meaning, or direction of the developments that they address—they contribute to a broad, repetitive discourse
of loss connected to networked media. For it is a narrative rule that a grim
present, or indeed a grim future, requires a better state of affairs to be articulated against: a time when the things that are currently in crisis or already
lost were still available is, by necessity, a past one. Douglas Coupland (2014)
argues as much when spelling out the rationale of his 2012 poster slogan
project I MISS MY PRE-INTERNET BRAIN:

> I'm discombobulated this morning: I forgot my iPhone, so have that homesick,
> disconnected feeling you get when you realise you're phoneless. . . . Time is mov-
> ing too quickly these days—and yet, at the same time, it's moving too slowly. And
> it's not just that I'm growing older. Quite simply, my brain no longer feels the
> way it used to; my sense of time is distinctly different from what it once was, and
> I miss my pre-internet brain. The internet has burrowed inside my head and laid
> eggs, and it feels as though they're all hatching.

Known for popularizing the term "Generation X" in the early 1990s,
Coupland frames his project in terms of loss. He misses his pre-internet
brain and the earlier tempo of life in which it thrived. The current one is
both too fast *and* too slow, and it suffers from what he terms "omniscience
fatigue": "Thanks to Google and Wikipedia, for the first time in the history of humanity, it's possible to find the answer to almost any question,
and the net effect of this is that information has become slightly boring."

The abundance of information then results in something of a destructive maelstrom: "Our attention spans are collapsing: we want movies; we want music; we want unfiltered information. ... And we want it all now" (Coupland 2014). Coupland's project communicates longing for forms of experience that were available before ubiquitous networked connectivity took hold: for a time when the sense of time felt less warped, when attention spans were more sustained, when information took longer to acquire and therefore held more interest, when the imperative of immediacy had not yet come to govern, and when things felt less boring.

Adding to this narrative of loss with rhetorical flair, Geert Lovink (2019, 11–12) describes social media as generating boredom, anxiety, and despair. For him, the addictive apps we use are basically designed to make us sad while the thrills they promise eat away at our capacities to relate and live: "As a result, we're dead inside. We feel defeated, overwhelmed, stressed, anxious, nervous, stupid, silly, useless" (Lovink 2019, 35). Hopelessly hooked, we

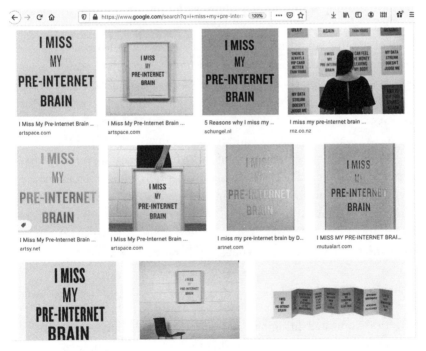

Google Images search results for "I miss my pre-internet brain," https://www.google.com/search?q=I+miss+my+pre-internet+brain.

stumble about in the world in sad, meaningless ways: "There is the sense of worthlessness, blankness, joylessness, the fear of accelerating boredom, the feeling of nothingness, plain self-hatred while trying to get off drug dependency, those lapses of self-esteem ... those moments of being overtaken by a sense of dread and alienation, up to your neck in crippling anxiety" (Lovink 2019, 50). Dominic Pettman (2016, 121) further maps out the affective terrain of social media: "Compulsion. Distraction. Procrastination. Addiction. The four courses of the apocalypse."

The current conjuncture may, then, seem bleak indeed—as may the very title of this book, *Dependent, Distracted, Bored*. The three affective formations examined here encapsulate the key argument repeated in narratives of loss connected to networked media: *that we are hopelessly addicted to devices and apps that distract us to boredom*. Focusing on addiction, distraction, and boredom as affective formations, I set out to explore a different narrative trajectory instead, one foregrounding ambiguity and contextual nuance over generalizations and reductive conclusions. While sharing the general premise running through the analyses addressed above—that media technologies are not mere instrumental tools for communication but shape our ways of sensing, being present in, and making sense of the world—this book steers clear of cultural pessimism and dystopian romanticism dwelling over, and lamenting, things lost, and refuses the fixity and firmness of the discursive templates that are most readily on offer. My aim is to make a critical intervention in how we imagine both the present and the past, and in how we conceptualize experiences and routines of everyday life in the context of ubiquitous connectivity. Moving away from binary divisions between dependence and agency, distraction and attention, boredom and enchantment, I foreground ambiguity and movement instead. Within the affective formations examined in this book, frustration and pleasure, dependence and sense of possibility, distraction and attention, boredom, interest, and excitement enmesh, oscillate, enable, and depend on one another.

Working with Ambiguity

Affect, as indicated in emojis and social media reaction buttons, or as diagnosed in zeitgeist analyses veering to the sad side, is routinely divided into the positive and the negative registers in ways implying that the good and the bad can be distinctly pried apart. A similar division between the positive (as that which we tend toward) and the negative (as that which we try to minimize or avoid) has meandered through affect inquiry ever since Baruch Spinoza's seventeenth-century consideration of affectations as either increasing or diminishing the body's power to exist and to act (Spinoza 1992; see also Paasonen 2018c, 41–42). When considered more closely, this was, however, never a binary, for "the one and the same thing can be at the same time good and bad, and also indifferent" (Spinoza 1992, 153). Following this line of thinking, the same object—be it a smart device, an app, an animated GIF, a hardcore porn clip, or a social media update— can result in virtually any kind of an affective encounter, and the ensuing affectations can be ambivalent indeed. An affective intensity that is enlivening (and in this sense positive) can come in all kinds of hues and be cut through by ripples that are far from enjoyable. Boredom, as flatness of feeling, may yield excitement as well as result in stupor, just as distractions can bore, fascinate, irritate, or enchant, possibly simultaneously so.

Starting from and working with ambiguity, *Dependent, Distracted, Bored* argues that cultural inquiry has to be able to hold seemingly contradictory things together in dynamic tension if it is to understand that which it studies with sufficient degrees of granularity. Holding on to irreconcilable tensions without the aim of resolving them makes it possible to grasp how things appearing to be diametrically opposed and mutually contradictory are in effect codependent, or give rise to one another (see also Bem 2019, 3, 22). Writing on contemporary dominant aesthetic categories, Sianne Ngai (2015, 19, 23) sees the interesting as feeding boredom, aggression and tenderness as intermingling in cuteness, and playfulness as fusing with desperation in zaniness. For Ngai (2015, 14), these aesthetic categories in fact characterize social media "with its zany blogs, cute tweets, and interesting wikis." While Ngai's project is distinctly different from the line of inquiry pursued here (her interest is in aesthetic categories, styles, and judgment and hence focuses on specific objects of analysis rather than on forms and dynamics of experience), her approach makes it possible to see everyday affect as equivocal, as made of mixed feelings, and as requiring forms of analysis capable of accommodating such ambiguity.

In order to work with ambiguity and irreconcilable tensions, I build on Jacques Derrida's (1981, 1993) discussion of the *pharmakon*—namely, objects that can operate as both the poison and the cure, and which are fundamentally ambivalent in their potentialities, meanings, and uses:

pharmakon is, to borrow Spinoza's terms, "good and bad, and also indifferent." The figure of the pharmakon—along with that of the *pharmakos*, scapegoat—weaves in and out of the following chapters that discuss how networked media is identified as locations of potentiality, as that which keeps potentialities from being actualized, and as that which can be blamed for a range of social developments. The pharmakon undoes binary division such as good or bad, the remedy and the toxin, the inside and the outside, and offers a productive analytical tool foregrounding complexity, cohabitation, and simultaneity instead. This makes it helpful in thinking through experiences of living with networked media beyond diagnoses lamenting the current moment as flat, lifeless, and pretty much doomed.

Dependent, Distracted, Bored asks how the culture of ubiquitous connectivity and data traffic is sensed and made sense of, remaining wary of how critiques of networked media risk being both simplifying and totalizing either because of their level of generalization or because of their disinterest toward how things are felt and lived with. All kinds of elementary differences among human subjects, routines of technology use, bodily abilities, identity markers, social attachments, political passions and actions disappear in overarching analyses of the current socio-technological moment. As the structural level of the macro is highlighted at the expense of the micro, contextual nuances, contradictions, and ambiguities—the very stuff that this book sets out to explore—fade from view. Yet as Kathleen Stewart (2007) argues, ordinary affects form contact zones on which everyday lives, both social and personal, take shape: potentiality emerges from the mundane.

If one is to take to heart the argument running through this book, that transformations in media technology—always tied to economic and political frameworks—are intimately connected to available ways of thinking, acting in, understanding, and feeling out the world, then one also has to consider the option that these transformations can be ambivalent, not always toward the worse for all involved, and not easy at all to pin down in their social ramifications. Networked media can contribute to greater social equality in the form of information resources, historical references, social connections, or, simply, add to enjoyment taken in by life through diversions catering to one's specific niche desires. At the same time, it builds on exploitative working practices, causes broad environmental harm, and fuels monetization, commodification, and affective manipulation within data capitalism, the effects of which are far from equalizing, democratic, or transparent (West 2019).

In his discussion of social media, Pettman (2016, xi, 123) sees it as allowing for escapes from paying attention to the unhappy state of the world— for burying one's head in the digital sand, so to speak. As an addictive cure or "new opium for the masses," social media, for Pettman (2016, x), dulls the pain. Writing on the addictive, seductive rhythms of Twitter, journalist Richard Seymour (2019) chimes in: "The user has already dropped out of work, a boring lunch or an anxious social situation to enter into a different, timeless zone. What we do on the Twittering Machine has as much to do with what we are avoiding as what we find when we log in—which, after all, is often not that exciting." While such accounts identify social media as a site of escape, for many, platforms like Twitter are key sources of knowledge concerning the world: from news headlines to petitions, to personal witness accounts, to event invitations, to heated debates, and beyond. Social media—even including the hegemonic data giant, Facebook—play diverse roles in and for social activism, horizontal self-organization, and the formation of affective publics, from political uprisings (Papacharissi 2015) to the Black Lives Matter and #MeToo movements (Garza 2014; Rickford 2016; Sundén and Paasonen 2020) and to global climate strikes (Fisher 2019).

As I am finalizing this book in March 2020 in self-isolation during a state of emergency in the midst of the global coronavirus outbreak, it is evident that social media serves multiple purposes from peer support to diversion to information just as it captures people in seemingly endless, immobilizing loops of news items, statistics, and predictions concerning the pandemic. The overarching narrative of addicted, distracted, bored, and empty users simply does not hold or account for the multiplicity of things at play. Strong narratives of loss and erosion have obvious appeal, yet they ultimately come across as an easy solution in making it possible to turn away from the kind of complexity, contradiction, and ambiguity that everyday lives are made of. In the definite outcomes that they allow for, strong narratives of loss are, in effect, compatible with the clickbait economy that lives off of snappy sound bites and harbors affective intensities clear-cut enough to be encapsulated in available sets of reaction options and emojis.

Within the social media economy, moods, intensities, and affective formations are monetized in complex ways. If, as argued in this book, affect is a fuel that motivates multiple uses of networked media, it is also the case that corporate entities are increasingly keen, as well as intrusive, in their attempts to identify and manipulate such dynamics. And, as Shoshana Zuboff (2019a) argues, the current moment where commercial apps are key to the operability of everyday lives—from monitoring health to booking flights or practicing mindfulness to alleviate the stress of work—departs from previous forms of market capitalism in challenging democratic norms and forms of governance. As apps leak data to third parties, data giants are able to track, monitor, analyze, and predict people's behavior in notable detail, making the need for critical studies of the affective data economy pressingly acute. The multiple means of collecting, analyzing, and applying user data are increasingly recognized, debated, and critiqued—particularly so in the aftermath of the 2018 Cambridge Analytica scandal (discussed in more detail in chapter 3). While the users of apps and sites may have misgivings about the harvesting of their personal data, such unease largely fails to result in their opting out. Handing over their data—with more or less explicit consent—affords people access to platforms, the uses of which have grown habitual, and which hold affective value.

Networked media reproduces, feeds, and accelerates capitalist accumulation within the data economy, yet this does not exhaust its meanings, functions, or political potentialities (see also Jarrett 2015a, 76). This economy, variously identified as "digital capitalism" (Wajcman 2014), "communicative capitalism" (Dean 2005, 2010), "platform capitalism" (Srnicek 2017), "big data capitalism" (Fuchs and Chandler 2019), "cognitive capitalism" (Lemmens 2011; Parikka 2014; Stiegler 2013, 102), and "surveillance capitalism" (Zuboff 2015, 2019a, 2019b) is one where user data circulates increasingly through and as property of corporate giants such as Google/Alphabet, Facebook, Amazon, and Apple. Like any preceding form of capitalism, this one is not a particularly happy place to live in. My point is that there never was a happy place; that a happy place for some may be a living hell for others; and, most importantly, that imaginary happier places of the kind necessitated in broad narratives of loss are simply not productive rhetorical tools in and for critical inquiry (this argument is fully formulated in chapter 5). Critiques of the contemporary, for which there is certainly much need, have to start from somewhere else and be mindful of whose past, present, and future is being laid out, whose losses are being recounted and how, and what attachments and experiences are being ignored or effaced in the process. Critical inquiry, in sum, has to be both contextual and attuned to ambiguity.

Social media, convergent with the spread of smartphones and the mobile internet, have brought forth transformations in how sociability is organized and conceptualized—and, indeed, in how individual agency comes about. Within a relatively short period of time, smart devices have become integral to the management of social ties and information resources to the degree that, should we be deprived of them, our lives would not be the same. While focusing largely on social media, my inquiry is then situated within the broader context where network connectivity has grown *infrastructural* (Couldry and Mejias 2019, 337; Race 2015a, 2015b; van Dijck 2013, 4, 155). In using the term "infrastructural," I am referring to facilities and backbones—both material and organizational—which "shape the conditions for relational life" (Wilson 2016, 247). Like electricity, which makes networked communications possible to begin with, connectivity is more of a necessity than the kind of added experiential and communicative layer that it was some two decades ago.

Any networked media event is dependent on material computational and connective infrastructures, such as data centers, cell phone towers, and fiber optic data cables (e.g., Bratton 2015; Farman 2015). As Ara Wilson (2016, 271) notes, the notion of "infra" points to that which is below: "hidden from the view of most users: pipes beneath ground, wires behind walls, or satellites orbiting out of sight." This book takes a somewhat different approach by considering the infrastructural functions and roles of network connectivity and personal devices, rather than by examining the technological infrastructures necessary for their operability as such. Building on media theory, cultural theory, affect inquiry, actor-network theory (ANT), feminist media studies, and internet research, I map out the affective formations connected to networked media by examining social media platforms, mindfulness apps, clickbait sites, self-help resources, research reports, journalistic accounts, and academic assessments, as well as student accounts of moments of mundane technological failure. In doing so, I do not try to counterbalance the optimism of the tech sector through soberly dark countervailing examples, nor am I trying to pep up critical diagnoses of data capitalism with fuzzy, warm accounts of personal feeling. Rather, I consider networked media platforms, devices, and apps as constitutive (and not merely as representational or

ordering, patterning, and shaping of sensation that come about in encounters between people, apps, devices, and services (cf. Levine 2017, 3, 49). Formations occur in "defined patterns of interconnection and exchange that organize social and aesthetic experience" (Levine 2017, 113). Importantly, the affective formations addressed in this book do not assume any sameness in how their intensities and rhythms become registered or made sense of. For Michel Foucault (1982, 31, 38), discursive formations—that is, discourses identifiable through their recurrent themes, perspectives, and concerns—result from mutually disconnected micro-instances, rather than from any singular or centralized structure (see also Mittell 2004, 11–12). Discursive formations come into being on multiple sites that need not be interconnected yet share similar features to the point of being recognizable as patterns of a larger whole. The micro, then, gives rise to something like macro—or, perhaps better, helps to identify the analytical shortcomings of this very division (Sampson 2012, 39). I similarly address affective formations as surfacing in repetitive, mundane microevents—a search here, a meme, a tweet, or a video clip there—as something tangible and societally resonant enough to result in the kind of zeitgeist diagnoses that I began this chapter with.

As I discuss in more detail in the following chapters, zeitgeist diagnoses focusing on the current moment and aiming to identify budding trends that are not yet fully present or articulated reiterate concerns that have in fact been voiced for decades, and even for more than a century—as in the case of distracted, bored, and anxious modernity where technological advances have been seen to speed up the sense of time in ways impossible for people to cope with. Were such concerns be examined in terms of, or as indicative of, structures of feeling, they should be somehow identified as residual, dominant, or emergent—so that the emergent, for example, resists the dominant—yet such a periodization does not work here. It is more the case that similar concerns and stories of loss have been articulated at regular intervals and in diverse socio-technological contexts at least since the mid-1850s, giving rise to contingent affective formations where repetitions occurring over time become eclipsed by diagnoses of the very present.

This book addresses affect, in its more fleeting and lingering forms, as intensities that emerge in and give shape to relations between human and nonhuman bodies, and make them matter. As both a precognitive force and a contingent sense of connection and relation, affect translates as vibrancy varying in intensity and register (Featherstone 2010; Paasonen 2011; Seigworth and Gregg 2010). Affect is a matter—and capacity—of impact that builds up in and modulates daily encounters with the world. As such, it can be conceptualized as an "unstructured non-conscious experience transmitted between bodies, which has the capacity to create affective resonances below the threshold of articulated meaning" (Featherstone 2010, 199; see also Ahmed 2004; Coleman 2018). While preceding cognitive processing, affect is also a force registered in individual bodies—and hence something to be retrospectively named, interpreted, articulated, and situated along an emotional spectrum. Things can then get meta as affect becomes an object of reflection and we get "bored with pleasure, angry at being fearful, worried that we don't care, optimistic about depression, curious about our own insistent questioning, and enjoy being confused" (Coyne 2016, 99). It is important to note that, as affective formations, dependence, distraction, and boredom are cognitive inasmuch as they are discursive. They are experienced as visceral intensities and contingent bodily states, but they equally come about as objects of reflection and concern in cultural and social analyses, in autobiographical accounts, and in theorizations of capitalism. In mapping some of the affective qualities connected to networked media, this book remains focused on how these become analyzed, explained, and diagnosed. My discussion of affect is therefore much less about precognitive and presubjective intensities of the kind that Brian Massumi (2002) and other authors building on the work of Gilles Deleuze and Félix Guattari foreground. I remain interested in the affective economies of social media as comprising people's investments, their perceived losses and gains, and the broader social reverberations that all this entails.

Conceptualizing affect as networked (Paasonen, Hillis, and Petit 2015) means focusing on its circulation and oscillation involving a range of actors, from individual users to inanimate objects and collective and hybrid assemblages. Networked affect takes shape and ripples through devices, platforms, apps, interfaces, files, and threads. Drawing on Spinoza (1992), we can conceptualize networked devices as bodies that affect human bodies: through such engagements, our life forces and capacities to act may increase or diminish, slow down or speed up (Deleuze 1988, 125). As a constitutive element of contemporary life, networked media enables connections and disconnections, both creates and cuts down potentialities for action (Karppi

2018). This conceptual framing does not situate networked affect as either visceral gut reactions (that is, as specific to any singular individual) or as a broad nonhuman potentiality. Rather, it allows for an examination of how affective intensities shape our networked exchanges and become registered in bodies as they pass from one state to another.

Silvan S. Tomkins foregrounds affect as that which propels people forward, motivates their actions, and makes things matter. Affect is aroused in ways and through factors that individuals can scarcely control, yet without it "nothing else matters—and with its amplification, anything else *can* matter. It thus combines *urgency* and *generality*. It lends power to memory, to perception, to thought, and to action" (Tomkins 2008, 620, emphasis in original). Excitement, in particular, is that which invests things with a sense of magic and—in fact—defines the self: "*I am, above all, what excites me*" (Tomkins 2008, 191, emphasis added). At the same time, excitement remains fickle as it waxes, wanes, and weakens in the course of repetition and familiarity (Tomkins 2008, 193). Following this line of thought, excitement, as elusive as it may be, is that which is sought out when browsing Tinder, Grindr, and Bumble profiles or when checking Twitter, Jodel, Instagram, FetLife, TikTok, Snapchat, Twitch, Facebook, PornHub, Reddit, and WhatsApp—even when such routines are habitual and possibly end up being boring in themselves. As the affective fuel of user actions, excitement can remain a promise unfulfilled; it can be experienced in mild hues of interest, or its promise may come into being through its lack and absence in disappointing flatness of feeling.

Writing on mobile media, Richard Coyne (2016, 10) identifies its transmissions of data as equally "media for the circulation of moods." Moods "carry us into the world" and "carry the world within us" (Thiele 1997, 497); they are atmospheres that envelop people and attune them to one another and to their material environments and circumstances of life (Coyne 2016, 44, 51). Moods, in Coyne's (2016, 32) discussion, involve affect without an object. Affect, unlike mood, can be objectless *and* have an object. It can be peripheral and vague *and* focal and intense. It can be prolonged as a murmur *and* as visceral as a clap of thunder. For James A. Russell (2009, 1264), "Affect is part of, but not the whole of, what are called moods and emotions." Likewise, moods (and emotions) are part of, but not the whole of, affective formations. My take on affective formations departs from the Heideggerian notion of mood in focusing on bodies and the encounters that animate, grab, and transform them. These bodies are particular and feel out the world differently—and, consequently, are differently moved by moods as they catch on, linger, or slide by.

Dependence, distraction, and boredom, as discussed in this book, are not affects as such. As affective formations, they are also discursive and come into being in a range of cultural diagnoses both past and present. Like discourses for Foucault more broadly, they give shape to that which they describe. In order to have cultural resonance—to be recognizable as something *felt*—discursive formations need to tap into structures of feeling: they have to be "able not only to address a social experience that is not adequately understood, named, or categorized but also to 'frame' it in adequately explanatory ways" (Illouz 2014, 23). Affective formations, then, entail both amalgamations of feeling and the persistent creation of meaning.

Attention Ecologies

In the framework of media studies, it is obvious to identify the internet as a medium in the sense of a technological solution for transmitting messages as signals from senders to recipients. It is a technical solution and a channel for communication. Yet if one conceptualizes network connectivity as a matter of infrastructure, and the internet—as the network of networks, and as shorthand for a range of actors from hardware to cables to protocols—as that which allows for the current range and width of data circulation, then the notion of a medium can be applied to more specific means of organizing content, engaging with it, and interacting with interfaces, algorithms, and people. In other words, platforms, sites, apps, and services can be understood as media forms in how they differ from one another in their affordances, rhythms, and patterns of communication. As argued in chapter 3, the speeds and lengths of attention are contextual and situational and vary according to interface, platform, context, and interest alike. Hence the rhythms of browsing apps, for example, cannot be extended to diagnoses concerning more general rhythms of attention, despite the seeming ease with which this seems to happen. Pettman (2016, 95) similarly points out that online attention economy tends to be addressed as somewhat monolithic when the issue is rather one of diverse attention ecologies, "each with its own ecosystem and microclimate." Totalizing and reductive analyses on the impact of smart devices and ubiquitous connectivity on everyday lives nevertheless fail to accommodate such multifariousness.

This book's general starting point, the coconstitution of media technologies and ways of perceiving the world and acting within it, broadly builds on media ecology. Marshall McLuhan (1964, 2011) conceptualized media as extensions of the human sensorium both requiring and fueling different kinds of engagement, participation, and focus. While McLuhan saw the overall shift from print to electronic media as involving a loss of linearity as well as a reworking of our nervous system and forms of sensation and perception, his was no narrative of loss. Rather, he saw this shift as entailing a bombardment of stimuli that opens up possibilities for less hierarchical and multisited forms of knowledge. For McLuhan, what was at stake was no simple erosion of rationality or focus but an open-ended transformation in forms of perception and interaction: "the way we think and act—the way we perceive the world" (McLuhan and Fiore 1967, 41). While I do not wholeheartedly embrace McLuhan's theorization of media and society, I find the openness of alternatives connected to different, parallel, and overlapping media forms a fruitful starting point, not least since much ensuing critical media theory has tended to close such alternatives down.

A focus on the rhythms, speeds, and sensations connected to networked media makes it possible to tease out both specificities and common features in a landscape characterized by the promiscuous circulation of content, as well as the promiscuous movements of users across platforms (Payne 2014). This also entails reframing the notion of "the user" less as someone in control of devices and apps than as an actor whose agency is dependent on multiple networks comprised of both human and nonhuman actors (Latour 2011; chapter 2). Online exchanges are dependent on the ever-increasing performance level of server farms and the capacity of underwater cables, as well as the operability of material devices and applications. As such nonhuman actors in the network become inactive, drop out, or change, the user's possibilities to act are reconfigured. Transformations can be gradual enough to almost fail to be noticed or drastic enough to disorient, yet contingency is the norm as networks seldom stand still.

Sarah Kember and Joanna Zylinska (2012, 13) argue that "It is not simply the case that 'we'—that is, autonomously existing humans—live in a complex technological environment that we can manage, control, and use. Rather,

we are—physically and ontologically—part of the technological environment, and it makes no more sense to talk of *us* using *it*, than it does of *it*
using *us*." In their theorization of mediation, Kember and Zylinska depart
from studies of "mediatization" examining the social impact of media (e.g.,
Hepp, Hjarvard, and Lundby 2015; Lundby 2009), framing it as an issue
of dynamic human and nonhuman liveliness where the boundaries of
subjects and objects, events and media, have grown porous at best. This
perspective does not assume the mastery of technology over culture, or
vice versa, emphasizing their coconstitution instead. This is also my point
of departure for thinking through the affective ecologies and economies
of networked media as ones entailing shifting machine-human assemblages of people and desires, devices and networks, algorithms and software, spaces and times.

A Contextual Note

Zeitgeist diagnoses of the addictions, distractions, and boring qualities of
networked media are not necessarily connected to, or built on, empirical
inquiry. The flat, sad, empty, anxious, unfocused, and amnesiac subjects
evoked in these accounts are regularly paradigmatic, abstract placeholders
necessary for outlining expansive social, cultural, and technological developments. Meanwhile, empirical research focusing on people's views and
practices points to things being more complex, as in negotiations concerning algorithmic processes that are hard to grasp (Bucher 2018) or in failures
to experience presumedly distracting media as such (Wajcman 2014, 101).
Empirical lines of inquiry open up something of a parallel story which,
while equally tackling affective formations, resists confinement in categorical diagnoses and adds crucial nuance to cultural inquiry.

My analysis of affective formations builds on a very specific set of research
material: 174 student essays describing experiences of failure in media and
communication, composed for my undergraduate media studies classes at
the University of Turku, Finland, in 2012–2018. These self-reflective essays
have been written by students born between the years 1970 and 1998, the
majority of them belonging to the age group diversely identified as "digital natives" (Bennett et al. 2008; Prensky 2001), millennials (Howe and
Strauss 2000), and Generation Y (although Generations X and Z are also
represented). Most of the students have had access to computers, mobile

phones, and the internet for virtually their entire lives, and their accounts offer vignettes into experiences of living in and growing up with ubiquitous network connectivity.

Courtesy of government-driven information society agendas of the 1990s securing online access for all through public institutions such as schools and libraries, and being the home of the (now collapsed) mobile phone giant Nokia that introduced texting (SMS) to the world, Finland has been a highly wired nation for more than two decades. In 2018, there were 154 mobile broadband subscriptions per 100 inhabitants in the country (OECD Data 2018). Of people ages 16 to 44, 100 percent use the internet, 97 percent access it several times a day, and 98 percent do so with a smartphone—the volume of mobile data used per capita being the highest in the world (Statistics Finland 2018).

The essays, then, communicate the experiences of privileged, predominantly white young people living in the Global North. Instead of proposing that these accounts function as imaginary common templates of experience, I explore their repetitive features and resonant points as illustrative of the affective formations connected to networked media with an overall aim of challenging the generality of zeitgeist diagnoses concerning networked lives.

My interest in and motivation for working with the essays have to do with the frequency with which the heterogeneous category of "young people," from children to teenagers to young adults, is used as a rhetorical figure of worry. As Tina Kendall (2018, 85) points out, adolescents in particular but also the young more generally "are mobilised to illustrate concerns about shrinking attention spans, and to rehearse arguments about what happens when the human capacity to endure boredom is eroded in an era of digital networks." It is young people whose capacity to hold attention is argued to be either atrophied or unformed, whose quality of life is seen to suffer most from the pressures of fear of missing out (FOMO), who are positioned as particularly susceptible to the addictive effects of media technology, and who are seen as canaries in the virtual coal mine, pointing toward a bleak future for all (e.g., Lovink 2019, 10). All this involves generational generalizations over those "whose capacity for sustained critical reflection is imagined to be most at risk in the dangerous new regime of hyper-attention" (Kendall 2018, 86). As I discuss further in chapter 2, the accounts I draw on are reflexive, intelligent, ironic, contextualized, diverse, and actively resistant to diagnoses of shriveled-up attention spans, shallow learning, or the lack of critical capacity. As such, they help in coining a more nuanced story of things currently underway.

The students writing the essays operate in multiple registers across networked media. Some use many and others few social media platforms. Some are aspiring social media influencers while others participate with reluctance or opt out. Some rely heavily on Instagram, others occasionally, and yet others have deleted the app or have never been users to begin with. Some are highly critical of data capitalism and engage in social activism while others plan careers in social media marketing, branding, and consultancy. The students describe mundane attachments to networked media as ranging from hours of online gaming to random, vacuous browsing, to quotidian practicalities and social necessities, to the obligations of study and work. By building on these essays, it is possible to resist the kind of age and generation-based othering that runs rife in public debates on attention, distraction, boredom, and network connectivity.

All the Feels!

The rest of this book is organized into four interconnected chapters. By drawing on the student essays describing sharp affective ripples evoked by technological failure, chapter 2, "Dependent: Agency and Infrastructure," addresses the mundane infrastructural roles of networked media. Engagements with devices and platforms can be smooth, hardly noticeable, routine-like, or animated by visceral dissonance in moments of rupture where frustration, helplessness, and rage abound. Social media scholars have addressed FOMO as an ambivalent social glue that keeps young people online, yet I argue that something more substantial is at work in the role that information networks and smart devices play in everyday lives. The chapter further argues that network connectivity comprises an infrastructure of intimacy that is vital to the creation and maintenance of friendships and sexual arrangements, as well as a range of other mundane attachments and dependencies (see also Race 2015b; Wilson 2016). In doing so, it problematizes diagnoses of internet and social media addiction and conceptualizes dependence as inseparable from agency.

Chapter 3, "Distracted: Affective Value and Fickle Focus," explores the dynamics of distraction and attention in the context of social media's attention economy. By focusing on clickbait sites and Facebook in particular, it inquires after the value of distraction, as well as its functions in the affective management conducted on and by social media platforms. The chapter examines concerns voiced over distraction and the shortening of attention spans while also addressing value creation within the affective economy of clicks, likes, and shares. Rather than conceptualizing attention and distraction as mutually opposing dynamics, the chapter frames them as rhythmic patterns in the affective fabric specific to the contemporary landscape of ubiquitous connectivity. In doing so, it both foregrounds discussions of rhythm and tempo in social media research and questions dystopian accounts of the distracted present.

Chapter 4, "Bored: Flatness and Enchantment," moves to sensations of blandness, flatness, and boredom connected to networked media, inquiring how the quest of fighting boredom through the distraction on offer is seen as boring in itself. By examining mundane microevents involving minor enchantments, the chapter argues for understanding boredom and excitement (interest, pleasure, and fascination) as two sides of the same coin. Like attraction and distraction, they give rise to rhythms ranging from flatness and lull to intense focus and sharpness. The chapter discusses this dynamic in the context of cultural and social theory that has defined boredom as a markedly modern phenomenon generated by an overflow of stimuli. Countering the narrative of "disenchanted modernity," the chapter further asks what may emerge from the speeds and affective ripples of network culture, what productive captivations and intensities it may engender, as well as what pleasures boredom itself may afford.

Finally, the concluding chapter, chapter 5, "Nostalgia: A Toxic Pursuit," returns to the narrative of loss cutting through the book, asking whose losses are being presumed and foregrounded within it and whose voices and perspectives become eclipsed in the process. Focusing on the notion of nostalgia and drawing on student accounts, the chapter critically examines the notion of authenticity associated with less media-saturated lives lived off the grid. Connecting this to a critique of generational othering and the scapegoating of smart devices, it engages with popular diagnoses casting young people as unhappy and nefariously impacted by networked media, foregrounding a contextual, reflexive approach instead. The chapter equally returns to the notion of the pharmakon, highlighting the necessity of working with and through ambiguity in cultural inquiry, and of acknowledging the diverse intensities and potentialities that affective formations entail.

Now, with all this said, let us move onward: dependence, distraction, and boredom await.

2 Dependent: Agency and Infrastructure

Without net access, I feel some sort of feeling of emptiness and lack, since without it it's impossible to do schoolwork, for example. ... The lack of access breaks down the regular rhythm of the day that of course involves checking Facebook, e-mail, work stuff, and certain discussion forums at regular interval. It feels intolerable and depressing to know that connections are cut. Measures therefore follow: sitting by the computer and trying to diagnose the error until the net [connection] either comes back or it feels like a vein is bursting in my frontal lobe. (male, b. 1989)

Net use has become such an elementary part of my everyday life that I don't even notice all the things I use it for until the connection stops functioning or doesn't exist. I recognize my increasing ineptness when, for one reason or another, I can't check baking recipes or bus schedules online. (female, b. 1991)

In these casual accounts, Finnish students recount their experiences of network failure and lack of online access as leading to diminished modes of existence. All kinds of ordinary routines and connections with partners, friends, acquaintances, colleagues, and family are paced and maintained through networked devices, apps, and services that both generate and leak data (e.g., Lasén and Casado 2012; Race 2015a, 2015b; Wilson 2016; Wise 2015). Whether resulting from a software bug, ruptured cable, hardware malfunction, signal failure, or one's own negligence and forgetfulness, the lack of network access cuts people off from their socio-technical networks and gives rise to unease, anxiety, and frustration that can fast flare up into blind rage. Following theorizations of the transmission of affect (Brennan 2004) and its intensification through social circulation (Ahmed 2004), affect, as qualities of connection and sensation, comes into being in encounters between bodies—be these those of people or those of other animals, inanimate objects, values, ideas, or objects—and its intensity feeds on circulation, interaction, and connectivity between these bodies. Affective intensity nevertheless surfaces rapidly and abruptly in instances of technological nonfunction when circulation comes to a halt and interaction is disabled. Intensities become further amplified through delays, lags, and waiting; messages left undelivered or unreceived; web searches aborted; and documents not downloading. More than an irritating glitch, lack of access can reconfigure available ways of being in the world: "Without access, one's capacities to act become truncated in ways that can give rise to seemingly excruciating sensations of frustration" (female, b. 1993).

Building on student essays, this chapter maps out the affective formation of dependence as it becomes tangible as mundane connections, insecurities, and ambiguities and as it yields pleasures and frustrations alike. Dependence signifies "the quality or state of being influenced or determined by or subject to another" (*Merriam-Webster*, hereafter MW), pointing to the capacity to be affected in a broadly Spinozian vein. Standing for "the state of needing the help and support of somebody/something in order to survive or be successful" (*Oxford English Dictionary*, hereafter OED), it further points to lack of autonomous subjectivity and agency. This chapter addresses dependence as descriptive of mundane infrastructural connections and, therefore, as not synonymous with addiction. The rationale of this chapter is to tease out ambivalences in human-machine relations and the heterogeneous actor networks within which everyday lives are lived. Framing the issue in media ecological terms as prosthetic connections and infrastructural dependencies that shape ways of thinking, relating, and being in the world, it explores how such dependencies are articulated, experienced, and reflected upon.

On Method

The essays that form the backbone of this chapter, each one to three pages long, were written between 2012 and 2018 by students in my compulsory undergraduate-level course "Media and Networks" at the department of Media Studies, University of Turku. The course has moved from histories of media networks (telegraphy, telephony, radio, television, internet, social media) to conceptual work on media convergence, remix, intermediality, materiality, and affect, and with readings ranging from Marshall McLuhan to Bruno Latour and beyond. In the assignment in question, handed in during the third week of class, students were simply asked to describe how failures in media and communication technology feel. While mentions of printers and media players occurred, especially during the first years when the exercise was introduced, the vast majority of the essays focus on mobile phones, computers, and network connections failing.

Pedagogically, the essays have served two main functions: first, they have provided the students with a possibility to reflect on their overall relationships with, and attachments to media technology. Second, excerpts from these accounts have been used in class to help explain and flesh out theoretical accounts of the entanglement of human and nonhuman agency that may otherwise seem too abstract, or just opaque—such as ANT and affect theory that we moved to discussing soon after the exercise in question. In these sessions, anonymized quotes from the essays frame readings of ANT, discussions of planned obsolescence, and the key principles of affect inquiry, bridging the personally felt together with the more general. When theoretical arguments are presented through the words of the students themselves, they tend to come across as more easily relatable.

The essays are "requested stories," knowingly crafted, often ironic, largely witty, and designed for the instructor (me) to read (Tuuva-Hongisto 2007; Paasonen 2015a). Some essays resort to hyperbole in describing the affectations involved while others remain laconic and report-like in their delivery. While compulsory to hand in, they have been free in their form of execution, they have not been graded, and they have been treated anonymously both in class and for research purposes for which the students have given informed consent. As the excerpts offered above illustrate, I cite the essays without added pseudonyms and by mentioning the gender and year of birth of the student in question in order to broadly situate the author. The students have been informed of how their essays are identified, and none have provided a nonbinary gender marker—which, of course, is not to say that their self-identifications may not be more complex than the markers "f" and "m" allow for. The overwhelming majority of this student body is white and speaks Finnish as their first language. There is nevertheless diversity as to socioeconomic background, as facilitated by an equalitarian public school system and the lack of tuition fees in higher education. For this book, I have coded the essays for instances addressing dependence on or addiction to networked media, describing the role of networked media and disruptions therein in everyday life and detailing the affective intensities of failure, as well as elaborating on the distracting and boring qualities of networked lives. I have tried to avoid repeat citations from the same essays, although some exceptions do apply. All translations from Finnish are mine and made with the attempt of conveying the original tone and style of writing, even though nuances are bound to get lost in translation.

To perhaps state the obvious, the essays do not facilitate access to affective intensity as such. As self-curated, selective narrations of feeling, orientation, and relationality, they are retrospective reflections and investigations of sensation after the fact and translate the visceral and the embodied into linguistic form. Following Brian Massumi (2002, 28), autobiographical reflections limit conceptualizations of affect to the level of emotions as "intensity owned and recognized." Unqualified intensities can be retrospectively described, named, and translated into distinct emotive states such as frustration, anxiety, and rage—examples of which abound in the essays. This naming reorders affective intensities to emotions that can be represented, hence both limiting and enabling inquiry into sensation (Massumi 2002, 25–27). At the same time, such recollections are among the only available means for tackling affectation on the level of experience—and for possibly making affect inquiry more concrete in the process. In the student accounts, the immediacy of sensation gets retrospectively registered, reflected upon, and contextualized, allowing for empirical ways of working with and through affect.

Another point concerning the pedagogical nature of the exercises is that students often deliver what they believe instructors want to read: they understandably aim to act according to assignment in order to get a certain grade and to acquire the study credits involved. It is therefore not impossible that exercises can ask students, for example, to affirm that they are addicted to their smartphones or that their attention spans have been completely busted, and to find them fully articulate on the subject. If used as research evidence, such material provides evidence for precisely that which the teacher designing the exercises has been looking for, leading to a circular loop that fails to provide much proof of anything. This is precisely why the essay assignment was free in format and focused squarely on the students' experiences, thoughts, and feelings in instances of technological failure. These students should not, at any instance, be mistaken for ventriloquist's dummies mouthing that which I, as their teacher, have scripted.

In describing intensities and qualities of feeling, the essays render legible dependencies on devices, connections, and information resources. Asking students to describe in writing how instances of failure feel pushes them to tackle the elusive yet tangible affective and somatic underpinnings connected to media technology, with the premise that these most readily manifest in moments of rupture. In doing so, the essays help to connect the personal and the anecdotal with the social, the structural, and the theoretical. Should the excerpts cited seem repetitive, this would be a key point. I suggest that such repetition makes it possible to outline, and to grasp, the affective formation of dependence connected with networked media. In this sense, the essays are both anecdotal and, in pointing to repetitive patterns of sensing and making sense, definitely not.

Infrastructural Dependencies

Daily lives are lived and intimacies surface and wither in networks composed of both human and nonhuman actors in ways that are not merely metaphorical. These networks facilitate and condition work obligations, studies, the creation and maintenance of friendships, sexual arrangements, and affairs of the heart. Within them, network connectivity is not so much a neutral mediating factor or "channel" of communication as a crucial mundane socio-technical affordance—an infrastructure. Some of this is evident in how the essays describe disruptions in connectivity as ruptures in everyday life and potentialities for action: "Disorder in network connectivity was more than a technological malfunction, it cut off connections to the world and social relationships. ... Loss of connection felt like isolation and the inability to do anything about it was distressing. I could only wait for it to come back at some point" (male, b. 1987). "As the computer went for maintenance I felt as if completely cut off from the world" (female, b. 1990).

> I notice that I've amassed smart devices, digital players, consumer electronics, and other gadgets around me that suddenly seem fragile and perishable. When devices start to slowly turn off, they can't necessarily be replaced with new ones anymore. The perishability of gadgets makes me think of their meaning—would

I remain the same without television, synthesizer, vinyl player, or would they merely leave behind the unpleasant silence of a broken radio?

Technological devices are built to make everyday life easier but at the same time they've created a network of mutually codependent parts where one suitable piece breaking down feels like being returned back to the Stone Age at one go. I've accidentally dropped my phone already once and I suspect the second time to be like the first domino block that makes me once more thoroughly rearrange my everyday life. (male, born 1993)

This description of everyday life as a "network of mutually codependent parts" resonates with ANT—although it had not yet been addressed in the class by the time these essay assignments were handed in. In ANT, individual users are seen as actors defined through the networks of which they form a part, through their connections to and their reverberations in networks of people, technologies, and practices (Latour 2011, 806). Consequently, agency is not a matter of individual intention or enterprise but redistributed, networked, and emergent in its forms and effects. Actors are in a continuous state of interaction, learning, and becoming and are, as such, necessarily connected to and reliant on others (Gomart and Hennion 1999, 224–225; Latour 1999a, 17–19). Connections between different actors (or nodes, or elements) within any network can be stronger and weaker, and their intensities may vary. Yet should one key actor—such as a smartphone—fail, one's capacity to act is transformed. In its horizontal treatment of human and nonhuman actors, ANT helps in articulating, even if not fully untangling, the crucial role that network connectivity plays in everyday life. For their part, the student essays describe mundane dependencies and routines that, in fact, make the self:

Technological failures can completely ruin my schoolwork and possibilities to manage my university studies. They can remove all relevant, content-producing hobbies and sources of entertainment from life. They can ruin my friendships and romantic relationship. It's pretty obvious that I'm fully dependent on the possibilities that media and technology offer and without them there wouldn't be me either. (male, b. 1995)

Reading and sending messages on, and following social media and news is my way of keeping track of events in the world and in the lives of close ones. This is why their lack causes a feeling of helplessness and isolation, as if I were alone, completely unaware, outside of everything.

Last year my cell phone didn't work for a few days and it wasn't connected to a GSM network. It's considerably more difficult to be without a cell phone than without the net but the anxiety is probably due to the same reason. It's hard to reach anyone without a cell phone and you even feel unsafe. I have my cell phone with me practically always. I don't even go and take out the garbage without the phone. At home it's usually in the same room, in my bag, pocket, and very often in my hand when I'm somewhere else. Even during lectures, the phone is usually in front of me on the desk. I always keep the phone close by although I know that I probably won't need it for anything just that moment, and without the cell phone I feel downright naked. (female, born 1992)

The lives described in the essays are saturated by networked media in ways that clearly depart from articulations of media use as rational exertion of instrumental control over technology of the kind that were long influential in human–computer interaction (HCI) research and that continue to underpin optimistic views of social and individual empowerment through technology, as offered by the corporate sector in particular. In contrast, the essays outline user agency as ambivalent and often precarious (see also van Dijck 2009). As routinely noted in science and technology studies, the degree of mundane dependencies on technological solutions becomes most evident in moments of failure. When smooth operability comes to a halt, users are left with little to operate. Failure of a single device, or even lack of access to a single platform, may feel like a sharp rupture in one's everyday life. Or, as Jenny Sundén (2018, 64) puts it, "The break has the potential to bring forth what constant connectivity means, and how it feels" (see also Karppi 2018; Sundén 2015a). One's degree of dependency on network connectivity becomes viscerally evident when it is lost: "Without internet connection it feels like living in darkness. As if anything can happen, I have no means of finding out about it" (female, b. 1983). The essays describe the sense of agency unraveling especially if smartphones are unavailable: "When it's taken away, one no longer knows what to do" (female, b. 1990).

In the Finnish context, as in much of the Global North, both public and private services—from banking to doing taxes—are rendered accessible primarily, or even exclusively, through online platforms. Meanwhile, continuous connectivity has, for many, become if not precisely a civic duty, at least a social obligation of sorts. Within this relational geography, "we are constantly—while at the same time never completely, or securely— reachable" (Sundén 2018, 64). Connectivity does not, therefore, simply speak of privilege (as discussions on the digital divide frame it), nor is it unequivocally a personal choice. It can even be argued that the precarious need to remain the most connected if they are to find out about possible gigs and available work shifts which cannot be chosen or planned ahead. Correspondingly, *not* being constantly connected and reachable, or having someone else do the work of connectivity instead, is a sign of privilege and practiced among business executives, politicians, and celebrities.

In this context, the infrastructural role of connectivity makes it similar to utilities such as electricity, gas, running water, and heat, in highly literal ways: "Each time... [the lack of connectivity] has obviously angered me and simultaneously it's felt unreal. *A thing taken for granted was no longer available, as if my flat suddenly had no toilet*" (female, b. 1991, emphasis added). Some students even prioritize online connectivity over other infrastructural factors:

> My phone just got an upgrade where you can check how much the phone is used on average daily and weekly. My average is around four hours a day and, in a week, I've spent nine hours browsing Instagram and Snapchat alone. So, the phone is a very central component of my everyday life. ...
>
> One morning, I woke up to my apartment having no electricity. I'd even forgotten to charge my phone the night before so that when I woke up, the battery was almost empty. I panicked. Of course the internet didn't work on my computer and my phone was almost out of power. The first thing I did was call my brother and tell him that I was coming over immediately to charge my phone. ... I was only interested in how I could remain present in social media and connected to my friends without a break. (female, b. 1995)

Following ANT, the lack of connectivity means being detached from the multiple networks that enable individual agency. Connectivity is essential for all kinds of daily routines—from online learning platforms to shopping, access to news and entertainment resources, map services, dating, and hooking up—and cuts through the different social networks within which we operate, and which define the self:

> If my phone won't momentarily work, different kinds of concerns awake in my mind: what if someone is trying to reach me, but I can't respond? What if my friends are discussing something important and I'm left outside? What if all my photos disappeared and I hadn't had the time to upload them to a cloud service? What if I get lost, where do I find a map or a bus schedule? ... It's not uplifting to notice that I'd no longer know how to be without my smartphone. (female, b. 1997)
>
> Since I live in continuous symbiosis with technology, possible malfunctions in tech have much greater impact on my life than food suddenly running out or

water being cut. ... Technology has given me and made possible my romantic relationship, a range of friendships, school, entertainment, and my ways of consuming media and art. Glitches in these huge parts of my life would mean a major
glitch in my life in general. (male, b. 1995)

Hooked?

According to thesaurus definitions, dependence bleeds into addiction
when growing in intensity to "the state of being addicted to something (=
unable to stop taking or using it)" (OED). The term "addiction" is widely
used to describe a range of dependencies on, attachments to, and investments made in media, not least in the context of smartphones and social
media. In tandem with the mainstreaming of fandom as a general affective media relation, expansive uses of the terminology of addiction—as in
the vernacular of being "hooked" on TV shows, games, applications, and
devices—implies the fundamental ubiquity of such attachments, as well as
their promotion in a media economy where the ideal consumer is "active,
emotionally engaged, and socially networked" and, hence, already hooked
to a degree on what she or he consumes (Jenkins 2006, 20; see also Hellman 2009). It even seems that the notion of addiction can be applied to
virtually any activity geared toward enjoyment that draws us back again
and again as "a kind of streetwise colloquial overstatement to which any
of us could subscribe" (Coyne 2016, 129; see also Chan 2008). "Facebook
addiction," for example, may merely refer to people checking their news
feed numerous times a day—which many of us do without considering it
as compulsive overuse comparable to substance abuse (see Andreassen et al.
2012; Griffiths 2012).

Meanwhile, media dependency is very much inbuilt in the pedagogical
practice and curricula of contemporary academia. Students need to create,
modify, upload, and download files; share and comment on them; access
e-mail; and log into intranets, databases, and online learning platforms
on a daily basis: as the semiglobal shift from face-to-face to online learning during the COVID-19 epidemic shows, computer abstinence is simply
not an option. Combined with the social expectation to be reachable, this
results in lives heavily dependent on network connectivity. In describing
this, the essays make use of the Finnish terms *riippuvuus* and *riippuvaisuus*,
which are mutually interchangeable and translate as both dependency and

addiction (see also Suominen 2006): "My own dependency on [*or addiction to*] the functioning of the internet would be almost amusing if removing the possibility of its use wasn't so stressful" (female, b. 1990). Dependence, then, comes across as the default effect of network connectivity experienced as infrastructural:

> I'm scared to even think of how many of my waking hours I spend with different media and how dependent I'm on [*or how addicted I am to*] them. So, while on the one hand I miss the days preceding the "dominance" of media and technology, I've grown so dependent on [*or addicted to*] them that I wouldn't know what to do without them, on the other. This also evokes dismay and fear. (female, b. 1990)

> In the beginning of the day, I have breakfast while reading the news, I choose my bus through a mobile app, I choose my lunch place at Unica's [*student cafeteria*] site, I message in-between lectures with my friends and set up meetings, after class I again choose a bus with the right app, after which I use different websites for example for work and fun. This list is very simplified but gives a good picture of how many possibilities there are for technological malfunctions to make the course of my day more difficult. (female, b. 1996)

> We have such routine in using our smartphones, for example, that most of us would feel like being in direct trouble if we left the gadget behind for the workday or school day. Without drawing any larger conclusions, it's interesting to compare these notions to different dependencies [*or addictions*]: the necessity of a telephone is considered normal but if someone has trouble surviving half a day without intoxicating substances or gambling, for example, one is discussing a serious problem. (male, b. 1996)

Popular accounts of smartphone and internet dependency assume a continuing ideological—and, at this particular point in time, false—division between online and offline worlds. This division, however central to internet inquiry in the 1990s, has lost most of its analytical edge with high-speed mobile internet and broadband connections, and as news updates, posts, messages, and notifications perforate routines of work, entertainment, and intimate interaction alike. In framing common engagements with networked media in pathological terms, addiction discourse in fact comes across as anachronistic. Consider, for example, the Internet Addiction Test developed by Kimberly Young, the founder of the resource site Netaddiction.com. "How do you know if you're already addicted or rapidly tumbling toward trouble?," the site's 2018 version asked, further listing 20 questions, including:

How often do you block out disturbing thoughts about your life with soothing thoughts of the Internet?

How often do you find yourself anticipating when you will go online again?

How often do you fear that life without the Internet would be boring, empty, and joyless?

...

How often do you try to cut down the amount of time you spend online and fail?

How often do you try to hide how long you've been online?

...

How often do you feel depressed, moody, or nervous when you are off-line, which goes away once you are back online?

Established in 1995, Netaddiction.com promotes itself as an educational resource for fighting addiction: "It provides treatment for Internet addiction using CBT-IA, Young's specialized Cognitive Behavioral Therapy for Internet addiction is the first evidenced-based Digital Detox™ recovery program." The Internet Addiction Test follows the general guidelines for identifying addiction in the context of drugs, alcohol, and other forms of substance abuse. In doing so, it does not distinguish among different forms of or motivations for online access: it is the abstract object of the internet itself, rather than the multiple entangled networks of potentiality, exchange, investment, and obligation that it entails, which becomes framed as an addictive substance (Johansson and Götestam 2004; Karaiskos et al. 2010). The internet is, then, discursively positioned as similar to drugs and, in turn, the compulsion felt toward them. This discursive framing, where dopamine hits hook people to apps and interfaces, is certainly widespread (Stjernfelt and Lauritzen 2019; Syvertsen and Enli 2019), as is the positioning of internet users as akin to the users of other addictive substances who can thus benefit from detox (Karppi 2018, 67). Like alcoholics or drug addicts, pathological internet users are, in the questionnaire, imagined to fantasize about next logging in, to alienate themselves from those around them who might try to intervene, and to escape their worldly obligations with the aid of the addictive substance. Like an alcoholic dreaming of drink and hiding the empty bottles, a net addict is seen to disguise the extent of his or her addictive desire, unable to cut down the use.

Some of the questions set forth in the Internet Addiction Test, such as "How often do you find yourself anticipating when you will go online again?" and "How often do you try to hide how long you've been online?," make little sense for people constantly connected through mobile devices. The questionnaire was launched well over two decades ago when online connectivity depended on dial-up modems, required logging in, was slow, and was far from continuous. Despite drastic contextual differences in the quality of network connectivity and the roles that it plays in everyday life, the questionnaire remains in active use: a Google search shows it to have been translated into several languages and taken up globally by psychologists. Completing the questionnaire collectively in class, as was an exercise for a number of years, generally resulted in the diagnosis of moderate internet addiction: "You are experiencing occasional or frequent problems because of the Internet. You should consider their full impact on your life." Fair enough.

The students contributing to these exercises, however, perceive themselves as needing the internet to successfully navigate their daily life and describe network connectivity as a glue holding it together: "Although there is life outside the internet, too, for most of my life I'm in almost constant connection with the net either actively or passively. When technology doesn't work as expected, it creates a sense of insecurity as you never know when the situation will 'get back to normal'" (female, b. 1997). It is crucial to resist overarching and simplifying accounts framing such dependencies in terms of addiction, as these lack the nuance necessary for distinguishing between uneasy and ambiguous experiences of dependency and pathological behavior impairing one's capacity to act, be, and relate. Despite the impulses and motivations for network access being an admixture, the frame of addiction associates them all with a quest for pleasure. Thus decontextualized, internet use is framed as insular activity driven by the desire for online access per se—and the internet becomes an addictive substance in itself. This kind of undifferentiated treatment of both addiction and internet use circumvents the multiple conditions and forms of dependency related to network connectivity, reducing them to issues of individual choice motivated by a quest for pleasure instead. It then makes no difference whether a person is online in order to finish his or her work tasks, to find himself or herself on the map, to check up on an ill parent, to read the latest news on a pandemic, or to hunt down a recipe for the fluffiest of scones: the mere desire to be online means that the user is hooked and possibly addicted (see Korkeila et al. 2010).

The notion of addiction implies the loss of individual autonomy and rational control. Eve Kosofsky Sedgwick (1993) conceptualizes addiction as assumedly insufficient freedom of will: "Losing it," addicts are seen as driven by external forces beyond their control. The discourse of addiction, Sedgwick (1993, 130–132) further argues, is connected to the demonization of "foreign substances" whereby the affective, somatic, and cognitive modulation that these afford, impacting one's degrees of concentration, alertness, sense of bodily rhythm or temporality, is framed as polluting and corrosive. All this involves the "propaganda of free will" premised on subjects that are autonomous, self-contained, and freely choosing, yet frequently unable to choose appropriately or freely enough (Sedgwick 1993, 133). As both will and compulsion are seen as internal and emanating from within subjects themselves, those depending on external stimuli simply fail to be proper subjects. At the same time, both the ubiquity and the notable flexibility of the discourse of addiction, as it is currently deployed, ultimately results in a moral judgment separating artificial and artificially stimulating substances from so-called organic ones (Reith 2019; Sedgwick 1993, 136). The division between time spent online and offline, where the former should be monitored, controlled, and kept under control, can be seen to speak of such boundary work between authenticity (as organic, natural, and beneficial) and the external (as artificial, addictive, and potentially harmful).

While there is much contingency to definitions of addiction in their expansive contemporary uses, it can be understood as "repetitive activities that fail to reproduce much else besides addiction" (Ruckenstein 2012, 108). Minna Ruckenstein (2012, 117) suggests that such compulsive loops are fundamentally an issue of temporality: "When the balancing of time cycles and everyday rhythms fails, bodily reactions are inevitable: people feel stressed, they lose sleep, suffer from high blood pressure, or start to engage in a compulsive manner with some activity. People respond to, and are shaped by, daily practices and rhythms." Understood in this vein, addiction is a response to disruptions in everyday rhythms of life that further fuels lack of synchronicity with the surrounding world as people become immersed in their substance of choice.

For their part, Bennett Foddy and Julian Savulescu (2007, 29) argue that "addictive desires are merely desires for a source of pleasure." Addiction then entails the quest for pleasure, coupled to the difficulty of managing or achieving it, that is experienced as a problem or a hindrance. The user's engagement with addictive substances and objects both enables and blocks his or her life forces as things that are intended to excite fail to do so, and as the intensities sought out fail to materialize (Bjerg 2008; Weinberg 2002). When satiation remains inaccessible, the addict's life forces are diminished rather than strengthened. In both promising pleasurable release and eating away at the pleasure of life, addictive substances function as a pharmakon— the cure and the toxin wrapped in one (Derrida 1993).

If, following Silvan Tomkins, "I am, above all, what excites me," then any quest for pleasurable excitement involves the making of the self and possibly comes with degrees of addictive desire, making it hard to determine just where and when addiction begins and ends and what it encompasses. To the degree that the rhetoric of addiction involves the recognition that "there is a power (or powers) greater than the self that shape(s) the individual's life" (McGee 2005, 186), and that one abandons oneself to such a power (Gomart and Hennion 1999), compromised agency is in fact something of a human condition. Human agency is shaped by contingent networks and forces beyond our control—from bodily realities of thirst and hunger to electricity to running water to roadways to economy to climate and to law—that condition who we are, what we can do in, and how we can relate to, the world.

Uneasy Users

Checking messages, clicking on links promising images of cuddly kittens, following status updates from former lovers, uploading overdue coursework, searching for information about this and then that, users are attracted to the accessibility of information and sense of contact. Without access, anxiety soon builds up, and any binary division made between the user (as the subject) and the technology (as the object operated) unravels. A student describes the experience of having no mobile internet access:

> Occasionally I hear a voice in my head saying, "browse Facebook." I'm just about to do so when I remember that it's not possible. Being without a smartphone can be distressing. Now we're so used to being constantly accessible. When the phone is left at home or breaks down, availability ceases. It feels like being isolated from the whole world. (female, b. 1992)

According to the expectation of constant and immediate access connected to smartphones, information, goods, services, and people are equally and instantly available (Gardner and Davis 2013). Lags, delays, and glitches interfere with this ideal of frictionless use, forcing a discontinuous rhythm to one's interactions and occasionally giving rise to sharp ripples of irritation: "I consider myself a pretty patient person but when the net is both extremely slow and cuts off, it's hard to remain calm" (female, b. 1992). Although a slower speed of access would have been not only tolerable but something to be expected not so many years ago—recently enough for many of the students to recall—the immediacy of high-speed connectivity has since become ingrained in the rhythms of daily life:

> Waiting doesn't go together with contemporary high tempo, information-glutted life, neither does "slowing down" as a concept for that matter. Even philosophers and yoga teachers talking about slowing down want technology to work without fault, and fast. (female, b. 1990)

> I've … noticed the effect that if pages open more quickly on the computer, it also helps me to better focus on what I'm doing. If it takes more than five seconds for a page to open, I've already had the time to put on my workout gear and I'm ready to do something completely else than study. (female, b. 1993)

Contra accounts of the stresses and costs associated with the speeding up of life that focus largely on the toll of media environments rife with too much numbing stimuli (e.g., Crary 2014), the students cited here foreground the stress and toll of *forced slowness* that is incompatible with their overall rhythm of life and, as such, is highly frustrating. While partly aligning themselves with diagnoses on the acceleration of culture (e.g., Rosa 2003, 2013), the students frame the issues at stake differently: for it is not the speediness that is the problem but the speed slowing down against one's will, design, and interest. Slowdowns not only limit options for social engagement but impair one's very ways of thinking and being. Speediness is a matter of habit that provides the rhythm for mundane routines:

> The best quality of current technology is its speed. … I'm so used to technology working quickly and effortlessly that even the smallest of problems causes a great sense of frustration, even ridiculously so. I've noticed my habit of picking up the phone whenever I need to wait for the computer to work longer than usual. Sometimes it takes more than a second for pages to load. I then immediately grow bored and frustrated. … Mobile data is mostly fast and functional in Finland, but for example on trains and in rural areas connections grow glitchy. The sense of irritation that the slowdown gives rise to is completely absurd and ridiculous. Through it, I've learned to reflect on my relationship with technology, and social media in particular. Although I'm not the worst of addicts, even this degree of fixation on media technology occasionally causes great anxiety. (female, b. 1996)

Contemporary technology is so fast by default that you expect it to work that way without exception. Information exchange and communication should be immediate and user shouldn't need to wait for a page, picture, or even a large video file to download. (male, b. 1996)

What mostly frustrates me in technological devices is their slowness. If they don't work fast, I grow angry and may yell at them (not in public though). So, I'm of the generation that's been pampered with fast technology and for whom technology should work in the blink of an eye. This applies especially to web browsing. If pages are slow to load or don't work at all, I get a little empty feeling inside. As if something was missing and I wouldn't get the daily dose of information that I'm looking for. (male, b. 1993)

Rather than pathologizing such a "little empty feeling inside" as indicative of addiction and unfulfilled pleasure seeking requiring diagnosis and intervention, these accounts can be more productively considered as speaking of matters of habit (see also Coyne 2016, 129–130; Mowlabocus 2016). Habits are learned and hence make people similar to one another while also being deeply personal (Chun 2016, xi). Ingrained in sensory schema as a matter of habit, high-speed connectivity has become the expected state as an infrastructural affordance. For those attuned to information immediacy, the forced slowness of lagging connections results in unsavory affective dissonance where the subject judges the situation as simply not being quite right.

Wendy Hui Kyong Chun (2016) argues that networked media matter most not when they are novel and just introduced but when they do not seem to matter much at all—namely, once they have become habituated as matters of mundane routine that require little conscious thought. "Through habits users become their machines: they stream, update, capture, upload, share, grind, link, verify, map, save, trash, and troll. Repetition breeds expertise, even as it breeds boredom" (Chun 2016, 1). As such, habit—"both mechanical and creative; individual and collective; human and nonhuman; inside and outside; irrational and necessary"—can be considered as a form of dependency (Chun 2016, 6, 8). Following this line of thought, dependency on devices, apps, platforms, and the diverse socio-technological networks that they afford is an issue of habitus: ingrained habits, skills, dispositions, and practices repeated "without any deliberate pursuit of coherence…without any conscious concentration" (Bourdieu 1984, 17, 173), as in casual mobile phone use:

Occasionally, when reading an exam book, for example, I become aware of having picked up my phone and opening one of the social media channels. In this situation my primary feeling is surprise since I've taken the phone in my hand entirely unawares. On the other hand, this goes to show how dependent I ultimately am on the phone. However, if I for example turn off the phone or leave it in another room, soon I don't remember to miss it anymore. (female, b. 1994)

As Ingrid Richardson (2005) notes, applications, devices, and bodies are covalent participants in the making of meaning and environment that continuously intermesh as forms of "techno-soma." Mobile devices in particular have grown crucial to our ways of feeling out the world. Similarly to Chun's discussion of habitual media, the notion of techno-soma points to the degree to which devices and apps are part of the rhythms and motions of everyday life. They arouse and orient the affective and the somatic; this is a central source of their attraction and appeal. To quote Sundén (2018, 69), "The pace of our digital devices blends with the rhythms of our bodies, as a speeding up, or a slowing down, of how our bodies compose with those of others, fostering new rhythms and relations." In relations of connectivity and impact, technologies press themselves on the people engaging with them. Devices and applications are the loci of potentiality that may or may not be available and that influence—increase, sustain, and diminish—one's capacities to act. The issue is one of prosthetic connectivity ingrained in techno-soma and translating as dependency: "I don't understand how I was able to live before Google but apparently I did so until I was 30" (female, b. 1970).

All in all, the student essays describe affective intensity as resulting from and intensifying with weak signals, network failures, slowness, and connections abruptly broken or never established, pointing to the degree to which "disconnect, rather than operating as a decrease, a dis-composition, or a cool down … essentially makes digital connectivity heat up and, with a burning sensation, circulate through bodies and networks" (Sundén 2018, 75). Since the students were asked to recount their experiences of technology failing, it is only to be expected that the intensities they describe revolve overwhelmingly in the negative registers of dismay, horror, pain, distress, infuriation, fury, and helplessness, with frustration being a key sensation: "I was so frustrated that I can't recall when I last had such sensations. The malfunction of the network broke the camel's back: suddenly I felt the walls cave in, and nothing worked anymore" (female, b. 1991).

Mundane errors, breakdowns, disruptions, and delays are more than familiar for the users of consumer electronics (Hayles 2012, 2; Uotinen 2010, 161). Computers, mobile phones, modems, printers, and tablets have limited life spans inbuilt as planned obsolescence (Bulow 1986; Guiltinan 2008), in addition to which they regularly malfunction or just break down (Lundemo 2003, 13). Failure equally results from people's inability to operate technology and to understand the logic of systems, programs, and services. Rupture may also be caused by external conditions such as power cuts or random accidents such as phones dropped in water and laptops falling off tables. Failure brings planned tasks to a halt as user actions and commands are interrupted. From the perspective of HCI, the issue is one of noncommunication: of a program, protocol, signal, or device not responding, not being understandable, or not being accessible to the user (e.g., Lindgaard and Dudek 2003; Tractinsky and Zmiri 2006). In HCI, error messages, dropped network connections, long download times, and hard-to-find features have been long identified as key frustrations (Ceaparu et al. 2004). When such experiences repeat, their affective intensities grow, speaking to the dual shape of affect as both encounter and impact (Ahmed 2004, 66; Coleman 2012). A singular frustrating experience may leave little mark while its recurrence soon lends human–technology relations a tenacious negative affective charge. As a male student born in 1991 exclaims, "All my experiences of failure in media technology are connected by the same, almost unbearable sense of frustration and annoyance."

In the tradition of cybernetics—the science of communication and control in human and machine systems—that underlies both modern computing and classic media models such as Claude Shannon's 1948 mathematical theory of communication, as later elaborated by Warren Weaver, the user is understood as the operator, and the machine as the tool operated (Weaver and Shannon 1963). The Greek root of the term "cybernetics," *kybernētēs*, translates as governor, pilot, or steersman (Wiener 1999). It can be argued that a similar view of the user as masterful operator of smart devices remains influential in contemporary discourses—academic, journalistic, promotional, and popular alike—where our relationships with technologies are premised not on failure and frustration but on control over applications and, more broadly, on human control over the world (Wise 2015).

The student essays nevertheless narrate the uses of media and communication technology as unending balancing between control and helplessness where no level of user skill ultimately suffices to guarantee smooth operability: "The greatest dismay stems perhaps from my own ineptitude: either I don't know what to do or I don't know what to do in order to figure out what I should do" (male, b. 1991). "Frustration was considerable once I realized there was nothing to do. The worst thing about the feeling was the knowledge that even if you give everything you've got, and no matter how good you are with computer technology, it still isn't enough" (male, b. 1991). Visceral responses to technological failure are intimately tied to the uncertainty of users' sense of control in ways that effectively call into question the very notion of "the user" itself. It may be the case that the term "actor"—as theorized in ANT—has greater analytical value in conceptualizing the situation at hand. As actors in networked exchanges, we can be active, passive, proactive, intentional, or random, but our agency is far from autonomous, let alone innate. Such ambiguity is already inherent in the notion of the user itself, signifying "a person who uses or operates something," "a person who takes illegal drugs; an addict," as well as "a person who exploits others" (OED).

In her research on digital gambling machines, Natasha Dow Schüll (2008, 2012) argues that the pleasures of compulsive gambling lie in the tactile interaction with the machines and their mechanical rhythms. The gambler "plays" the machine and is "played" by the machine in return. The students cited are similarly both playing and being played by the devices and applications they engage with. As in Schüll's analysis of "addiction by design," social media apps and smart devices are designed with the principle of attracting as much and as continuous use as possible for the purposes of optimized data traffic, collection, and analysis. As we play with smart devices, apps, and random online content, our locations, operating systems, clicks, searches, shares, and downloads are tracked and archived as data. And as we grab online content by sharing, tagging, remixing, and commenting on it, platforms aim to grab not merely our data but our sustained attention, preferably repeatedly and for extended periods of time (on the notion of grab, see Senft 2008). Notable conceptual and contextual gaps nevertheless exist between the tactics of attaching users to platforms through compelling design, infrastructural (functional, affective) dependencies experienced in connection with smart devices, and diagnoses of addiction. When the BBC TV documentary *Panorama: Smartphones? The Dark Side* (2018) simply identifies smartphones as "the new cocaine," something elementary is amiss.

The perceived validity of diagnoses of addiction builds on their positioning subjects as pushed and pulled by powers beyond their control. If, however, we understand agency as resulting from heterogeneous actor networks—and, as such, as consisting of all kinds of dependencies on factors and powers beyond our control—then such pushes and pulls are merely the stuff of life. While the student essays largely describe the user as the controller and technology as the instrument operated, this human-as-controller/technology-as-tool relationship is ultimately understood as an unattainable ideal not quite of this world. The same applies to the ideal of smooth and frictionless technologically mediated communication more generally (see Sundén 2015a). As these two students fantasize, "I only want a device that works. And serves just me, just the way I want it to" (female, b. 1992); "Good technology would be such that you wouldn't notice it. It would just always work and enable a life rich in experience" (male, b. 1983). The students articulate their agency as users with great degrees of uncertainty as it seems that failure, rather than function, is an oft-expected outcome.

A customer fairly enough expects for a new car to work, a new oven to heat up, and pants not to come apart at the seams when first worn. This does not seem to be fully the case, however, with smart devices. As the design and operations of high technology grow ever more complex and as the knowledge involved in their manufacture becomes more specialized, the inner operations of devices are increasingly inaccessible for the majority of their users (Gell 1992, 62; Lupton 1995, 106). As Latour (1999b, 158, 192) points out, complex technologies are "blackboxed" in the sense that their inner operations are hidden inside and therefore impossible for the user to affect: gadgets just work, until they do not (see also Goddard 2015). Black boxes are defined through their operations and functions—their input and output. In moments of failure, such operations come to a halt as the flow of input and output is severed, and as the mysteries of the machine, at least to a degree, evaporate. Alternatively, it can be argued that devices become black boxes in the second degree in that their now unavailable operations remain equally, if not increasingly, difficult to grasp, and certainly impossible to affect. Black boxes are, after all, defined through their overall lack of transparency (Bucher 2018, 41). The positioning of the user as the masterful operator, "steersman," or "governor" is effaced, rendering the user as something of a helpless outside observer instead. Such second-degree black boxes are complex yet unusable, and hence already close to debris.

Black boxing regularly results in guarded, self-deprecating, and even pessimistic approaches to technology: "Ultimately it feels like media devices are never worth the trust, yet one trusts them with many functions, trusting everything to go perfectly" (female, b. 1994); "I've generally always had a reserved, lukewarm approach to technology. My preconception is often that nothing will work as it should anyway, or that if problems occur, I can do nothing to fix them" (female, b. 1994). While daily dependency on networked media characterizes virtually all essay submissions cited here, it is noteworthy that such wary and suspicious responses were more commonly coined by female students expressing frustration over not being able to cope with, or to solve, technological malfunctions:

> I hate gender stereotypes more than anything else and even more than that I hate it if I somehow support these stereotypes with my own being. It's therefore enraging to admit that I'm rather bad when it comes to electronics, and I often need help in this. I'm a typical woman who can't even set up a net connection, and that bugs me. It may also be one of the reasons why the breakdown of net connectivity really made me lose my nerves. (female, b. 1991)

Here, resentment felt toward cultural stereotypes of female impotence vis-à-vis technology intensifies the frustration experienced, amplifying its overall valence. Amplified through self-consciousness, aversion toward gender clichés adds to the felt intensity of failure as that which sticks not only on the technology but also on the user in question. It is nevertheless the category of generation, more than that of gender, that reoccurs as a point of distinction and identification in the essays. The students regularly self-identify as digital natives who "have been surrounded by different media and communication technologies all their life" (female, b. 1992) and are so used to this "that they feel unsafe and insecure without their external extensions" (female, b. 1992). The term "digital native" has been much debated (Bennett et al. 2008), yet students make use of it in order to conceptualize their dependencies on technological objects and networks as specific not only to the historical moment they inhabit but equally to their generation, as largely defined against older people.

Prosthetic Entanglement

> Different communication and media technologies have been molded into extensions of the senses. ... One can consider them as third legs of sorts, without which we feel castrated. We constantly stick our hand into our pants just to check if it's still there: we glimpse Facebook and WhatsApp on our phones, waiting for something, checking that the connection still works, that it's still there. (male, b. 1993)

Ubiquitous connectivity facilitated by smart devices and the mobile internet has, in this florid account, become incorporated into bodily schema as
gestures and motions repeated both purposefully and routinely (see also
Karppi 2018, 5). On the one hand, this account explicitly gestures toward
familiarity with McLuhan's conceptualization of media as extensions of
the central nervous system—this is, after all, a media studies major who
had, as part of the class in question, read excerpts from his *Understanding
Media*. On the other hand, Finnish teenagers identified mobile phones as
intimate, organic parts of their everyday lives—and as body parts—already
around the turn of the millennium, and certainly without any exposure
to McLuhan (Oksman and Rautiainen 2003). A prosthetic framing is further echoed in the Finnish terms used for mobile phones. Officially known
as "travel phones" (*matkapuhelin*), these devices have long been discussed
and marketed as "little hands" (*känny*; *kännykkä*)—the term being originally
introduced by a Nokia engineer in reference to extensions of a child's hand
(Mäenpää 2005, 267; Paasonen 2009, 19).

It is erroneous, therefore, to assume that the student describing prosthetic
connections with media technology is doing so simply by virtue of being
inspired by scholarly discourse. Rather, it seems that his experiences resonate
with a broader notion of media-as-prosthesis, as is the case with numerous
other essays: "One currently considers a smartphone almost as an extension
of the hand. It's such a self-evident part of everyday life that one no longer
even pays attention to a smartphone—unless it's suddenly missing" (female,
b. 1996); "If net connection is cut or if messages stop going through, or
if Spotify for example won't repeat music as it should, it feels as if my legs
stopped working, to exaggerate a little" (male, b. 1994); "Mobile phone is
such a big part of everyday life that it's actually an extension of the hand.
When it's taken away, one no longer knows what to do" (female, b. 1990).

> One doesn't unconsciously consider computers, printers, typewriters, etc., as
> mere tools but as extensions of one's body and mind. That's why when a device
> fails it feels as if a part of me has turned against itself. A bit like a hand grown
> numb that suddenly feels strange. Although unlike with electronic devices, one
> doesn't feel like throwing the hand at the wall; perhaps like slapping it a bit at
> best. It then follows that we develop somehow amazingly humane relationships
> of respect, fear, and control with technological devices. (male, b. 1991)

> Dependency on for example the functionality of cell phone networks…generates
> a submissive relationship of sorts. It feels as if communication technologies such

as mobile phones really are some sort of an extension of man but, to exaggerate slightly, with malfunction they change into some sort of a malicious entity. (female, b. 1992)

Before my phone broke down, I hadn't thought how dependent you can be on one small gadget and in this case on one of the gadget's functions. A little like a body part, the functionality of which is so taken for granted that you get all confused when it's damaged. (female, b. 1989)

Ingrained in techno-soma, devices become experienced as prosthetic extensions of the human sensorium: as the means of contact and engagement with the world and as *aides de mémoire*. As part of our corporeal organization, or schema, devices and applications are part of our, and function as externalized memory archives of people, moments, and places (Gehl 2011; Pybus 2015). In the student essays, involuntary effacement of mediated memories is described as particularly unnerving, equated with the loss and effacement of one's actual past: "Photographs, music, and text messages disappear with devices, which feels as if memories themselves disappear when they're no longer concretely visible" (female, b. 1991). "Having the phone's memory card destroyed is a little like throwing into a fire not just my address book but a bunch of letters, a photo album, alarm clock, and a few albums of music. The phone is like an archive for me" (female, b. 1989).

The worst thing about the situation is that it's so surprising, and the loss of unsaved photos, videos, and discussions. Especially in my teens a certain carelessness in transferring photos to the computer or a cloud service made me lose them. Thinking about this still causes sorrow and longing. It feels bad to lose memories connected to my course of life that I've taken myself. As if the past was torn apart or got permanently lost and I fear forgetting situations. From this reaction I notice how attached to photos and video memories themselves are through media. Photos make broad tangles of memories surface. (female, b. 1994)

Mundane, prosthetic connections to and dependencies on technologies (devices, software, apps, and so forth) blur the kinds of divisions of inside and outside, the inner and the outer, the human and the machine that diagnoses of internet addiction operate with. We are dependent on these technologies that shape and condition our ways of thinking and relating, and which affect a range of quotidian microlevel operations. All this translates as dependencies that yield pleasure and displeasure, confidence and apprehension alike (Lupton and Noble 1997).

Writing of her emotional connections to computer technology in the mid-1990s, Deborah Lupton (1995, 97–98) describes feelings of impatience, anger, panic, anxiety, and frustration when it fails to work. These oscillating intensities are, for Lupton, tied to her dependence on computers for the act of writing. More than instruments, they are intimate companions "to think with" (Turkle 2007). The nonlinear word processing possibilities of cut, paste, delete, and add have grown integral to the processes of thought and writing, and it is unlikely that any of the students composing the essays—any more than I as their instructor—could write anything much lengthier than a page or two without them (see also Kirschenbaum 2016). Should we suddenly be deprived of ways of thinking, as enabled through word processing, there might, for many of us, not remain much textual craft at all.

For people writing in their second language (as I am doing here), online dictionaries and search functions connected to syntax and grammar are integral parts of the writing process without which words remaining on the tip of the tongue would remain just that. The uses of prepositions would be wobblier, and expressions would lack the degrees of nuance afforded by translation apps and online dictionaries. Without network access it is, in fact, difficult for me to write. This was not always the case yet currently remains a fact—one that runs parallel to the broader development of computers having become internet terminals by default. While online connectivity was, for a large part of the 1990s, and certainly before, an additional feature of personal computing, an offline computer now comes across as lacking, and even to a degree unusable. Transformations in habitual uses of media technology can be relatively fast just as they can be profound. When viewed on an individual level, they can nevertheless be difficult to perceive and identify as steady streams of novelties, upgrades, and updates constantly alter the state of things.

At the time of Lupton's article, online connectivity was mainly facilitated by dial-up modems with a downstream speed of maximum 56 kb/s, resulting in lengthy download times. The shift from desktop computers with dedicated Ethernet cables to portable devices operating on high-speed Wi-Fi transmission marks obvious transformations in the mundane presence of networked media, giving rise to the routines of googling information on the spot. Cut to the current average Finnish broadband connectivity speed of 64 mb/s:

I wonder if a general impatience in the face of technological malfunction is worse every year. In the 1990s, for example, when the internet was in its early days [sic], it could take five to ten minutes for an image or a video to download, with videos even half an hour if they were exceptionally long. Nowadays I think that many users go to another site if it takes even several minutes for media to download. (female, b. 1986)

I seldom have the patience to wait for a web page to download, which is a pretty big transformation from the early days of the internet. I think I had better patience with waiting before I got a smartphone: now I have to see everything right away or it's already old news. If I don't see something immediately, I'll skip it. One can still bypass news, but it's the worst if a lovely dog video hits a glitch or the loading symbol of Netflix just spins around. (female, b. 1991)

Love, Hate, and Ambiguity

All this considered, it is unsurprising that the student essays speak of networked media in ambiguous terms of love, hate, possibility, anxiety, enjoyment, and dependency—as balancing acts between frustrated helplessness and the desire for smooth operability: "I take the internet for granted. 'How difficult can it be to get one net to work?,' I wonder. 'It's the 2000s, as self-evident a thing as the internet simply can't not work!'" (female, b. 1989). "When media and communication technology don't work, it *pisses me off....*My personal experience of being pissed off by technology oscillates from aggression to hopelessness, from action to despair" (male, b. 1998). In the essays, smart devices come across as elementary in that which they afford but also as replaceable material objects that are seldom loved in themselves, or held onto for sentimental reasons alone. Exceptions do, of course, apply:

My soulmate smartphone got lost into thin air during the last weekend's festivities, making me feel as if I'd moved back to the Stone Age. You have to actually go through trouble to see the time, it's impossible really to be in contact with anyone since my phone also functions as Wi-Fi hotspot for my laptop, and my pockets somehow feel all too spacious. What most gnaws at me however is that I'll never see my phone again. It's somehow worrying and sad that I've formed some kind of an emotional bond with this electronic gadget. I looked at videos on YouTube that compared my now-former phone to a new phone I'm considering and seeing my former phone on the screen caused a true sense of longing inside. I'm absolutely a materialist person and I become all too easily, as well as too deeply, attached to my things. (female, b. 1993)

As love of technology, technophilia involves intimacy with machines while technophobia indicates the opposite—aversion, fear, and aggression felt toward them. Both tropes describe seemingly clear-cut affective relations toward, and investments made in, technology. Examining accounts of intimate attachments to technological objects, Jaakko Suominen (2011, 18–19) identifies them as "technological romances" of longing, fascination, and attachment that may even follow the generic patterns of romantic relationships in their highlights, frustrations, and disappointments. When loving devices and applications, users attach hopes, promises, and desires to them. When feared, technology is described as that which can, or is even likely to, cause harm. Furthermore, love and fear more than easily intermesh. Lauren Berlant (2006, 21) points out that investments in objects "and projections onto them are less about them [insert *devices*] than about a cluster of desires and affects we manage to keep magnetized to them." Therefore, "we are really talking about a cluster of promises we want someone or something to make to us and make possible for us." Following Berlant, attachments to technological objects are ultimately optimistic, despite all the disappointments that they may cause. Laden with promise, devices evoke yet also block potentiality through access to networks, resources, and affective attachments: generating "new modes of material participation … new forms of community and speculative practices" (Race 2015a, 269). As malfunction is always a possibility, and ultimately inevitable, devices nevertheless occupy an ambiguous position as both promise and threat, cure and toxin.

In a neatly dualistic framework, the affective intensities experienced when a smartphone cannot access a network or when a computer crashes could be explained as technophobic impulses revealing themselves in moments of operational rupture or as disappointment when the objects of our affection fail us. What is at stake, however, is a more ambivalent clustering of intensities and desires that surround devices operating both as objects of dependency and as actors in the networks underpinning our very agency (as potential to act):

> I was so shocked about what had happened, and a freezing fear crept to the back of my head, such that I had to go and buy a new computer. It's almost impossible to put these feelings into words. The horror of having ruined a computer. The fear that it'll never come back to life and the pain of needing to purchase a new one, all crisscrossed. (female, b. 1976)

Having unsuccessfully tried to reformat her old PC's hard drive, this student describes her subsequent trepidation and guilt. As her agency seems to dissolve, she is left only with the option of purchasing a new device. At the same time, she invests the now defunct PC with agency and liveliness as that which—to her horror—might never revive.

Such anthropomorphic qualities emerge in a range of essays, where "the computer won't even agree to turn on," mobile phones play "the most incredible tricks," electronics gain consciousness "only in order to mess with me," and computers possess a "spark of life." Such vitalistic formulations are both matters of essayist literary effect and telling of the fundamental entanglement of human and nonhuman agency. The sharpness of affect brought forth by technological failure that nullifies one's agency as user can even lead one to physically assault the disappointing device:

> My pent-up anger quickly turns to rage. After insulting my USB modem for minutes to no avail my fury usually evolves into physical assault. I really don't remember ever having experienced similar rage than when the network connection doesn't work. I find my actions difficult to justify, but the frustration and rage are simply overpowering. (female, b. 1991)

> I don't otherwise become upset very easily in life but all kinds of malfunctions really make me upset and agitated from zero to a hundred in a matter of seconds. Profanities are yelled and my fist moves. I have no nerves whatsoever when it comes to these malfunctions. ...
>
> I've also beat the keyboard of my laptop with my fists multiple times when the net has been patchy or the connection too slow. I also quickly lose my nerves when connection is too slow. (female, b. 1984)

> I've ... also experienced rage if the net hasn't worked ... [and] my mind has accelerated from zero to a hundred. I compare this fury connected to nonfunctioning Net to the concept of *road rage* where altogether regular sensible people become rabid fanatics at the steering wheel of a car. (female, b. 1989, emphasis and the English term in the original)

Overwhelming frustration and rage can make physical aggression seem like the only available release (see also Uotinen 2010). Some of this is captured in a well-known scene from the 1999 Mike Judge film *Office Space* in which three long-suffering low-tier open office employees kidnap a printer. Throughout the film, the printer has been jamming and malfunctioning, frustrating and infuriating the employees. Once kidnapped, the printer is carried out to a field where the three men continue to ceremoniously kick it and hit it with a baseball bat, courteously handing the tool from one to

another and assaulting the printer with gusto. Accompanied by the rap song
Still by the Geto Boys (with the chorus line "Cause it's die muthafuckas, die
muthafuckas"), one of the men ultimately loses himself in the moment and
starts pounding the printer—in shambles by now—with his fists until the
two others drag him away.

The modality of the scene is one of humorous and violent catharsis—of
breaking away from the mundane frustrations of office work, the humili-
ations faced from the lower management, and the unpleasantness of the
social ties cultivated at work due to conditions beyond one's control. Yet
the printer—the object of this seemingly blind act of violence—is much
more than a passive symbol or metaphor for such frustrations. It is a key
agent in the assemblage of things that has rendered the lives of the office
workers unlivable, day in and day out. Randomly functioning, stubbornly
jamming, and acutely error prone, it is a central node in the dynamics of
the office: employees gather around the machine, cursing, as work tasks
fail and frustrations build up, and as they try to make it operate again.
If feelings "are how objects create impressions in shared spaces of dwelling" (Ahmed 2010, 14), then the printer impresses the employees daily in

Google Images search results for *office space printer*, https://www.google.com/search
?q=office+space+printer.

concrete ways. As it continues to malfunction, these impressions grow, saturate the technological object with affect, and ultimately drive the employees to annihilate it as a violent ritual of revenge.

The catharsis of the scene would perhaps not be recognized as one, were not frustrations with poorly functioning printers a fact faced by many within office work. Jams, feed errors, and flashing error code lights are more than familiar, as is the frustration, unease, helplessness, and anger building up when interfacing with such machines. Before electronic documents caught on, gathering around a dysfunctional printer, trying out different tricks, and comparing the episode to the ones previously witnessed was the stuff of social bonding at the academic workplace. The itchiness of dysfunction may decrease and abate as frustrations are shared and negotiated—or it may well become amplified, as in the fictitious yet emotionally realistic scene from *Office Space*. Sensations caused by technology failing just like that, when facing them all alone, can be equally intense, not least when there is nothing to be done about it:

> Mundane malfunctions in communication and media technology are infuriating, frustrating, and cause constant disappointments … [they] cause similar sensations as the actions of a close person against [one's] will … it's enraging, you feel like throwing something at someone, and hard. … In the emotional scale caused by malfunction, technology gets the dimensions of a sentient being. "Why are you doing this to me?" and other similar feelings comparable to self-pity and frustration emerge. …
>
> Surely the necessity of technological devices is an important cause for the emotional scale caused by technological malfunction. If the net doesn't work, the poor person is separated from the external world. You can't update Facebook or Twitter, can't see e-mails arriving in real time, can't instantly report your sushi lunch on Instagram, or follow the news headlines popping up on the smart device's screen almost non-stop.
>
> In addition to spare time self-marketing, technology has also extended its tentacles to work, banking, sorting out kids' absences from school, and many other practical things directly influencing the operability of everyday life. Malfunctions in technological devices stop us from paying bills, doing taxes, calling a friend, and responding to a job interview invitation on e-mail. The lack of technology … makes us powerless: we're unable to influence our own affairs, unable to cook since recipes are also online, unable to watch TV as that's also been done online. (female, b. 1990)

Affective intensities surface in the monetary, affective, and temporal investments made in devices and apps; in tactile interactions with them;

and in moments of rupture that truncate the sense of user agency. Rage ripples to the surface when that which is experienced as a necessity is unavailable: in such instances, infrastructures defined through their perceived invisibility are at least momentarily rendered evident.

Intimacies

Smart devices enable relational presence and "salient and transitory modes of intimacy" (Hjorth and Lim 2012, 477) of the kind that may be cumbersome or plain impossible to construct through other means (Clark and Sywyj 2012; Ito and Okabe 2005; Sundén 2018; Wallis 2015). The notion of intimacy is most commonly used to refer to closeness, familiarity, affection, and the potential for sexual contact (Wilson 2016, 249). Berlant, however, conceptualizes it more expansively as "connections that *impact* on people, and on which they depend for living" (Berlant 2000, 4, emphasis in original). Understood in this vein, intimacy is infrastructural as networks that our everyday lives depend upon (Coleman 2018, 610). It then follows that intimacies are not limited to human connections but equally involve networked environments in which such connections unfold: these all impact on people, and people depend on them for living. Considerations of intimacy as connections and networks that matter thus need to extend to the infrastructural role of digital technologies in the functionality of personal, social, occupational, and collective lives (Paasonen 2018b).

Mobile phones have been seen to engender compulsory connectedness (Gardner and Davis 2013) and "intimacy and a feeling of being permanently tethered to loved ones" (Vincent 2006, 39). The simultaneous desire for and obligation of reachability is galvanized by an orientation toward that which is possibly within reach, or possible to occur. These potentialities are centrally about personal contact and the risks of missing out on it—as well as missing out on the events taking place in the world more broadly. Defined as "a pervasive apprehension that others might be having rewarding experiences from which one is absent," FOMO (associated with social media in particular) has been identified as a "desire to stay continually connected with what others are doing" even when this is inconvenient (Przybylski et al. 2013, 1841; see also Fox and Moreland 2015). Given the ubiquity with which FOMO is discussed in public, it is not surprising that the students situate their own experiences in relation to it:

On the basis of my own experience and the stories from my inner circle I feel that my generation also suffers from a fear of missing out in the context of the digital world. Malfunction in media and communication technology then causes different degrees of anxiety as one fears that something of importance is taking place when being offline. Fear of technological malfunction even seeps into dreams. Sometimes I dream of meeting my idol yet being unable to document the moment. In my dream my cell phone camera won't work or the photo is blurry. (female, b. 1997)

If, for example, I can't browse social media at night before going to sleep, it feels as if my daily routine hasn't been filled. It feels odd to fall asleep without this electronic stimulus—usually I start sleeping when my eyes start to close, browsing the web. Without mobile internet I feel orphaned and idle at night when going to sleep. This sense of lack in routine due to an inability to engage with social media also evokes *fear of missing out*. (male, b. 1997, English term in the original)

This fear of missing out is of course connected to the inability to access WhatsApp discussions without a net connection. A fear emerges that I'm missing out on some important or interesting message and that others can't reach me with their important business.... All in all, it feels that digital devices are one part of my existence and if they don't work, I have to act without routine and in alien ways. This sense of exception is of course irritating as it makes my ordinary everyday life more difficult. (female, b. 1994)

There is a violent edge to experiences of being suddenly cut off against one's will: to connections lagging, exchanges freezing up, mediated presence fading into frozen pixels, and possibilities for intimacy aborted (Sundén 2018). If one goes offline or off the grid, a message from a lover or friend may go unnoticed, one may be left out of social engagements, and new connections may fail to come about. This virtual sense of the possible involves investments and imaginations concerning both the present and the shape of things soon to come. The virtual, then, orients and motivates the actual uses of smart devices (cf. Deleuze 2002). Without network access, expectations fail as the virtual remains separate from and inaccessible to the actual, resulting in experiences of isolation and diminished capacity to act, as well as in sensations of dismay, irritation, and rage:

The situation feels a little like losing a mobile phone. I've been cut off from all my social networks, I'm truly alone. The internet represents at least for me some kind of electronic presence, constant reachability. Being separated from that against one's will comes as a bit of a shock. (male, b. 1991)

Problems related to cell phones are particularly irksome since one has grown somewhat dependent on one's phone and the possibility of constant communication.

The thought that I can't be reached or that I can't reach others at the moment of my own choosing...feels difficult and even odious. (female, b. 1991)

When the mobile phone is left at home or breaks down, reachability ceases. It feels like being isolated from the whole world. Often in moments like this I imagine that of course everyone is missing me right now when I don't have my phone with me. And when I finally get hold of the phone again, I notice that nobody has tried to reach me all day. (female, b. 1992)

This orientation and mood of endless expectation has to do with routine, obligation, and concern. The social expectation of uninterrupted mediated presence and reachability may be experienced as stressful, but so can the failure to act accordingly (Fox and Moreland 2015). And while escapes from connectivity can be tempting, they are far from alluring when unchosen (see also chapter 5) as this may even make it hard to operate as a citizen: "Immediate reachability enabled by the phone is also somehow connected to a sense of belonging to a society. For example, through certain social media apps you avoid becoming an outsider on some level" (female, b. 1994). "Without technology I'd also be alone. Since so much of my human contact takes place with the aid of technology, I wouldn't even be able to be in contact with many of my friends since I don't know where they live" (male, b. 1995).

Inability to access the net may occasionally cause certain experiences of disappointment if, for example, you've waited for messages from friends or want to follow news about things important to you. One may imagine being left out of something and fear isolation from the online world but also from society on some level. These days, full membership in society seems to also involve a certain requirement of participation facilitated by the internet in particular. (female, b. 1990)

Rather than FOMO, the essays address the networked infrastructural underpinning in how everyday lives are managed. Without connectivity, one simply risks as if falling out of sync with the world. In contrast to the kinds of ambiguities that run rife in our engagements with and attachments to communication partners, devices, apps, and services, much firmer narratives of loss and isolation concerning networked culture nevertheless hold obvious, steady appeal. According to a predominant narrative variation, in the course of ubiquitous connectivity, relationships have grown increasingly shallow, feeble, and commodified, and people are feeling increasingly lonely as they isolate themselves behind screens rather than engage in more direct interaction with one another (see Gardner and Davis 2013). Sherry Turkle (2012, 1), for example, opens her widely read *Alone Together* by arguing that "technology proposes itself as the architect of our intimacies" yet "networked life allows us to hide from each other, even as we are tethered to one another." She continues to elaborate on how the navigation of emotional lives though smart devices and social media applications leaves us lonely and lacking in the kinds of intimacies that physical proximity and face-to-face communication allow (see also Lovink 2019). A similar perspective is evoked in studies exploring the "dark side" of social media that correlate its high use with a lower quality of life, lower self-esteem, and feelings of distress (Fox and Moreland 2015, 169). When setting out to explore the so-called dark side of social media, one is likely to discover such a side, just as studies examining the sunnier side likely will find something happy, bright, and cheery indeed. If one opts for ambiguity instead, as is the rationale of this book, things are much less decisive and firm.

In a media historical perspective, the narrative of eroding sociability rings familiar. Television, after all, was broadly diagnosed as a medium that isolates family members from one another—and facilitates novel forms of togetherness and sharing (Spigel 1992; Tichi 1991). Broad yet selective narratives of loss connected to media and communication technology, such as the one proposed by Turkle, position devices as if taking over the role of human partners, and media content as if replacing and destroying more immediate face-to-face forms of communication. In doing so, they eschew the complex assemblages of human and nonhuman actors, social roles and obligations, aims and interests, and times and spaces of communication that compose the exchanges involved. Relationships and intimacies managed through networked media are always part of a broader nexus of social proximities and distances, mediated presences and absences bleeding well beyond any binary divisions between the online and the offline.

Connections made and maintained with networked media are by default an issue of disconnections. Tero Karppi (2014, 28) makes use of disconnection as an analytical prism for understanding the ambivalent appeal of social media services and the difficulties of fully detaching from them, arguing that "through disconnection it is possible to see how the offline and online are brought together, remixed and contemplated." Ben Light (2014), again, is interested in the disconnections that people plan and execute in social media toward the people they know and the spaces and contexts that they inhabit through friending, liking, unfriending, blocking, and limiting the accessibility of updates. The work of social media connectivity involves the crafting of proximities but equally the management and creation of distances, boundaries, and detachments. Disconnection can be seen as a default effect of connectivity, or as "part of what it means to connect, to relate, to depend in the first place" (Sundén 2018, 74). Furthermore, "there are different types of disconnection, attached to different affective tendencies," from abrupt breaks to being left hanging in midair in zones of uncertain connectivity which, while possibly yielding frustration and anxiety, nevertheless continue to carry the promise of connection restored (Sundén 2018, 71).

The student essays addressed in this chapter are not accounts of intimacy amputated, disrupted, or skewed by technology; rather, they point to the roles that devices and applications play in the maintenance of intimate connections past, present, and future. During earlier decades and past centuries, mediated interpersonal communications depended on infrastructural factors such as the postal system, the telegraph, and the telephone network, all involving their own speeds and tempos. Letter exchange had a rotation of days—and, historically, that of weeks—during which one could do little else else than wait. The synchronicity of telephony since the late nineteenth century did away with such lengthy waits while also tying communication to specific devices that were, before the era of mobile phones, literally bound to physical spaces (Fischer 1994; Wilson 2016). As horizons of possibility, media technologies open up forms of connection and exchange while replacing or even closing down others and crafting spaces for disconnection. In doing so, they build on previous solutions and routines of communication—as in the shift from paper mail to electronic mail—while fundamentally transforming their forms, rhythms, and avenues.

Sensory attunement to the presence and functionality of personal devices and the information networks they are connected to shapes everyday life in ways not characteristic of telephony or much of computing culture preceding the 1990s. The development toward ubiquitous connectivity has been gradual, just as it has been both speedy and drastic in its implications. The mood of expectation involved in the imperative of constant connectivity is tied to the rhythm of devices' notifications of new messages, posts, and updates. As these punctuate and puncture daily life, one's focus keeps on shifting, moving, and altering as forms of distracted attention of the kind discussed in the following chapter. As Rebecca Coleman (2018, 601) argues, the temporality of networked media is "focused on the now and immediate, and is also on-going and open-ended. This is therefore a temporality that is not unified or cohesive, but rather is multiple, diverse and changing." The perpetual "nowness" involved in this can be experienced as disruptive and disturbing, yet there is also a mood of expectation to it. Looking forward to that which is about to come about—be it a direct message, a news item, or a nude selfie—is steeped in degrees of optimism, or at least in those of hopefulness. The anticipatory orientation of waiting for things to happen then comes with a hopeful edge.

We are dependent on all kinds of things, networked media included, and the devices we live with help to craft out both connections and disconnections with the world. The student essays, in describing lack of network connectivity as causing one to feel as if one is being cut off from the world and the people within it, speak to how dependence on network connectivity, which some are ready to willingly diagnose as an addiction—and hence as something debilitating—is central to one's very sense of agency. As an affective formation, dependency then becomes entangled with agency and potentiality. Rife with ambivalence and steeped in optimism and frustration alike, it emerges from the infrastructural roles and functions of network connectivity that underpin our capacities to act in the world.

3 Distracted: Affective Value and Fickle Focus

Focusing on news, entertainment, and pop culture, the clickbait site Distractify (est. 2013), faithful to its name, trades in distraction: "Distractify was created for you by a diverse set of Internet junkies who want wasting time to be more than just a waste of time. Through highly shareable video, trending news, and listicles, Distractify draws over 30 million people away from something boring (like waiting for the bus), tedious (like doing homework) or pointless (like every conference call) each month." Similarly to competing clickbaits such as Upworthy, BuzzFeed, Bored Panda, and ViralNova, Distractify traffics in spreadable media with the aim of capturing user attention and inspiring the further circulation of the content provided (Jenkins, Ford, and Green 2013). In a 2013 *Business Insider* interview, Quinn Hu, then the CEO of Distractify, explained the site's rationale: "The idea is to bring people closer through a shared experience…to make people feel an emotion that's universal. 'There's no agenda outside of that,' Hu says" (Dickey 2013). Despite Hu framing it as something of a modest proposal, the agenda of evoking universal, shared emotion is in effect a monumental one.

If one were to choose one key diagnosis recurring in debates concerning social media and networked communication more broadly, it would be that of distraction: for it is the power of social media and apps to distract that lies at the heart of the zeitgeist analysis of our being addicted to things that distract us to boredom. Furthermore, as Hu's interview suggests, the art of distraction comes tied in with the production and potential manipulation of affect. Distraction is, in most available diagnoses, framed as unequivocally negative and erosive in its compelling dynamics. Beginning with these diagnoses, this chapter sets out to paint a more complex picture. Taking a cue from Fredric Jameson's (1981, ix) imperative to "always historicize!," it sets out to do two things. First, it looks at the lessons to be learned from history in thinking through the rhythms of networked media and the ways of experiencing the world. Second, by considering the economies of social media in particular, it examines how distraction gets monetized and how affect becomes translated into data in the process. Framing distraction as a matter of rhythms, speeds, intensities, and qualities of experience, this chapter resists and rejects an understanding of distraction as the simple polar opposite of attention while further examining the affective economies connected to attention capture. Asking how value is extracted from affect *and* how affect also escapes such forms of capture, it then considers attempts at distraction management through mindfulness applications and "digital detox" retreats, and the affective modulation and manipulation practiced by social media platforms.

Value, according to the *OED*, refers to "importance, worth and usefulness; to material and monetary worth; to principles of behavior and judgments over what is important." On the one hand, the value of distraction in social media is about the generation of monetary value—for example, the value of Distractify as a start-up and with Facebook as its main engine of traffic, or the value of user data extracted from this traffic. On the other hand, value also entails worthiness for the users as intensifications of experience, clusters of interest, titillations and frustrations of distraction, the pleasures of sharing, and the interactions that this may engender.

For almost to two decades, the capturing of attention has been a key goal and rationale of the social media economy. Social media companies analyze clicks, likes, and shares as indicative of both user attention and the reach of sponsored content with the aim of appropriately pricing their targeted advertising plans and, consequently, for establishing their own net worth. This attention economy is equally a distraction economy. As perception is fragmented across various screens, windows, and apps, the aspiration to capture restless attention has become a central aim. In this framework, attention is understood as a scarce resource in a media environment characterized by an excess of available content, a valuable yet elusive immaterial commodity in itself (Crogan and Kinsley 2012; Goldhaber 1997; Terranova 2012; Webster 2014). According to a common horizon of expectation, "there will always be something online more informative, surprising, funny, diverting, impressive than anything in one's immediate actual circumstances" (Crary 2014, 59). The challenge for the individual user is then to find such captivating nuggets of data among all other available options—a task that can well be challenging. For those aiming to make their online content seen, the challenge is to somehow capture users' attention by grabbing them by the eyeballs and to distract them from whatever it is that they are currently doing.

Machines of Distraction

There are several ways to understand the concept of distraction. The first, and possibly the most common one, sets it in tension with attraction, "a quality or feature that evokes interest, admiration, affection, or sympathy" (OED). Distraction is thus "the drawing away (of the mind or thoughts) from one point or course to another; diversion of the mind or attention. Usually in adverse sense" (OED). On the one hand, distraction signifies the reorientation of attention, in varying speeds and degrees, so that there cannot be attention without distraction, and vice versa. On the other hand, the landscape of social media's attention economy operates as something of a political economy of distraction. Within the explicitly political applications of this economy, tactics of diversion reorient, shift, and lift attention with the aim of rerouting online public debate and, possibly, the directions that public opinion, participation, and representation take: as in fake news and organized trolling campaigns. Distraction is also a diversionary technique used to call attention to something else and as such something of a pervasive feature of contemporary political discourse where, arguably, President Trump has helped reduce the collective attention span of US citizens to 280 characters with his Twitter habits (Houpt 2018).

A second understanding of distraction is a "state of mental uncertainty" (MW), "being drawn or pulled (physically or mentally) in different directions by conflicting forces or emotions" (OED). Synonyms for such distraction in include "bafflement, befuddlement, bewilderment, confusion, discombobulation, fog, muddle, tangle, whirl" (MW), states that resonate with cultural diagnoses concerning the nefarious effects of "data smog" (Shenk 1997) feeding cognitive overload. Here, distraction comes across as a state of fuzzy mental uncertainty wherein focus is split, thoughts get aborted or jammed, and connections between things become lost. A third understanding connects distraction to heightened affective intensity as a "state of wildly excited activity or emotion" (MW) and "violent perturbation or disturbance of mind or feelings, approaching to temporary madness" (OED). In such states of inner turmoil, one may descend—or, depending on the perspective, ascend—into "agitation, delirium, feverishness, flap, frenzy, furor, fury, hysteria, rage, rampage, uproar" (MW). There is then a fair dollop of drama to the notion of distraction—as there is to its uses in cultural critique.

In his examination of distraction, Robert Hassan (2012, 191) argues that we are "becoming decimated by information" as the time scapes of immediacy and urgency, dominated by the imperatives of capital, make it impossible for reflexive discussion to evolve. Consequently, we are "condemned, through technological speed and social acceleration, to experience overstimulation and chronic distraction—a double negative that robs us, individually, of the knowledge that gives us power and agency and opportunity" (Hassan 2012, 160). For Hassan, as for many other critics, the speeds of online communication add to a dilapidating force that eats away not only at individual cognitive capacities but at the foundational principles of critical rational exchange on which modern societies are built (e.g., Lovink 2019; Pettman 2016). This zeitgeist narrative is nevertheless a strange one in that it now spans almost two centuries. Its contemporary reiterations build on a long trajectory of complaint concerning modernity and the diverse media technologies that it gave rise to, which have been seen to disturb, transform, and potentially destroy more authentic—and hence presumably more valuable—ways of being in the world. Diagnoses of distraction as a pervasive mode specific to industrial societies and urban cultures where things speed up too fast for human cognition to keep up have been on specifically ample offer.

Well ahead of the current textual wave, nineteenth-century critics expressed dis-ease toward what was then termed the "highway of thought" (Standage 1998, 1), namely, the electric telegraph. In his autobiographical reflection on living simply, American transcendentalist Henry David Thoreau (1854) complained how "our inventions are wont to be pretty toys, which distract our attention from serious things. They are but improved means to an unimproved end, an end which it was already but too easy to arrive at." At the time of his writing, the first cross-Atlantic telegraph cable was in the process of being set. Finalized in 1858, and after failure built again in 1866, the cable provided an alternative to written communication transported by ship between North America and Europe: electronic messaging that was startling in its unprecedented speed. For Thoreau, this emergent era of network connectivity—"the Victorian Internet" (Standage 1998)—was nevertheless not one of progress but rather one of distracted attention that fed an increasing trivialization of information. "We are eager to tunnel under the Atlantic and bring the old world some weeks nearer to the new; but perchance the first news that will leak through into the broad, flapping American ear will be that the Princess Adelaide has the whooping cough" (Thoreau 1854). In a similar fashion, German social critic Max Nordau (1898) decried the acceleration of temporality and its negative effect on the human body and psyche, from the speed of the railroad car to the mood of anticipation connected to newspapers fed by telegraphic information flows:

> All these activities…even the simplest, involve an effort of the nervous system and a wearing of tissue. Every line we read or write, every human face we see, every conversation we carry on, every scene we perceive through the window of the flying express, sets in activity our sensory nerves and our brain centres. Even the little shocks of railway travelling, … our suspense pending the sequel of progressing events, the constant expectation of the newspaper, of the postman, of visitors, cost our brains wear and tear.

In their tone and logic resonant with contemporary diagnoses of network culture, these nineteenth-century accounts point to the importance of historically grounded inquiry attending to repetitions and continuities—as well as gaps and novelties—in how the impact of media technology on "our sensory nerves and our brain," and on the society at large, is interpreted. They point to the necessity of veering away from contemporary exceptionalism by addressing both continuities and transformations in media culture and the ways in which it is being made sense of. This means building on, or at least working through, the tradition of (largely negative) critique of new media forms spanning from the telegraph to cinema, radio, television, social media platforms, and smart devices where the accelerating speeds of media are seen to feed focus that is fickle and fleeting at best. As Hartmut Rosa (2003, 3) argues, "Although there is a noticeable increase in the discourse about acceleration and the shortage of time in recent years, the feeling that history, culture, society, or even 'time itself' in some strange way *accelerates* is not new at all: it rather seems to be a constitutive trait of modernity as such."

In his 1903 essay "The Metropolis and Mental Life," Georg Simmel (2002, 110) outlined a modern urban affective formation where "stimulations, interests, and the taking up of time and attention, present themselves from all sides and carry it in a stream which scarcely requires any individual efforts for its ongoing." For Simmel, the acceleration of speeds of life in the modern city, combined with urbanization and mechanized forms of production and mediation, fed experiences of both distraction and boredom. Writing two decades later, Siegfried Kracauer (1995, 1998) theorized the "cult of distraction" as both an impediment to productivity and a form of pleasure within capitalist systems of mass production. Addicted to distraction, the urban masses fill "their day fully without making it more fulfilling" as cinematic "stimulations of the senses succeed one another with such rapidity that there is no room left between them for even the slightest contemplation" (Kracauer 1995, 325, 326). Kracauer, then, saw speed as erasing the capacity for reflection as people become hooked on the seductions of distracting films and radio shows. The mass culture connected to both the organization of labor and the media industry collapsed class-based distinctions between artful watching and mass consumption, resulting in a culture of sameness characterized by docile escapism. All this, for Kracauer (1998, 68, 91, 94), fed the uniformity of character and experience as general flatness where the propensity for distraction and glamour overrode deeper engagements with the world.

In a contemporaneous analysis, Walter Benjamin (2007) saw monotonous industrial work as giving rise to boredom, fatigue, and inattention while the forms of urban mass entertainment featuring eye-catching spectacles fueled the vagrant, flickering dynamics of distraction (see also Duttlinger 2007, 34). For Benjamin, distraction represented an absentminded mode of perception specific to modernity and its loops of mechanical reproduction. Both Benjamin and Kracauer considered film as facilitating novel forms of perception and sensation symptomatic to the fragmented, discontinuous, and accelerated speeds of modernity more generally (Poster 2002; Van Alphen 2007, 342–343). Benjamin, however, outlined distraction as an alternative mode of attentive engagement that teaches the audience to "take in the stimuli of modern life in a casual, detached state of distraction" (Duttlinger 2007, 42). For Benjamin, the tactile shocks catered by film went against the contemplative mode of reception characteristic of art forms such as painting. Arguing against the "ancient lament that the masses seek distraction whereas art demands concentration from the spectator," Benjamin (2007, 239) sought to understand these novel, casual, and distracted forms of perception:

The distracted person, too, can form habits. More, the ability to master certain tasks in a state of distraction proves that their solution has become a matter of habit.... Reception in a state of distraction, which is increasing noticeably in all fields of art and is symptomatic of profound changes in apperception, finds in the film its true means of exercise. The film with its shock effect meets this mode of reception halfway. The film makes the cult value recede into the background not only by putting the public in the position of the critic, but also by the fact that at the movies this position requires no attention. The public is an examiner, but an absent-minded one. (Benjamin 2007, 240–241)

Benjamin's conceptualization of cinema as a distraction-engendering medium prefigures some of the more recent analyses. His focus on the forms of attention afforded by media technology further resonates with Wendy Chun's (2016) discussion of habitual media as that which gains its impact in the course of mundane, routine use (see chapter 2). As different as such examinations are in their scope, context, and empirical evidence, they identify media as generative of modes of perception, experience, thought, and feeling. The concerns connected to distraction, as articulated in the context of diverse media technologies, share enough similarities to occasionally seem interchangeable, or at least to form a diagnostic narrative (and a very contingent affective formation) spanning almost two centuries. The media forms and technologies examined in such analyses are joined at the hip to capitalism, its organization of labor, and its forms of value production.

The late nineteenth century witnessed the birth of "neurasthenia" as a condition of nervous weakness and frenzy characterized by fatigue, irritability, and emotional unbalance caused by excessive stimulation within the accelerated money economy—something already hinted at in Nordau's complaint about the mental wear and tear brought forth by modern life. Coined in 1869 in the United States, the notion of neurasthenia signified the weakness of the "'nerve force,' that mysterious substance that gave vitality to the organism": "Many nineteenth-century physicians believed that the new urban way of life was producing generations of Americans with smaller reserves of nerve force and at the same time creating new and more intense strains, or precipitating causes, to threaten the individual from without" (Gosling 1987, x, 90). The causes and symptoms of neurasthenia were not entirely different from contemporary diagnoses of attention deficit/hyperactivity disorder (ADHD) and attention deficit disorder (ADD) identified as plaguing "digital natives," millennials, and younger people in particular (Aho 2007, 450–451; Duttlinger 2007, 33; O'Gorman 2015). Bernard Stiegler (2013, 82), like many others, sees the infantile psychic apparatus as being rendered fragile through "marketing...the armed wing of a financialized capitalism." Here, the industrialized exteriorization, materialization, and spatialization of memory connected to networked media are seen to cause novel, destructive forms of attention (and disorientation) that result in short-term attachments at the expense of long-term ones (Stiegler 2012a, 3; 2013, 83; see also Stiegler 2009). Stiegler (2013, 81) identifies digital networks as forms of psychopower producing "a constant industrial channelling of attention, and resulting in a new phenomenon: a massive destruction of attention, referred to by nosologists in the United States as 'attention deficit disorder.'" Considering 19th century neurasthenia, the current phenomenon diagnosed however seems less unique or novel.

In 1890, defining distraction as the opposite of attention, American psychologist William James (2012) characterized it as "a confused, dazed, scatterbrained state," saying, "As concentrated attention accelerates perception, so, conversely, perception of a stimulus is *retarded by anything which either baffles or distracts the attention* with which we await it" (James 2012, emphasis in original). James associated distraction with weakened capacities of perception as a retarding force that fiercely consumes attention spans. He did not, however, equate distraction with inattention or loss, as distraction could also inspire creative thought, passionate encounters, and affective connections with the distracting objects (see also Caliman 2006, 34). In his analysis of modernity and perception, Crary (1999) frames the issue somewhat differently by defining both attention and inattention as markedly modern notions connected to the forms of productivity operating within capitalism. Capitalist forms of production fuel incessant transformations and uncertainties in the workforce and in technologies of production yet simultaneously erode the possibilities of focused attention that capital's organization of labor requires. Capitalism, for Crary, generates attention as much as distraction through its accelerated speeds of circulation and sensory stimuli (see also Terranova 2012). These rhythms operate as if beneath the surface, on the level of infrastructure, modulating people's ways of being and fundamentally transforming social patterns and cultural practices in the process.

Modernity, for Crary—as for Simmel, Kracauer, and Benjamin—entails both novel speeds of perception and the accelerated circulation of sensory stimuli (see also North 2011). These require ceaseless adaptability on the part of individuals as part of an "ongoing and perpetually modulating process" that never pauses so that individual subjectivities can "catch up" (Crary 1999, 30; see also Adam 2003, 51; Bogard 2000). Such mutability requires continuing affective attunement and personal flexibility. Hassan (2012, 63) similarly argues that within capitalist markets operating in the perpetual present, "flexibility of the mind, the body, and attitude has grown imperative, resulting in rationalized and instrumental flexibility where the individual worker... is expected to correspond with and synchronize to the unpredictable and fast-flowing economic logic of neoliberal globalization." According to these assessments, both the restlessness of attention and the necessity to keep it in focus are built into the rhythms of capitalism (in both its contemporary and historical forms). When the sense of both the present and the future remains mutable, attention hovers around available options, calibrating potentialities that are, by necessity, distracting.

Shifting their focus among posts, GIFs, and video clips, social media users similarly enter zones of attention and distraction operating in fast registers of immediate, shifting parallel choices. In this landscape, distraction and attention intermesh to the degree of being virtually impossible to tell apart. In any case, as Crary (1999, 15) states, distraction and attention cannot "be thought outside of a continuum in which the two ceaselessly flow into one another, as part of a social field in which the same imperatives and forces incite one and the other." Understood thusly, attention and distraction are not antonyms or opposites but variations in the intensities and zones that perception and experience take. Writing on human perception, Lauren Berlant further points to attention's transience: "Attention travels and takes naps, cruises and makes tracks, puts a foot in the water and holds back demonstrably, wanders, and trespasses" (2015, 199). In other words, human attention is not steady and does not easily remain centered on one object alone. We automatically and continuously track changes in our environment which, in its digitally networked dimensions, operates in the logic of updates, refreshes, and alerts. Distraction is therefore something of a constant and is separable from attention only as degrees of intensity and speeds of attachment.

Are We Like Goldfish, or Even Worse Off?

A 2015 Microsoft research report on online marketing that deployed insights from neuroscience in order to measure Canadians' attention spans was covered in *Time* magazine with the catchy headline, "You Now Have a Shorter Attention Span Than a Goldfish" (McSpadden 2015). According to the report, between 2000 and 2013, human attention spans decreased from twelve to eight seconds whereas the average attention of a goldfish remained stable at nine. The report argues that multiscreening makes it more difficult to filter out distractions, fueling bottomless hunger for novelty. The erosion of long-term focus is seen as particularly severe among early tech adopters and heavy users of social media ages 18 to 24 (Microsoft Canada 2015, 4).

These findings would seem to support the more pessimistic accounts of human mental capacities decomposing to less than the level of a decorative fish: the report dramatically warns that "Social media can drain one's resources, reducing the ability to allocate attention, connect with content on an emotional level, and process information" (Microsoft Canada 2015, 40). Other neurological studies similarly indicate that heavy use of social media results in "memory deficits, attention disorders and emotional flattening," especially among young people (O'Gorman 2015). The rhetorically compelling comparison of attentiveness between people and goldfish alone rendered the report's findings the kind of distracting content that fuels social media traffic to begin with. This, again, speaks of the appeal of a *narrative* of loss crisis as compelling, clickbait-compatible content. Despite the broad, quick coverage that the report reached, the research data cited in it has been critiqued for vagueness (Miller 2016). Commenting on the study in a 2017 BBC interview, psychologist Emma Biggs further argues that "'average attention span' is pretty meaningless. 'It's very much task-dependent. How much attention we apply to a task will vary depending on what the task demand is'" (in Maybin 2017). If there is no average attention span to be measured, attention is situational and connected to a person's expectations, investments, interests, and attachments. "Some also suggest that evidence of ever-shorter shot lengths in films shows attention spans are dwindling. But the academic behind that research says all it shows is that film-makers have got better at trying to grab our attention" (Maybin 2017). Business writer Jason Miller (2016) similarly sees the trope of diminishing attention spans as a myth: "The overriding conclusion of the science on this is pretty clear: our attention isn't diminishing; it's becoming more demanding."

In the research Microsoft conducted, the capacity to filter out distractions and to sustain selective attention was not seen as affected *unless* multiple screens were involved. The ability to move among different tasks actually increased through multiscreening and heavy use of digital media correlated with improved alternating attention (Microsoft Canada 2015, 30, 37, 39). According to the report, those suffering from a lack of prolonged focus have increased short bursts of high attention and are better at processing and encoding information to memory (Microsoft Canada 2015, 19, 23). It then suggests that while sustained attention is growing more strained and elusive, especially among heavy users and multitaskers (see also Wajcman 2014, 104), the ability to process information simultaneously from multiple sources is on the increase. Its foreword certainly veers away from lament: "If there's no need to stay tuned in, why not move onto the next new and exciting thing for another hit of dopamine?" (Microsoft Canada 2015, 2).

The report, like much of the public debate connected to networked media, is concerned with neuroplasticity—namely, the basic ability of the brain to change throughout a person's life. Whereas authors such as Nicholas Carr (2010) associate such plasticity with the loss of cognitive capacity (Terranova 2012), this is by no means the only interpretative avenue available. For her part, N. Katherine Hayles (2007, 187) proposes that deep, extended attention on a singular object or task of the kind traditionally valued in learning is giving way to hyperattention as "switching focus rapidly among different tasks, preferring multiple information streams, seeking a high level of stimulation, and having a low tolerance for boredom." In her take on the contemporary overload of available information, Kristin Veel (2011, 308) equally refuses the narrative of cognitive erosion and digital dementia, arguing instead that "we often thrive with multiple inputs at a fast pace, whereas less input potentially results in distraction and boredom." It is also the case that different media forms and platforms involve specific speeds and patterns of attention that are off sync with one another. Although overarching diagnoses of neurological rewiring and the erosion of cognitive capacity propose otherwise, the rhythms of engagement, perception, and focus alter from one media form and interface to another. They vary both among different people and within their engagement with smartphones, tablets, and laptops; apps and sites; content ranging from long reads to animated GIFs; and from one instance and context to another. The same person can be minutely mindful or pay no attention whatsoever; be transient or immersed in his or her focus; be engaged in interaction or remain a detached lurker. One can move restlessly within and between sites in search for something to momentarily alleviate boredom, enjoy intensive marathon-like sprees of binge-watching entire seasons of series on Netflix, spend hours crafting a perfect mash-up video to be shared on YouTube, or engage in online multiplayer gaming sessions of *Fortnite* requiring hours of sustained, repeated attention. Different platforms organize temporalities in distinct ways, allowing for a range of rhythms of experience as "infrastructures of feeling" (Coleman 2018, 614; see also Pilipets 2019).

Those clicking and swiping in search of potentially fascinating nuggets of data at high speeds can then be equally immersed in best-selling novels, the lengths of which have not exactly collapsed during recent years: J. K. Rowling's seven *Harry Potter* novels (1997–2007) topping the sales charts with some 500 million sold copies span approximately 3,500 pages; E L James's *50 Shades of Grey* trilogy (2011–2012) extends to 1,700 pages; Stephanie Meyer's four *Twilight* books (2005–2008) encompass over 2,500 pages; and, in a commercially more modest framing, Karl Ove Knausgård's six-volume *My Struggle* (2009–2011), published in 22 languages, is 3,600 pages long. Reading these, whether on paper or on the screen of an e-reader, involves serious temporal commitment and stretches of focus; as audiobooks, they take as long as five and a half days straight, 24/7, to listen to. Unlike concerns over drastically atrophied attention spans would suggest, the lengths of Hollywood blockbusters have not shortened either: *Avengers: Endgame* (2019), the highest grossing film ever before *Joker* (2019, 122 minutes), runs for 182 minutes, the second runner-up, *Avatar* (2009), for a paltry 162. Meanwhile, authors lamenting the mass erosion of attention spans often do so in book length, as if indicating either their own immunity to such powers or their heroic fortitude in sticking with extended linear accounts in an age arguably characterized by their demise.

Should the narrative of digital dementia stand true, such long formats could no longer be popular, yet the contrary is the case: there is a multiplicity of overlapping intensities of attention at play. Radio and television, for example, can be turned on for background noise for domestic tasks or a session of laptop labor so that their presence is ambient, aiding a sense of focus. We can acutely pay attention to the programming or shift in and out of focus while fiddling with apps and searches. We can tweet and message when watching a TV show, a practice encouraged by producers themselves keen to insert interaction options into their programing formats. We zoom and zone in and out, engage with a range of devices, multitask, and prioritize the media objects we engage with. Acknowledging the persistent focus on distraction in cultural theory, Kristin Veel (2011, 310) identifies a qualitative difference between its nineteenth-century and contemporary organization: "It is only with the advent of ubiquitous digital information technology that the concept of attention takes on its present form, in which the ability to focus on more than one thing at the same time becomes so habitual that it can be regarded as a prerequisite of concentration rather than its opposite." Attention, then, is both divided and multidirectional at once, and hence always already to a degree distracted. As Jenny Sundén (2018, 70) further points out, in this techno-somatic context, divided attention allows for multiple parallel connections mixed in with distraction that "do not demand our full attention, but nonetheless make their marks." If the pervasiveness of media technology induces transformations in how we process, store, and share information, then the loss of focus, memory, or fullness of experience is not the only imaginable outcome. Some cognitive capacities may weaken and others strengthen. And, given the range of different media and applications involving their specific rhythms and speeds that people interact with on a daily basis, such transformations cannot be either simple or singular.

Writing on mobile telephony, Larissa Hjorth and Ingrid Richardson (2009, 32) address distraction as a state where "our attention becomes divided when we speak on the phone, send or receive a text message, or play a game on the mobile. It suggests that the locus of our perception is divided between the 'here' and 'there,' such that we can *know* different times and spaces simultaneously, an effect that shifts the boundaries of what immediacy is, and how it is defined and experienced." In this framing, distraction is less about the narrowing down or truncation of experience than it is about the multiplicity and simultaneity of experience as attention becomes attached to, and shifts between, multiple objects at once. In discussing interviews with habitual mobile phone users, Sharif Mowlabocus (2016) quotes their description of the distracted rhythms of scrolling and swiping as "meditative" and "comforting." Following this line of thinking, multiple impulses and parallel actions facilitate forms of focus, richness of experience included (a path of investigation continued in chapter 4).

In the following essay excerpt, composed by a then-22-year-old Finnish female student in 2014, the act of web browsing is pleasurable in its speeds and rhythms, yet simultaneously blasé or flat in its general disaffected modality: "Often when I have nothing to do, I surf online jaded. Occasionally I won't have the patience to do one thing at a time and online I usually have at least three, sometimes more than ten tabs open. Compared to that, it feels frustratingly slow and monotonous to focus on just one thing." Writing today, she might have way more than three to ten tabs open, yet the point would remain essentially the same: one of horizontally shifting focus searching for jolts of excitement. A sense of multiplicity, more than twoness, remains persistent within network culture: in multitasking, in the focus on a screen that lets us divide our attention between here and there, "in the caress of the point-and-click interface" affording conflation of routine chores and entertainment, and in the offer and expectation of both archival availability and immediacy (Petit 2015, 171). Parallel to the allure of abounding accounts on the erosive qualities this fosters, there is undeniable pleasure to the speeds and rhythms of divided attention.

The Microsoft research report concludes with tips targeted at online advertisers: "Be clear, personal, relevant, and get to the point"; "Defy expectations, keep it moving, and use simplicity to focus on your message"; "Embed calls to action, be interactive, continue experiences onto other screens, and use sequential messaging" (Microsoft Canada 2015, 47). The report provides highly concrete guidelines for creating value out of the rhythms of user experience as it oscillates between attention and distraction, or somewhere in between as gradations of fickle focus—that which Tiziana Terranova (2004, 19, 140) defines as distracted perception characteristic of network culture. Brian Massumi (2002, 139–140) similarly sees such the rhythms as particular to web browsing: "Link after link we click ourselves into a lull. But suddenly something else clicks in, and our attention awakens, perhaps even with a raised eyebrow. Surfing sets up a rhythm of attention and distraction." If, following Stiegler (2013, 81), we understand attention as connected to care, then the lack thereof translates as negligent, inattentive carelessness—the difference between the two being connected to how much we care, or are interested, in the exchanges taking place.

Making Things Sticky

One of Microsoft's proposed strategies involves grabbing attention by catering to the fascination for continuous stimulation: "When consumers are looking for something to care about at every moment, rapid fire tactics like branded content, native advertising and generally useful, entertaining, and shareable content are best" (Microsoft Canada 2015, 24). In addition to providing so-called sticky content for social—and optimally viral—circulation, advertisers are told to aim for clarity and catch users by standing out. Since attention is a commodity, user "preference for higher levels of stimulation" (Hayles 2007, 189) is obviously something to both fuel and monetize. Addressing virality, Tony D. Sampson (2012, 14) explains its contagious attraction of "mesmeric fascinations, passionate interests and joyful encounters"—that is, in instances of affective intensity. Although this perspective may be less pronounced in marketing discourses, the more negative registers of dismay, disgust, anger, and outrage can play an equally key role in how we engage with online content and contribute to its viral circulation: we can love to hate, and to express our hate together, just as we can navigate toward things promising to shock and appall.

Jodi Dean (2010) argues that uses of social media are more broadly driven by a search for affective intensity, which orients and provokes the interest and curiosity of users to move across sites and apps, to click, share, and comment. Intensity, or that which Dean, in her Lacanian framework, discusses as the drive, is the affective fuel for our actions. Understood in this vein, networked exchanges involve quests for some kind of jolt, a moment of interest, amusement, empathy, anger, or disgust—some kind of a shiver, some kind of a thrill. Such micro-instances of affective intensity are valuable in the sense of being desirable and having importance, no matter how fleeting, as well as in the sense of making things matter (Paasonen 2018a). The promise of such thrills is nevertheless contingent and regularly fails to deliver.

When things fail to tickle or distract, they are unlikely to grab any degree of attention—possibly resulting in flat sensations of boredom and disaffect (discussed further in chapter 4). Both affective and cognitive, desired and undesired, chosen and difficult to control, the patterns of distraction remain in flux. This ambiguity is where much of distraction's attraction and irksome force both lie. When browsing through Instagram, Chaturbate, Snapchat, xHamster, WhatsApp, Tinder, Facebook, Mashable, Grinder, Twitter, Distractify—or whatever it is that currently tickles one's fancy—attention quickly and constantly shifts, cruising and taking naps (Berlant 2015, 199). Much of the attraction of networked media derives from its power to divert, a point that Distractify's name already aptly encapsulates.

The principles of value generation connected to all this, while diverse, revolve around the pursuit of stickiness: as Tero Karppi (2018, 117) points out, "Social media are a factory of affect that actively configures the interactions and encounters happening on the platform." Simply put, the stickiness of sites and their circulated content is based on the ability to make people pay attention and engage (Hassan 2012). Building on Sara Ahmed (2004), stickiness is a matter of affective value that accumulates through the circulation of objects and signs. The more spreadable media circulates and the more people comment on it, the higher the affective value it can accrue. From the perspective of users, sticky content is that which does not simply slide by: the sensations it evokes cluster rather than dissipate. From the perspective of social media platforms, stickiness is key to harvest in order to give rise to "affective bonds" that keep users coming back (Karppi 2018). Understood in this vein, stickiness is a question of attention, appeal, investment, and circulation, and it results in the generation of affective, monetary, social, and/or political value. And distractions, of course, can be highly sticky as such.

The life span of memes, some of which go viral and the overwhelming majority of which fail to, is only one example of the dynamics of stickiness in action. As individual, aberrant, or "off" images or videos, or as potentially absurd variations on a set theme (Milner 2016; Phillips 2015; Shifman 2013), memes are primarily circulated in social media as diverting content that creates value for the platforms in question, and that can both challenge and conform to hegemonic cultural scripts (Vickery 2014). The stickiest of memes, from Grumpy Cat to Doge and beyond, increase in their value by becoming internationally recognizable brands that feed into material production as coffee mugs, fridge magnets, and T-shirts. The topic of distraction has inspired a plethora of memes itself, from the text-based "If I had a dollar for every time I got distracted, I wish I had a puppy," to *Toy Story*'s Buzz Lightyear pointing out to a grimacing Woody the "distractions, distractions everywhere," to a "first-world problems" meme where a woman in tears "went to the library to study to avoid distraction—smartphone has internet," and to a *Lord of the Rings*–inspired "One does not simply go to Mordor" meme with Boromir firmly stating, "One does simply study without being distracted by the internet." Coming in a broad range of variations, these memes position network access as a source of sought-after distraction that is hard to resist, and that is at once both titillating and dissatisfying.

Google Images search results for "distraction meme," https://www.google.com/search ?q=distraction+meme.

The temporality of social media is centrally geared toward the potential: things just around the corner. It is this imminent future promise, that which Massumi (2015, 60) identifies as having "a kind of felt presence, an affective presence, as an attractor," that drives us to check for updates, reactions, comments, and replies, time and time again, over and over, from one day to next. In this sense, social media foregrounds quick, near-immediate affective exchanges focusing on the present—as in the form of status updates descriptive of that which users are doing or thinking at this very minute (Gehl 2011, 1234). "What's on your mind?," Facebook asks its users. "What's happening?," Twitter wants to know. This present sense of things going on bleeds into the immediate future as anticipation of events, updates, and fascinating nuggets of data to come: distraction, after all, involves both the very present and that which is almost at one's fingertips. And as things keep on changing in the course of updates, new tweets, posts, and messages, both present and future possibilities remain under recalibration, resulting in what Rebecca Coleman (2018, 604) identifies as "the multiplicity of the present" involving constant movement, change, and flow.

Social media, like clickbait content, caters fast jolts while user attention tends to veer toward forthcoming tickles. Once experienced, such tickles will not, for the most part, be revisited: like old jokes, old memes and updates seldom retain their allure, and attachments to them are hence transitory. For their part, memes gain in resonance by circulating from one platform, audience, and user to another, as well as from the generation of new variations on a theme and template—not so much from users sticking with the same content or paying it much attention after the initial encounter. The temporalities of Facebook and Instagram stories, Snapchat, Jodel, and Periscope are connected to the liveness and transience, even if the data exchanged may linger and become repurposed. According to diagnoses of digital dementia and amnesia, the modality of distracted engagement, in its attachment to the contemporary and the imminent, involves no small degree of oblivion. Meanwhile, video sharing platforms, from YouTube to PornHub, comprise vast, unsteady archives where content available today may be gone tomorrow, where historical footage meets video clips just shot, and where novelties fight for attention with popular sticky content garnering millions of views.

Social media platforms equally function as personal prosthetic memory reserves of events, locations, and people stretching from the current moment to both the future and the more or less recent past as user data documenting interactions continues to accumulate. Jennifer Pybus (2015, 240) points out that the archives comprised of Facebook accounts "are highly specific, fragmented, and ultimately resist the coherence of a linear narrative." All this may involve frailness of remembrance in comparison to how it has more traditionally been considered, but also a tangible permanence of archived records of past actions and events, at least for as long as the platform in question exists. At the same time, the permanence and volume of data speak explicitly of how platforms track and analyze user actions over extended periods of time (Zuboff 2019a). As the current social media market leader with some two and a half billion active users, Facebook serves as a prime example of this affective economy. Despite its hegemonic status as a social media platform further enforced by the company's ownership of Instagram and WhatsApp, Facebook does not form a singular object but rather encompasses a range of practices, economies, and purposes, not all of which are organically connected to one another (see also Miller 2011), even as there is hardly reason to underestimate the service's degrees of governance over its users. Encapsulated in algorithmic operations and in end-user license agreements and community standards delimiting appropriate engagements, governance impacts how and what content becomes visible to users, how their data is mined, analyzed, applied, and sold, and how people can relate through screens (Gillespie 2018).

On the microlevel of quotidian use, the computational externalization of memory results in automated reminders that jerk back nuggets of data once posted back into the present, assigning them with potential relevance independent of their content or subjectively felt value. Events and posts layer on a personal Facebook timeline as linearly accessible for future engagement. Meanwhile, the platform literally feeds back past events and, in doing so, makes visible some of the tenacity of the data recorded. Users are invited to enjoy summaries of their Facebook year in review, to look back on their top images and posts of the year, to watch and share automatically generated videos of their monthly actions and interactions with friends, and to put past events into recirculation with first-person invitations, such as "We care about you and the memories that you share here. We thought that you'd like to look back at this post from 7 years ago." Invitations to look back and share past posts, links, and pictures shared, or to celebrate the anniversaries of Facebook friendships, appear uninvited in news feeds, and, should the user choose to use the "memory" function, they can be consumed as a daily digest. By re-invoking past events and posts that people may well have forgotten, Facebook frames all user activities as memories in the making that, once preserved in the corporate database, become eternally accessible for reminiscence. The automated pushing back of past data aims to increase the affective stickiness of the objects (and signs) suggestive of social ties, intimacies, moments, places, and settings as ones that have mattered, and that continue to matter—and that generate further clicks as indexes of attention—once back in circulation.

Such reemergence of things otherwise buried in steadily accumulating archives of posts, events, shares, and photos is an issue of algorithmic serendipity. As Karppi (2015, 225) argues, Facebook aims to cater serendipitous "happy accidents" that people may not know to expect and that they do not need to actively search for. In his essay on distraction for *The New Yorker*, journalist Sam Anderson (2009) writes of randomness as a defining feature of the internet more generally as it "dispenses its never-ending little shots of positivity—a life-changing e-mail here, a funny YouTube video there—in gloriously unpredictable cycles." The feedback loop of serendipitously reevoked Facebook memories aims precisely at such affective modulation, or amplification, in the positive register (Karppi 2018, 55–58; see also Massumi 2015, 31). These accidents cannot, however, all be happy ones. A post that Facebook invites one to look back at may well be written during

(partly owned by Robert Mercer, an American billionaire with close ties to President Trump). In addition, a reportedly limited number of people had also consented to the app accessing their personal timelines and personal messages (Revell 2018). While the majority of the users whose data was harvested illegally were American, Cambridge Analytica also amassed data useful to those organizing the leave campaign in the United Kingdom referendum, since known as Brexit.

News of the massive data breach led to Congressional hearings with Facebook CEO Mark Zuckerberg on the company's privacy policies, and the company's share price fell sharply. The degree of public, international dismay connected to the traffic in and the utilization of user data speak of disconnections in how the operating principles of the social media economy are known, understood, and made sense of. Despite the costs involved in having one's data leaked and sold, no massive Facebook exodus followed the controversy as such, even if people within the Global North (such as the students whose narratives are explored in this book) use Facebook less than they used to, despite the user base continuing to grow on a global level (Perrin 2018). Writing on the gay hookup app, Gaydar, Elija Cassidy (2016, 2614) uses the term "participatory reluctance" to describe voluntary engagement "when we would actually prefer not to or would rather do so under altered circumstances." People may have misgivings about a platform's entertainment value or data policy; they may dislike its specific interface design or its interaction options such as hashtags, stickers, emojis, or Pusheens; and they may merely feel too tied to its rhythm of updates, notifications, and messages. All this, however, does not mean that the people just stop using the service or app in question.

The affective intensities surfacing and fostered in social media both motivate people's actions and "contribute directly to the economic value of the media platform in question" (Jarrett 2015b, 205). In the framework of Marxist and autonomist theory, this dynamic has been identified as the exploitation of user labor for the extraction of surplus value (e.g., Fuchs 2011; Jarrett 2015a). Mark Andrejevic (2011, 279) sees exploitation for the joint purposes of fiscal profit and commercial surveillance as key to the forms of "alienation, manipulation, and control associated with the interactive economy." Manipulation, as evoked here, translates as exploitative control and unfair advantage, but equally as skillful planning, execution, arrangement, and play (see also Couldry and Mejias 2019). As the creation of value through attachment, intimacy, connection, and community, affective labor (Hardt and Negri 2001, 293) has been seen as key to how platforms aim to glue users to their interfaces. As voluntary content producers and affective laborers, users provide and share their data; the corporation profits. Meanwhile, the people updating photos of their lunches, pets, or muscle tone on Instagram may, of course, not identify their efforts as labor of any kind but rather as recreational, distractive, and enjoyable activities routinely pursued at the expense of, or parallel to, paid work tasks.

Nick Srnicek (2017, 40, 89) points out that on advertising platforms such as Facebook user data is the raw material to be extracted and processed, while user activities are the natural source of this material. The issue can be framed in terms of data colonialism, namely, the appropriation of "life as raw material *whether or not* it is actually labor, or even labor-like" (Couldry and Mejias 2019, 338). In this landscape, the capture of personal data is naturalized on platforms "that produce a new type of 'social' for capital: that is, the social in a form that can be continuously tracked, captured, sorted, and counted for value as 'data'" (Couldry and Mejias 2019, 341). As Nick Couldry and Ulises A. Mejias (2019, 346) emphasize, data collection and use are not a problem as such, but the problem lies in their exploitative applications.

Considerations of exploitation (as the extraction of surplus value or as a means of social control) are key in analyzing the politics and routines of monetization in social media, as they are in understanding the broad ramifications of the datafication of culture. The affective formations examined in this book emerge from this context, yet in order to more fully understand their ambiguities, it is necessary move toward the microlevel of mundane use. The clicks, shares, and likes made are always implicated in, and feed, an online economy where individual users operate "above all as boredom managers—agents who are responsible for, and capable of coordinating, the affective texture of their own experience as it unfolds in real time" (Kendall 2018, 81). Yet, following David Hesmondhalgh (2010), not all unpaid labor (such as the affective labors of social media users) can be equated with exploitation in that it also holds value to the people involved—by, for example, giving rise to new experiences, skills, and encounters. I then propose attending to an additional notion of value and worth connected to affective lifts and amplifications that make lives more enjoyable to live (these are further discussed in chapter 4 through the notion of microevents).

From a corporate perspective, user data only has value when coming in sufficient mass, and it only does when enough users feel that they are gaining something from their engagement: otherwise, why bother? Despite the qualitative nuances of data mined from singular users, this becomes valuable as a commodity only in quantitative terms as data points. Organizations and companies wanting more visibility for their sponsored messages can pay for boosting them or advertise to select audiences of handcrafted specifications varying in terms of interests, locations, genders, age groups, or virtually any other quantifiable variables. Sponsored content comes with a specific price tag depending on the product—that is, the form of user data—desired. For the data giants and advertisers alike, this tag marks differences between the scales and types of reach sought and the degrees of granularity of user data extracted, cleaned, and analyzed for the purpose. There is then a disconnection between the value that data may hold in personal terms—as indicative of what one does or likes or with whom one interacts or who one *is*—and the monetary value that can be extracted from it when aggregated with other users' data.

The notion of exploitation refers to an unequal exchange situation where one participant gets more out of the exchange than the other, and where workers are not sufficiently compensated for that which they produce. If the exchange in question takes place with incommensurable goods—as is the case with the value of data archives and the personal value of the exchanges taking place in social media—then measures such as "more" or "less" cannot be neatly established or applied. There is no easy commensurability in what is being exchanged, or in what the different parties may gain from these exchanges as such. These gains can be financial, social, cultural, affective, political, or any combination thereof. All this, of course, does not mean that the issue is one of fair trade. There is no symmetry between the parties involved, a data giant such as Facebook being an actor, or player, of a disproportionately different scale and impact than any of its individual or collective users.

Even if their massive archives of user data, as fantastically vast databases of consumer preference, still remain to be fully capitalized, the value created on the stickiest of services is considerable. Just before the 2018 Cambridge Analytica scandal broke, for example, Facebook's net worth reached a high of 630 billion U.S. dollars. In 2007, the then social media giant MySpace—soon to be overshadowed by Facebook—had 300 million registered users, and it was valued at 12 billion U.S. dollars. By the time it was sold in 2011, the price was down to 35 million (Rushe 2011). Similarly, Tumblr, valued at 1.1 billion U.S. dollars in 2013, was sold for a mere three million in 2019 after its ban of sexual content led to a mass exodus of users (Marinova 2019). In a highly literal example of attention economy, when user logins, visits, views, and clicks slow down or grind to a halt, stickiness evaporates and the company's monetary value collapses.

Writing about MySpace, Mark Coté and Jennifer Pybus (2007) point out how the immaterial labor of its users involved creating value out of affect. A similar dynamic was already at play in 1990s e-commerce, which built on the affective investments that users made and the value that their actions engendered (Jarrett 2003, 341). During the first dozen years of the World Wide Web (circa 1993–2005), advertisement-based services existed alongside and overlapped with widespread applications of subscription and membership fees. Well before the era of broadband connections, dial-up access could be priced per second or by fixed monthly fees. People paid for hosting services as well as for accessing membership-only online social spaces, some of which were run by telecom companies wanting to optimize the time spent online and the volume of data downloaded. In the 1990s, web "content producer" was an ephemeral new media profession that involved writing articles and creating polls and other sticky content with the aim of attracting users to spend time on the site in question. In the course of the 2000s and the shift to Web 2.0 and social media, content production became the task of users themselves. As Terranova (2000, 33) argues, "voluntarily given and unwaged, enjoyed and exploited" labor has been central to the web—and, by extension, to network culture—from the start. The subsequent centrality of social media users uploading, sharing, remixing, posting, commenting, blogging and reblogging, tweeting and retweeting represents less an abrupt rupture in the principles of profitability than a variation in operations encompassing the relatively short yet eventful history of the web itself.

If social media platforms "produce and circulate affect as a binding technique" (Dean 2010, 95), then affective ripples, releases, and reattunements are central to understanding their compelling qualities. As exchanges, posts, and connections layer, their aggregated stickiness creates value for the site or app in question. Selling audiences to advertisers is the operating principle of all commercial media, yet the social media economy is clearly distinct in the nuances of targeted advertising that it allows (see also Gehl 2011, 1239; van Dijck 2013). As the field of social media keeps on growing, user attention is increasingly difficult to grab even as its monetization is crucial to corporate survival. Within this flickering landscape, some see media audiences as "frenetic, self-concerned, attention-challenged, and willing to allow advertisers to track them in response to being rewarded or treated as special" (Turow 2005, 103). Agreeing to be tracked is part of social media services' terms of use and fundamental to their business plans. This, however, does not mean that people are keen and willing for their personal data to leak toward unknown uses.

Creepy, Leaky Data

Writing on communicative capitalism premised on the circulation of data, Dean argues that its massive accumulating flows eclipse the content of any single post or message. As part of a data stream, posts become decoupled from content, sender, and recipient alike, none of which really matter (Dean 2005, 58). This broadly McLuhanesque articulation of the medium, rather than content, as mattering may come across as pessimistic. This logic is descriptive of data traffic in the monetization of social media use, but it does not, however, follow that specific messages do not matter for individual or collective users, given that such particularities largely motivate their engagements in the first place. During the years following Dean's initial work on communicative capitalism, the centrality of surveillant sites and apps monitoring and manipulating users, their affective states and degrees of attention, has grown ever more manifest, just as it has continued to remain opaque. Bots churn out tweets for audiences consisting of other bots on massive scales, yet this is not really what generates profit for the platform in question, or even for the enterprises running the bots, given that such content rarely has much of a social reach—and hence actual impact (Paasonen, Jarrett, and Light 2019, 19–23). Individual posts can stand out from vast constellations of data or, as is much more likely, be buried within them.

The richness and density of user data archived and mined, the increased ease of analyzing unprecedented masses of it, and, centrally, the tenacious linking back of data to individual users as data shadows, are all key to surveillance capitalism (Zuboff 2015). The archived traces of user action give rise to algorithmic composites that can be tracked with self-monitoring apps and devices enabling affective, even prosthetic, connections with users' "data doubles" (Kristensen and Ruckenstein 2018; Ruckenstein 2014). All data shadows track, and hence capture, some use patterns over others. In the context of social media, these shadows gain agency of sorts in contributing to what algorithms, on the basis of prediction, will feed back to users.

Roger Clarke, writing in the early 1990s, coined the term "digital persona" to describe "data collections about individuals that are sufficiently detailed to be used as a basis for decision-making in lieu of dealing with the individuals themselves" (Clarke 2014, 183). Parallel to digital personae stored in state databases of the kind that Clarke addressed, the data shadows of social media—encompassing professional and recreational pursuits; shopping tastes, political leanings, and religious beliefs; travels, check-ins, and physical whereabouts—are virtual figures of considerable gravity. Their accumulation represents a qualitative shift in the readily available, mundane technologies of surveillance and analysis (Andrejevic 2013, 30–36). Corporate-owned aggregated user data are not open to public access any more than proprietary applications are subject to public regulation or control, or their routes and leakages available for individuals to track. As Srnicek (2017, 45, 95) points out, the more users a platform has—the larger it grows, the more data it collects and processes, and the more valuable and monopolistic it grows—the more value users get out of it in the options and connections that they can access. A tendency for monopolistic growth is thus inbuilt in the logic of advertising platforms as that which contributes to the richer density and finer granularity of data shadows.

It is impossible for users to control data traffic and leakage, despite their possible attempts to do so: Facebook tracks call history and SMS data without users' knowledge (and has, on occasion, listened to and manually transcribed their calls) while Google's Android phone is reported to transmit geolocation data even when it has been turned off and the SIM card removed (Collins 2017). Leakiness, in short, applies to all user data, whether personal or not. Users grab data, data grabs users, and user data is automatically grabbed. Default data leakage is inbuilt in all kinds of devices and apps and, as Chun argues, it forms the very backbone of information networks: "*Our devices, our computers, constantly leak. They are wonderfully creepy.* ... This leaking is not accidental; it is central. Without this constant exchange of information, there would be no communication, no Internet" (Chun 2016, 52, emphasis in the original). Given that data leakage is the default condition, its perceived creepiness has to do with how, and the purposes toward which, leaks happen.

There is certainly creepiness to the persistent, ephemeral, and haunting permanence of data shadows already as such. Exploring experiences of creepiness among mobile phone app users, Irina Shklovski, Scott Mainwaring, Halla Hrund Skúladóttir, and Höskuldur Borgthorsson (2014, 2347) define it as "an emotional response to a sense of wrongness that is difficult to clearly articulate" in a landscape where devices and apps "collect personal, sometimes even intimate information." As the study points out, the tracking and surveillance of users for the purposes of targeted advertising, location-based services, and wellness and fitness apps, as well as the leakage of user data to third parties without their awareness, all contribute to sensations of unease and discomfort (Shklovski et al. 2014, 2349). Yet discomfort concerning the relations of exchange involved does not necessarily inspire users to uninstall applications or to opt out from using them. Rather, data surveillance comes across as something like the price paid (Shklovski et al. 2014, 2353–2354). Further examining this privacy paradox between people's concerns and their behavior, Chanda Pelan, Cliff Lampe, and Paul Resnick (2016, 5240) identify creepiness as intuitive gut feelings that are met with "a subsequent deliberate weighing of costs and benefits."

The overall balance of the exchange—the total price of it all—involves no small degrees of ambivalence and experiences of mistrust. There is persistent creepiness to data flows, as there is to leaky data shadows entailing a liveliness of their own. Cassidy's (2016) notion of participatory reluctance foregrounds such lingering unease and affective ambiguity in engagements with social media that the tropes of both autonomous user agency and exploited data serfdom are inept to cover. Quivers of creepiness are further amplified by awareness of how companies aim not to merely capture and divert user attention but to track, analyze, and manipulate their affective registers (see also Andrejevic 2013). Consider, for example, news leaked of Facebook's pending "emotion-based technology" patent application in 2017, well ahead of the Cambridge Analytica incident. The patent's rationale was to craft ever more tailored content and advertising by making use of laptop, tablet, and smartphone cameras to observe users without their awareness or explicit permission. Journalist James Billington (2017) explains, "The purpose behind the invasive idea is to analyze people through the camera in real time while they browse online and if it recognizes you looking happy, bored or sad, it would deliver an advert fitting your emotion. If you were forlorn, for example, it would be able to serve an ad to perk you up, or know what products you had previously looked at online and put them under your nose at just the right time." As the algorithm would recognize user moods and reactions to specific content—such as the ubiquitous kitten video—through visual tracking, it would learn either to feed or not to feed similar content in the future while also maneuvering opportune moments for targeting adverts to those appropriately attuned. Involving obvious ethical issues connected to user privacy, this patent is part of a larger constellation of affective tracking technologies either under planning or already in use. Facebook's listed patents include, for example, one connected to "a text messaging platform to detect a user's mood by measuring how hard and fast they were typing, then augment the message format, such as adding emojis or changing the font size, to match their emotion" (Billington 2017).

While these solutions remain virtual, the widely reported 2012 Facebook emotional contagion study made evident the weight and significance placed on affective management. The study, conducted by a team consisting of a Facebook staff member, a Cornell psychology professor, and a graduate student, involved experiments with 689,003 users and analysis of some three million posts consisting of 122 million words. The team tweaked the algorithms selecting the content visible in users' news feeds and manipulated them to show either more or less positive or negative posts. The overall aim was to assess how such manipulation affected the users' emotional states, which they would verbally express in their updates analyzed by the team. On publication, the study (Kramer, Guillory, and Hancock 2014) garnered unfavorable attention as it was conducted without the users' informed consent. For, contrary to the research group's claims, such deployments of data were not covered by Facebook's terms of use (see also Jarrett 2015a, 118–120).

According to the study's hypothesis, "emotional states can be transferred to others via emotional contagion, leading people to experience the same emotions without their awareness" (Kramer et al. 2014, 8788). The study divided emotions roughly into either negative or positive, by necessity obscuring nuance: irony and sarcasm, for example, are not easy to make sense of with text mining tools. The finding was that emotions—or moods—could be made to catch on, spread, and stick, even if the manipulation was conducted on a relatively modest scale. The experiment speaks of the routine and increasing trend of "digital mood modification" (Coyne 2016, 1–2) within social media whereby "technological platforms can be used to control and modulate intensities on a presubjective level" (Karppi 2018, 116). Such explicit attempts at transforming affect into data to be tracked, analyzed, circulated, manipulated, and monetized point to the centrality of affect within the social media economy (see Karppi 2018, 114–118; Sampson, Ellis, and Maddison 2018).

News of Facebook's emotional manipulation experiments and pending patents geared toward tracking and manipulating users have traveled widely through news and clickbait sites. As was the case with the Cambridge Analytica scandal, such news has been broadly shared, recirculated, and commented on via Facebook itself. In another reverberation of participatory reluctance and creepiness, people regularly use the very services that disturb them to complain and to express outrage over their policies, interests, and inclinations—generating additional data traffic and thus additional profit for the company.

Affective Modulation

In February 2016, Facebook introduced an additional range of reaction options in addition to the "Like" button that had been in use throughout the service's first decade. The novel options also allowed for reacting with "Love," "Haha," "Wow," "Sad," and "Angry." According to Facebook Product Manager Sammi Krug (2016):

> We've been listening to people and know that there should be more ways to easily and quickly express how something you see in News Feed makes you feel. That's why today we are launching Reactions, an extension of the Like button, to give you more ways to share your reaction to a post in a quick and easy way.
>
> Our goal with News Feed is to show you the stories that matter most to you. Initially, just as we do when someone likes a post, if someone uses a Reaction, we will infer they want to see more of that type of post. In the beginning, it won't matter if someone likes, "wows" or "sads" a post—we will initially use any Reaction similar to a Like to infer that you want to see more of that type of content. Over time we hope to learn how the different Reactions should be weighted differently by News Feed to do a better job of showing everyone the stories they most want to see.

As Krug points out, reaction options translate as markers of attention. At first, no distinction was to be drawn between the different options deployed when considering their attention value, yet the eventual purpose was to modulate users' news feeds toward showing more posts that they are predicted to react positively to: to ramp up those likes, loves, and hahas. The other obvious key aim was to identify finer granularity in users' engagements with commercial content. According to Krug, "We see this as an opportunity for businesses and publishers to better understand how people are responding to their content on Facebook."

Reaction buttons aim to qualify the affective dynamics of online exchanges and to render them into categorizable and analyzable data. The key goal is to harness these analyzable affective qualities for value production by helping commercial parties to fine-tune their advertising and PR campaigns, as well as by tweaking users' news feeds to prioritize content that they are likely to find sticky in a positive vein. *Tech.Mic* writer Jack Smith IV (2016) was quick to point out that "for every little inch of emotional nuance we gain from these buttons, Facebook gains a mile in the ways it can manipulate and keep tabs on us." By feeding users with more of that which they assumedly like or love, from the diversions of Distractify to news items resoundingly echoing one's own political sympathies, Facebook is likely to generate more of the same and, paradoxically, pave way for flattened affect by homogenizing accessible content. The principle of homophily, according to which similarity attracts (and, consequently, amplifies) similarity, is central to network science and, consequently, to how connections get organized in social media (e.g., Chun 2018; Grevet 2013; Leeker 2017; McPherson, Smith-Lovin, and Cook 2001). This, again, means the further amplification of filter bubbles and echo chambers as social connections and exchanges among the similarly minded who like the same posts and are outraged by similar content, allowing limited room for difference and conflict (Chun 2018, 86). There is certainly pleasure to be taken in sameness, yet it also comes with lackluster effects of predictability and dullness. And, as already suggested by the

Like   Love   Haha   Wow   Sad   Angry

Facebook's reaction options in 2016.

foregrounding of positive reaction options to Facebook content, in social media homophily comes steeped in, and geared toward, default positivity.

In a well-known 2013 incident, BuzzFeed's book editor, Isaac Fitzgerald, announced that negative reviews would not be published (Garfield 2013). The logic was that BuzzFeed caters to user satisfaction. It aims to please, this aim foreclosing other than positive engagements with literature. In a variation of the old repressive maxim to remain quiet unless you have something nice to say, if you do not like what you read, do not review it—or at least do not publish the review. This speaks of what Richard Grusin (2010, 4, 127) identifies as social media's general aim to minimize negative affect— for example, through the default reaction options of liking and loving. The steady accumulation of positive BuzzFeed reviews and uplifting clicks provides distractions from the grinding routines of school, family, and the office. In a world where good news seems to be hard to find, affective modulations divert attention away from the relentless flows of insecurity, fear, and sorrow connected to the news coverage of austerity politics, global terrorism, war, climate change, coronavirus, and tensions in international and domestic politics that otherwise haunt news feeds. They can make everyday lives more livable through small affective lifts, and as such they hold subjective value (Page 2017, 76; chapter 4).

At the time of President Trump's inauguration in January 2017, the affective landscape of Facebook had been divided and inflamed for months and has remained so in the years that have followed. The presidential race split and polarized users into distinct camps well beyond the borders of the United States while the circulation of fake news through social media was argued to have influenced the election outcome (in connection with the Cambridge Analytica scandal). The affective intensities fueled by news both fake and less so kept amplifying with the aid of filter bubbles, and with Trump's motions such as the introduction of the so-called Muslim travel ban, links soon began to circulate on "How to Block Political Posts on Facebook & Survive 2017" and "How to Block Annoying Facebook Political Posts." By this time, chain copypasta challenges on "occupying Facebook with art" had been in circulation for some years, with their themes ranging from music to poetry. In February 2017, yet another chain began to circulate, this time with the description "The idea is to occupy Facebook with art, breaking up all the political posts. Whoever 'likes' this post will be given an artist and has to post a piece by that artist, along with this text" (ACC Art Association 2017). This attempt at social, potentially viral, content management translated equally as affective management in that pictures of art blossoming across Facebook would allow for breaks from the otherwise strained and unhappy circuits of political coverage, making the environment lighter and, possibly, happier. A similar dynamic has been evident since the outbreak of the COVID-19 pandemic in the spring of 2020 as users share not only news items covering the latest of developments but also pictures of their pets and memes sarcastically commenting on the frantic hoarding of toilet paper for affective balance.

The rationale of the clickbait site Upworthy (est. 2012) has been to provide an alternative to the mundane flow of bad news of the kind mainly covered in the media by focusing on "stories that delight, uplift, surprise, evoke empathy, and motivate action" instead. Known for its left-leaning political tendencies that grew increasingly explicit after Trump's election, Upworthy was identified as the fastest growing media company in its year of launch (Williams 2015). Launched in 2019 with the musician David Byrne as its figurehead, Reasons to be Cheerful, an online editorial project described as "tonic for tumultuous times," follows a similar logic as "part magazine, part therapy session, part blueprint for a better world." Promising to offer rescues from the despair marking the current moment, the site hopes "to balance out some of the amplified negativity and show that things might not be as bad as we think" (in Arcand 2019). Upworthy and Reasons to be Cheerful both trade in cautious optimism connected to alternative means of social organization, offering positive affective modulation through curated links and editorial content aimed at viral circulation.

Efforts at affective modulation and manipulation are inseparable from the quest for attention capture that organizes the political economy of social media, from Facebook's practice of feeding past memories back to users to Microsoft's interest in advertising strategies catering to their fickle focus, and to diverse methods of diversion deployed on clickbaits, porn sites, shock sites, and beyond. Porn aggregator sites such as xHamster or Pornhub, for example, promise to cater to highly specific tastes through increasingly fine-grained search options afforded by metadata detailing the acts, positions, and performers within any video clip while also feeding users novelties and recommendations from their seemingly bottomless reservoirs of data. Shock sites like Specialfriedrice or Hai2U feature the intentionally disgusting and offensive to lure user attention by recursively attracting and repelling them—be it through gore, violence, or other displays of human bodies deemed disturbing (Paasonen 2011, 207–241). Meanwhile, enterprises focused on the cute, such as I Can Has Cheezburger?, offer avalanches of animal memes, images, and videos aiming at affective releases and lifts in the positive registers of affect (Page 2017). On clickbait sites, attention harvesting is equally tied in with affective management, or modulation possibly bordering on manipulation—as in Distractify's Hu's promotional entrepreneurial agenda to "make people feel an emotion that's universal." Despite drastic mutual differences in the forms of content offered and the affective ranges that these sites are designed to evoke, their overall logics of attention capture are akin to one another.

Clickbait content appears at the bottom of news sites as promoted links aggregated through advertising platforms such as Outbrain: as in "This Game Will Strain Your Brain to Think Strategically;" "50 Eye-Opening Facts About Europe 90% of People Don't Know;" and "Mac User Warning: The Only Providers You Should Trust To Protect Your Mac" algorithmically curated for my titillation via *The Guardian* at the time of this writing. Interested users understand that these elusive link galleries may be gone tomorrow: hence there is immediacy to knowing what most people do not know, or whom to trust with my laptop, lest these resources be soon gone. Clickbaits organize their affective address around compelling images of shelter dogs needing adoption, cats exhibiting idiosyncratic tendencies, tattoos and amateur baking projects gone horribly wrong, and tests making it possible to see which celebrity, fictional character, plant, or food one most closely resembles. Some clickbaits approximate shock sites, others rely on captivating headlines, and all aim at virality. Across their mutual differences, clickbaits gravitate toward that which might come across as surprising, amusing, disgusting, uplifting, or revolting enough to catch mercurial user interest.

The boundary between clickbaits, news and media websites, and journalistic news outlets—for example, that between Upworthy, BuzzFeed, the *Observer*, and *The New Yorker*—has grown convoluted in the sense that journalistic outlets fight for user attention with attention-grabbing headlines and clickbaits offer coverage of current events with the aim of doing the same. In its editorial outlook, Reasons to be Cheerful alone blurs such classifications. It is therefore central to understand the logic of clickbaits beyond the most common outlook, according to which they feed flatness, triviality, and distraction, achieving little else than detrimental effects. Clickbaits can certainly be flat, trivial, distracting, and irritating, yet this is not all they can be. Affective lifts or viral reach do not necessarily come at the expense of social engagement, and there can be considerable gravity to the temporal releases and affective reorientations that clickbaits offer. As Sharif Mowlabocus (2016) points out in the context of mobile telephony, "They are products of our environment, and they are the method by which we cope with that environment." There is fundamental ambiguity to all this.

Tracking Distraction and Happiness

Digital work, from video editing to writing and professional communication, is conducted on the same devices that provide distractions via social media. Notifications of new e-mails, messages, and posts call for attention during other engagements, and the active desire for jolts of interest, amusement, and diversion equally drive users' distracted attention from one source to another. The seductions involved in the splitting and shifting of attention are such that a number of work efficiency applications have been developed for shutting down online access for limited periods of time in order to ensure sufficient focus and performance (Gregg 2015). The names of these apps—from Freedom to Anti-Social, to LeechBlock, to RescueTime—promise freedom from social media that otherwise snags away our time and focus with its compellingly distracting force. Developed and marketed for the purposes of attention management, these apps are equally and interchangeably ones of distraction management. RescueTime beckons us to rescue time because "With so many distractions and possibilities in your digital life, it's easy to get scattered." We can further "Live a healthier, happier, more well-rested life with Headspace" as the always-on app tracks and provides pop-up advice on meditation and mindfulness.

Considered in the context of the accelerated rhythms and speeds of life, as addressed by Crary (1999), and the restless meandering forms of attention that they fuel (Wajcman 2014), these apps are valuable in temporarily cutting the user off from the flow of updates, requests, and fascinations. By barring online access, the apps truncate users' options for engaging with their devices and, by doing so, force degrees of focus upon their actions—suggesting that network connectivity itself constitutes something of a problem. This market comes intertwined with that of meditation, mindfulness, and happiness apps promising personal tools for coping with the fast tempo and routine of contemporary life.

MoodKit, for example, offers to help "boost your mood," to "discover unhealthy thought patterns," and to "change stress-inducing thoughts." Calm, again, features "guided meditations, nature sounds, and a step-by-step guide to finding that all-too-elusive peace of mind…when the fast-paced world gets a bit too much" (Johnson 2015). Spire, the by now defunct mindfulness and activity tracker, promised to help people de-stress and find calm by monitoring their breathing, stress, and activity levels. Ironically, given the degree to which alerts requiring, or grabbing, one's immediate attention are argued to cause stress as distractions, Spire operated by sending its users such alerts reminding them to do breathing exercises to ward off stress, as in "You seem tense. Time to clear your mind" (Choi 2015).

In accordance with the neoliberal imperative of personal productivity, Spire—like Mood Kit or Calm—promised to help individuals manage their lives, the speeds and conditions of which keep them from fully thriving. At the same time, such apps not only operate in accordance with these same speeds and conditions but build their market demand on them. Offering "proven techniques" developed by "leading scientists and experts," Happify is an app for achieving nothing less than control over one's affective and cognitive states with the aid of activities and games. "How you feel matters! Whether you're feeling sad, anxious, or stressed, Happify brings you effective tools and programs to help you take control over your feelings and thoughts." The rationale of Happify is to track and measure emotional well-being and to transform lives for the better by reducing stress and increasing positive emotions through the lessons of positive psychology, also known as "the science of happiness." Connected to a doctoral research project, the Track Your Happiness app similarly promises to unlock the secrets of happiness:

> For thousands of years, people have been trying to understand the causes of happiness. What is it that makes people happy? Yet it wasn't until very recently that science has turned its attention to this issue.
>
> Track Your Happiness is a new scientific research project that aims to use modern technology to help answer this age-old question. Using this site in conjunction with your iPhone, you can systematically track your happiness and find out what factors—for you personally—are associated with greater happiness. Your responses, along with those from other users of trackyourhappiness.org, will also help us learn more about the causes and correlates of happiness.

Like the permanently thriving market of self-help literature, a quintes-sentially American genre with global resonances (McGee 2005), these apps trade in affective management connected to the goal of self-improvement. They promise methods based on scientific evidence and systematic track-ing techniques for achieving the both alluring and normative goal of hap-piness. In her critical examination of the happiness imperative, Ahmed (2010, 7) argues that it gathers force through its factual unavailability. The quest for happiness has, for Ahmed, become something of a duty requiring both affective and moral labor, rendering happiness simultaneously a gen-eral wish, a social imperative, and an elusive pursuit. Happify and Sphere are instrumental tools, objects that "acquire their value as goods, as far as they point toward happiness.... If objects provide a means for making us happy, then in directing ourselves toward this or that object, we are aiming somewhere else: toward a happiness that is presumed to follow" (Ahmed 2010, 26).

Happiness and well-being apps are optimistic objects in promising path-ways to future happiness if properly and tenaciously used. Their monetary and moral value, as happiness goods and "happy objects," is based on the elusive pursuit of happiness-to-be through self-tracking, self-monitoring, and self-improvement taking place in the present. At the same time, happi-ness is something to be largely recognized in retrospect—as that which has already been, and which has since passed (Ahmed 2010, 27). Addressing the promises of a good life—and indeed, that of happiness—Berlant (2006, 2011) identifies "cruel optimism" at the core of neoliberalism. Cruel opti-mism refers to the fundamental ambiguity involved in affectively investing in objects that actually keep one from thriving—as in neoliberalism's prom-ises of the good life that it fails to cater. It does not require a vast associative leap to connect the markets of mindfulness and wellness apps with such promises which, both alluring and cruel, keep people in their aspirational clasp through promises of happiness within reach.

Mindfulness exercises, which have strongly entered the market of self-management tools as a variation of happiness goods, are introduced to employees of tech companies for finding calm and focus. Meanwhile, offline retreats are offered for the executives of such companies for restor-ing their work productivity that suffers from the stress and toll of devel-oping distracting devices and apps (Levy 2016; Syvertsen and Enli 2019). Companies such as The Digital Detox market off-the-grid experiences of

"growth, reflection, mindfulness, creativity, community and (dis)connec-
tion." With no access to smart devices, customers can do yoga and mindfulness exercises, go hiking, and enjoy organic meals, all under the slogan
"disconnect to reconnect" (see also Karppi 2018, 4, 109). The Digital Detox
offers a controlled break from ubiquitous connectivity where work pen-
etrates leisure or where boundaries between the two may have ceased to
exist. It further promises its customers "insight into personal lifestyle techniques and practices that keep them grounded and connected even in the
most stressed, overwhelming and technologically driven times."

In their discussion of digital detox discourse and the promise of authenticity, Trine Syvertsen and Gunn Enli (2019) note its similarities to traditions
of media and technological resistance connected to other communication
technologies for over a century while also highlighting the differences
involved. Rather than aiming to restrict harmful media content as such,
digital detox discourses "point more to individual responsibilization and
self-optimization," and, unlike shorter media fasts recommended in the
context of television, they "rest more on a presumption of balance that is
akin to mindfulness; temporary breaks are seen as a vehicle to heighten consciousness and learn self-regulation in order to reduce stress and increase
the presence here and now" (Syvertsen and Enli 2019, 2). Detox is promised
as solution to a felt shortage of time. In what Judy Wajcman (2014, 4) identifies as "a time-pressure paradox," feelings of harriedness lead to a sense
of acceleration where time simply feels to be running out even when the
"consensus among time-use researchers is that leisure time has, if anything,
increased."

The rhythms of work and leisure, tied in with uninterrupted connectivity, near-instantaneous communication, and the ready availability of data,
are beyond the powers of any single individual to influence or control.
As argued in chapter 2, the option of not operating within them—of simply opting out—remains inaccessible to most of us. It has nevertheless
become the responsibility of the individual to develop the necessary skills
and techniques required for coping and holding on (Hassan 2012, 81,
121). The demand for such life skills is understandably ample, not least
within the tech sector where professionals design alluring interfaces and
gamified forms of connecting with the aim of keeping users engaged, if not
hooked. Companies such as Digital Detox, just like the developers of mindfulness, happiness, and work efficiency apps, unavoidably draw their circle

of profitability from the very same distractions that they are promising to help their customers cope with. Just as mobile phones, for Mowlabocus (2016), support "the 'speed fetish' of late capitalism" while also providing "an escape mechanism from it (however illusory that escape might be)," the market of wellness and happiness apps operates with a circular logic.

To paraphrase Jacques Derrida (1981), there is then something pharmakon-like going on in the sense that the antidote resembles the drug, the cure offered is very much like the poison, and the cause is very similar to the remedy. A pharmakon, for Derrida (1981, 70), operates through seduction and comes with "this charm ... this power of fascination, [that] can be—alternatively or simultaneously—beneficial or maleficent." Consequently, it is "a force whose effects are hard to master, a dynamics that constantly surprises" those who aim to decipher it (Derrida 1981, 97). Mindfulness and wellness apps developed for sheltering users from the distracting pull of other applications act as distractions in themselves and operate with similar, engrossing techniques of self-tracking and self-quantification.

It can be further argued that networked media operate as both pharmakon and as *pharmakos*, scapegoat—an object or an actor that is seen as a symbol of corruption threatening societal order and well-being (Derrida 1981, 130; Stiegler 2013, 20). Apps can both erode and rejuvenate our attention spans while networked media in general, and social media in particular, takes the role of scapegoat for the broader conditions within which all this occurs—as in the zeitgeist narratives that this book examines. According to the overall premise of detox, these conditions can be ameliorated by purging individual and collective lives of digital content, attachments, and devices. Digital detoxes and cleanses are marketed as aids to contemporary malaise, with the idea that once the external pressures of connectivity are removed, one's inner, authentic self, along with authentic forms of sociability, can be restored (Syvertsen and Enli 2019).

However, as Derrida (1981, 103) argues, the pharmakon disturbs boundary maintenance between not only the remedy and the poison but equally between "good and evil, inside and outside, true and false, essence and appearance." If networked connections and smart devices are understood as prosthetic and habitual in their uses, and as infrastructural in their everyday functions, as argued at some length in the previous chapter, then a neat division between the inner and the outer cannot hold (see also Stiegler 2013, 108, 110). Contemporary infrastructural dependencies on networked media are such that few propose simply abandoning it in favor of other, earlier forms of communication and information management and retrieval. At the same time, as pharmakon, it is regularly perceived as toxic in ways requiring individualized regulation and rehabilitation (e.g., Seymour 2019).

Distraction and Affective Ambiguity

Distractify claims to generate universal, shared emotion, Upworthy and happiness apps aim to optimize positivity, and Facebook explicitly aims to track and modulate affect. Such attempts at the transmission of affect (Brennan 2004) are, however, necessarily volatile and disjointed. Reaction options or words written in a Facebook post, for example—of, say, loving or hating a song, a politician, or a specific dish—do not quite translate as, or speak of, how or what we feel, or what interests and attachments drive our actions, for all this is grounded in a much more complex nexus of personal histories, life events, surroundings, and encounters, many of which may not find their expression in language at all. Clicking "like," "love," "wow," "haha," or "care" on a post provides the platform with easily analyzable data, yet much of user experience remains permanently inaccessible to datafication (see also Jarrett 2014).

As a rich body of social media scholarship has shown, that which people disclose and share, with whom and how, results from strategies and decisions concerning audience management and self-presentation (e.g., Ellison and boyd 2013; Light 2014; Zhao et al. 2013). Social media updates, reactions, emojis, and comments are not transparent or immediate expressions of personal feeling as much as knowingly crafted displays of, and invitations to, certain forms of interaction. The modes that these interactions take can be studied, just as their affective tone can be modulated and monetized by platforms controlling the content available to users. All this does not, however, afford access to the nuances of experience, social ties, emotional investments, or affective intensities as such.

The distractions of social media cannot be confined to positive affective management for the reason that their allure owes equally to disturbing properties and mixed feelings. Writing on play, Miguel Sicart (2014, 3) points out how the pleasures it generates "are not always submissive to enjoyment, happiness, or positive traits." The same applies to social media, the attraction and value of which involve diverse intensifications of experience. These may involve the management of self-image, the hopeful pursuits of marketing, the tortuous dynamics of trolling or romancing, the heated waves of polarized political debate, or aggressive, collective displays of resentment felt toward a public figure (Paasonen 2015b). A joint object of hate alone sticks people fast and firmly together, motivates much posting, and fuels the flows of data (Chun 2018, 84–85). Contrary to any straightforward happiness imperative, the affective economy of social media is centrally one of diverting pleasures yet not necessarily one of sheer fun, for "joy and sadness, anticipation and anxiety intermingle in digital connectivity in ways that make them bleed and blend into each other" (Sundén 2018, 64). Pleasures, as intensities of feeling, can be elusive, strained, and dark; ambiguous and paradoxical—and this may well be where much of their appeal lies (see also Coyne 2016, 98–100). Attempts to ramp up positive affect within the compulsory promise of happiness do away with the entanglement of diverse, ambiguous intensities that make social media engaging.

The same goes for the affective formation of distraction. Distraction entails momentary intensifications of experience wherein attention gets disrupted and shifts. As such, it is connected to Silvan Tomkins's affective dynamic of "surprise–startle" orienting attention away from one thing to the next, and ranging in its intensity from mild surprise to the more intense and sharp forms of startle. For Tomkins (2008, 273), surprise–startle is a neutral affect that interrupts current activities and reorients one's focus. Startle is sharp, surprise less so, and both reset and reorient the body that can then continue to move within all kinds of affective registers. Clickbait sites and much other social media content aim at surprise—and, in the case of "shock and awe" content, at startle—and such intensities are very knowingly sought out. As discussed in the following chapter, all this can involve momentary releases from seemingly stifling boredom by resetting the body and adding to its overall sense of liveliness. These surprises and startles fuel data capitalism but also generate affective value that is not fully contained in its logics (Page 2017, 79).

The extraction of value from distraction, attention, and distracted attention takes many shapes and forms, some of which are more contorted than others: from digital detox retreats to mindfulness exercises and apps designed to help individuals cope with the dictates of constant accessibility. Value is equally extracted by grabbing user attention through marketing campaigns and by fostering the stickiness of apps and sites in order to increase the volume of clicks, likes, and shares. Such forms of value creation tap into the modulations of affect, from the feeding back and repackaging of previous user activities as memories to be cherished and recirculated, to attempts at manipulating the forms and tones that future encounters and connections take. Much of this modulation has to do with an imperative of positivity, as encapsulated in the like and love buttons used across social media, in clickbait sites' foregrounding of uplifting posts, or in the increase in positive feelings promised by happiness apps.

Attempts to map and modulate user experience make evident the forms of algorithmic affective governance operating in social media. Such governance, while involving human intention in setting the parameters, takes nonhuman forms in curating our sociability—basically, the ways in which we can relate to one another and to diverse nuggets of data, and how these interactions are optimized for the purposes of data mining and targeted advertising. They make it possible to grasp the degree to which this sociability is never merely human borne but a complex assemblage, or composite, of algorithms, information architecture, databases, links, and files, as well as the all too human investments of money, interest, curiosity, and care.

The affective formation of distraction gains shape through a plethora of cultural diagnoses—ones reaching toward the immediate future and others harking back to the nineteenth century—while also being urgently felt on an individual level. Both discursive and affective, distraction is associated with the crisis, rupture, and erosion of attention, yet, as suggested in this chapter, attention and distraction are better considered as matters of oscillating speeds, rhythms, and intensities. When understood as differences in degree rather than those in kind (Bergson 2007, 299), attention and distraction entail cadence, timbre, rhythm, and intensity through which focus moves, grows, and becomes diluted according to platform and context, resisting confinement as binary categories.

4 Bored: Flatness and Enchantment

"Why is social media so boring?" "Why am I so bored with my life? Why is social media so boring?" Posed anonymously on the question-and-answer site Quora, in January 2019, these two rather existential questions seek solutions to life lacking in excitement, with peer advice suggesting for the queriers to give up social media, to listen to classical music instead, or to just do social media in a better way. More than isolated cries of distress, the queries are connected to broader concerns about the affective affordances and effects of social media where the trope of boredom never looms far away. According to Tina Kendall (2018, 81), boredom comes across as a ubiquitous "condition of collective lethargy, flat affectivity, and stalled anticipation that we routinely experience, express and seek to displace through our engagements with networked media."

On the one hand, social media is broadly offered as a solution to boredom, as with the clickbait site Boredom Therapy, defining itself as "a media startup founded with the goal of *fighting boredom worldwide* by engaging our readers with incredibly sharable content. We are on a mission to discover the most extraordinary and inspiring stories from around the world, and share them with our audience." As Kendall (2018, 80) points out, Boredom Therapy, along with other similarly named clickbaits like Bored Panda and Boreburn, positions boredom "as a global epidemic that may strike anyone, anywhere, at any moment" while promising to dissolve the problem through its steady supply of spreadable, diverting content. In doing so, these sites "work to ensure that by the time we recognise that we are bored, we are always already-no-longer bored—or at least not in quite the same way" (Kendall 2018, 85). On the other hand, the habitual uses of networked media—and, as in the Quora questions

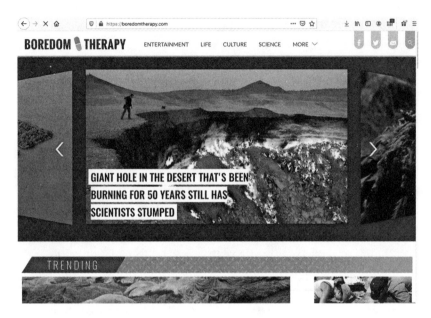

boredomtherapy.com.

cited above, social media—are regularly identified as being boring as such (e.g., Lorenz 2018).

In a yet another reverb of the pharmakon (and the pharmakos), networked media can then be the remedy, the poison, and the scapegoat all rolled into one, fluidly occupying multiple discursive positions at once (Derrida 1981, 125, 127, 152). Social media can promise rescues from boredom or be a fundamental bore; it can afford self-medication for those suffering from depression; it can be the root of depression itself; or, in a vicious cycle, do both (see Seymour 2019). As in diagnoses of distraction, the form of argumentation connected to boredom and networked media goes back decades to analyses presented in the context of cinema, television, and nineteenth- and twentieth-century modern urban life wherein boredom was considered prevalent and as characteristic of the historical moment. Networked media (like urban modernity) is seen to cause boredom through its excessive, distracting stimulations—by distracting us to boredom—while commercial actors are prone to frame it as a cure for the boredoms of life.

This chapter considers the affective formation of boredom through the grand narratives of modern urban disenchantment to more contemporary retellings, foregrounding the intertwining and mutually constitutive dynamics of affective flatness, interest, and enchantment. Setting out to challenge the bleakness and generality of most narratives on offer, it questions the ways in which their subjects and objects have been construed. Furthermore, by foregrounding microevents that rupture the boredom of everyday life, it examines how the flatness of feeling bleeds toward disaffect and enjoyment alike, and it sketches out instances of sensory richness connected to networked media. Finally, extending to the role of boredom in pedagogical practice, the chapter inquires after the productivity—or, put in less instrumental terms, the pleasures—of boredom. Throughout all this, I insist on the importance of holding onto ambiguity when disentangling the affective formation of boredom.

Modernity Was Boring, and So Is the Present

Boredom is generally conceived of as an affective desert comprised of flatness, nothingness, blandness, and blah. Most simply put, boredom signifies being "wearied, suffering from ennui" (OED); "having one's patience, interest, or pleasure exhausted;" being "fed up, jaded, sick, sick and tired, tired, wearied, weary" (MW). The bored may be waiting and wishing for a shift in the affective state—a change to something else, anything but this—yet nevertheless remain caught in a state that is as apathetic as it is uninterested; dejected and dispirited; drained and worn-out; frustrated and blasé; glutted and satiated. The mass of meanings connected to boredom, selectively presented here, map it out as simultaneous saturation, deflation, and exhaustion.

Scholars of boredom have a rather harmonious shared understanding of its symptoms. In boredom, "significance of world and self drain away, motivation ceases, and even the temporality of our existence is altered in a strange way: Nothing seems to happen and thus time seems to stand still" (Slaby 2010, 101). Boredom then involves liveliness, temporality, speed, and potentiality coming to a halt in "a situation where none of the possible things that a person can realistically do appeal to the person in question" (Mann and Robinson 2009, 243; see also Mann and Cadman 2014, 165). Life itself seems to be at risk of lessening (Anderson 2004, 740) to the degree that one can no longer quite act in the world. "To be bored is to be paralyzed: emotionally, spiritually, and perhaps even physically" (Thiele 1997,

492). Boredom amputates agency by sucking away interest and excitement: "The bored subject cannot make or does not find his or her situation meaningful. Such boredom is experienced as an irritating emptiness, a desire for something unknown to relieve the claustrophobic, enervating sense of time passing slowly. The experience of boredom is painful and agitating; it is a prolonged sensation of a hollow within or emptiness without" (Pease 2012, 4). In instances where the distractions of networked media seem dulling, nothing manages to lift the expanse of emptiness. As "a corporeal irritation or restlessness, an agitated inertia in response to a current situation that holds no interest, both temporally and spatially" (Hjorth and Richardson 2009, 32), boredom makes people feel uncomfortably stuck. For Ben Anderson (2004, 739), it "takes place as a suspension of a body's capacities to affect and be affected forged through an incapacity in habit." If, for Silvan Tomkins, *I am, above all, what excites me*, then boredom stands for the lack of excitement and, indeed, for a fundamental lack of appetite that undoes the self.

It then follows that boredom is not an affect but rather a matter of affective flatness, lack of intensity and interest that dilutes a sense of meaning from life. Psychological literature differentiates between "trait boredom," as the individual propensity for a given individual to experience boredom, and "state boredom," occurring "when an individual experiences both the (objective) neurological state of low arousal and the (subjective) psychological state of dissatisfaction, frustration, or disinterest in response to the low arousal" (Vogel-Walcutt et al. 2012, 102). This division delineates between individual capacities and contextual factors: some people are more easily bored than others, yet situations can be boring, too. Meanwhile, cultural theory tends to frame boredom as resulting from the speeds, rhythms, and possibilities specific to a historical moment, its societal organization, and its technological makeup, and hence as an issue and result of contextual circumstance. Boredom runs, in different shapes and forms, through cultural diagnoses connected to both media and modernity in ways suggesting it to be an affective formation in its own right.

During the 1964/1965 New York World's Fair, science fiction author Isaac Asimov (1965) offered a series of speculations about the world fifty years into the future: in 2014, he suggested, work will be automated, freeing people to live lives of leisure, yet mankind will suffer badly from the disease of boredom, a disease spreading more widely each year and growing in intensity. This will have serious mental, emotional and sociological consequences, and I dare say that psychiatry will be far and away the most important medical specialty in 2014. The lucky few who can be involved in creative work of any sort will be the true elite of mankind, for they alone will do more than serve a machine.

Indeed, the most somber speculation I can make about A.D. 2014 is that in a society of enforced leisure, the most glorious single word in the vocabulary will have become *work*!

Asimov's speculation sketches out boredom imposed on individuals as being caused by enforced leisure resulting in the lack of a meaningful, productive engagement with social and commercial worlds. The burdens currently faced seems quite different from those of Asimov's prediction, considering the range of work practices, forms of exploitation connected to them, and the felt infiltration of work into spheres of leisure through the flow of e-mails, updates, and alerts requiring attention, engagement, and response (Gregg 2011, 2018; Page 2017; Wajcman 2014). The age of automated labor and artificial intelligence servitude is not, after all, quite here yet.

Ubiquitous boredom connected to increasing automation of society, as proposed by Asimov, is in fact not a particularly bold or original future predication to make, given the recurrence with which it has been diagnosed in connection with modernization, urbanization, and modern capitalism. Boredom was diagnosed as a—or perhaps even *the*—major experience of modernity as the nineteenth-century *mal du siècle* (Anderson 2004; Goodstein 2005, 94, 137). The perceived acceleration of speeds of life was seen to not only distract but to bore, as in "the monotonous landscape of the railway journey, the numbing repetition of factory labor, the unnatural, hollow rhythms of unfamiliar urban life" (Goodstein 2005, 121, 160–161). For Walter Benjamin (2002, 108, 109), boredom as a mass phenomenon "began to be experienced in epidemic proportions in the 1840s" as "weariness with life, deep depressions, boredom" resonant with the rhythms of spinning and weaving mills. In her monumental analysis of boredom, Elizabeth Goodstein (2005, 1) defines it as an effect of modernity, "both the disaffection … that drives the search for change and … the malaise produced by living under a permanent speed-up." Understood in this vein, boredom signifies both a perceived lack of personal meaning and disaffection felt toward one's material conditions of existence (Goodstein 2005, 406).

Contemporaneous analyses characterized the late nineteenth century as involving a superabundance of stimulation where things moved at an ever-increasing pace, where time was money, and where, in Marx and Engels's famous phrasing, "all that is solid melts into air." Boredom, fatigue, melancholy, and neurasthenia all figured as symptoms of a crisis in desire and meaning (Goodstein 2005, 19, 94–95, 99). In examining "the intensification of emotional life due to the swift and continuous shift of external and internal stimuli" and the "rapid telescoping of changing images," Georg Simmel (2002, 103) saw them as resulting in boredom: as there was, at any given moment, too much to take in, nothing really stuck and therefore mattered. For Simmel (2002, 104), the fast tempo and the violent sensory disruptions of urban life, paired with a sense of emptiness caused by "the fluctuations and discontinuities" of the money economy, gave rise to a blasé outlook of indifference resulting from an inability to react and to engage (see also Wajcman 2014, 50–52). Such a state of "nervous indifference" (Aho 2007, 455) made it impossible to distinguish between different things encountered, bringing forth a sensory overload of sorts. The resulting indifference was seen to lead to a homogenization of sensation, lack of emotional response, and general flatness. As discussed in chapter 3, diagnoses of neurasthenia sprouted from this landscape as precursors to current conditions of ADHD as a disorder where attention keeps on splintering without holding onto a clear goal or target.

Martin Heidegger (1995, 108), a philosopher very much engaged with the topic of boredom, distinguished between "being bored by something and being bored with something," as well as a third variation, that of profound, existential boredom: "Boredom is still distant when it is only this book or that play, that business or this idleness, that drags on. It irrupts when 'one is bored.' Profound boredom, drifting here and there in the abysses of our existence like a muffling fog, removes all things and men and oneself along with it into a remarkable indifference. This boredom reveals beings as a whole" (Heidegger 1997, 99). Boredom, for Heidegger, was a matter of temporalities of existence that become transformed, or somehow warped, revealing something much more expansive about one's very existence, its nothingness and finitude (see also Slaby 2010). Rather than uncovering some unchanging essence or selfhood, deep boredom makes evident the degree to which moods "determine not only how the world matters to us, but, to a great extent, how this mattering will be played out" (Thiele 1997,

498). Heidegger, like many others before and after him, saw boredom as the "pervasive and dominant mood of our times" connected to "contemporary lust for technological innovation" (Thiele 1997, 490, 504). In yet another reiteration of the pharmakon, "Despite technology's vast capacity for generating novelty, it largely operates in collusion with boredom.... Technology feeds off this mood of boredom and at the same time suppresses the very opportunity for its overcoming" (Thiele 1997, 491). The solution, for Heidegger (1995, 79–81, 131), was not to escape or conquer boredom. He rather proposed facing it, along with anxiety, head-on, by reflecting one's conditions of existence.

For Goodstein (2005, 99), the frenetic rhythms of entertainment have merely increased since the early twentieth century, leading to a "contemporary terror of boredom, which testifies to its apparent inevitability." Kevin Aho (2007, 447) similarly argues that indifference, flatness, and boredom emerge from hyperstimulation and result in "a pervasive cultural craving for immediate amusement, risk, and peak sensations." Building on Simmel, Aho (2007, 459) sees modern disenchantment with the world as leading to a compulsive search of intensity through instant pleasures that nevertheless fall short of filling the emptiness of people's lives. According to this theory of desensitization and dumbing, "an existence based on experiencing intense pleasure quickly reaches the point of diminishing returns. In today's hyper-accelerated world, what is novel and exciting today no longer excites the nervous system tomorrow; yesterday's pleasures become boring and uninteresting" (Aho 2007, 457). The logic is similar to Schopenhauer's in identifying the satiation of desire that brings forth boredom: "Boredom is the consequence of the frustration of a peculiar desire to desire, or to be interested: the empty longing for a new desire is languor, boredom" (Reginster 2007, 22).

A focus on the unending anticipation of novelty was equally key to Neil Postman's (1985) account of the gradually increasing speeds of electronic communication, from the electric telegraph to television and the concomitant shift from a typographic print-based culture to one of televisual immediacy. For Postman, the birth of modern news media brought forth by the introduction of the telegraph involved a new conception of newsworthiness, one referring to current events across the world. Before the latter part of the nineteenth century, newsworthiness had to do with what was directly relevant in terms of a person's life, such as deaths and births in one's close vicinity and family, or drastic changes in the weather. Postman saw the new speed of electronic communication as paving way for a novel sense of meaningfulness and importance. As international or national news detached from the immediate life worlds of people became news, things happening far away, and hence impossible for one to influence, became newsworthy. With the invention of television, things, for Postman, only got worse, with people's attention spans shortening and their critical capacities being numbed by the hegemonic imperatives of entertainment. Things simply become clutter the faster the rhythms of media grow: according to Postman's well-known, decidedly pessimistic book title, we are "amusing ourselves to death." While a live political debate in the nineteenth century could last for a large part of the day and include elaborately scripted and memorized speeches, twentieth-century televised debates would last an hour or so, filled with interventions and quickly rotating snippets. It is more than easy to draw a connection to tweets, 280 characters in length, as a current form of political communication and exchange.

Writing on the speeds and mandatory updates that characterize new media, Wendy Chun (2016, 1) argues that these result in near-instantaneous cycles of obsolescence: demos are fascinating but, once launched, the actual products are not; interesting and definitive analysis always arrives too late as things have already moved on, and hence "We are forever trying to catch up … bored, overwhelmed, and anxious all at once." According to the argument spanning from mid-nineteenth century to the current day, nothing sticks as things fly by too quickly for us to grasp, and as the anticipation of novelty makes things within reach seem dull (see also Coyne 2016, 4). The overt saturation, pervasiveness, and accelerated speed of media environments have been lamented for decades, with the overall idea that the more stimulation there is, the flatter things get, the more difficult it is to focus, and the more boring everything becomes. Very well. But is this all there is to it? Why should the increase in available information and knowledge about the world be a matter of loss by definition? Why does there seem to be such uniformity of opinion so that all this involves a default loss in focus, rational capacity, and relevance? On what basis should we assume that premodern life free of electronic media was not experienced as boring, dull, or flat? How can it be argued that people's lives were simply fuller and more meaningful before the introduction of electricity or networked media?

Against a Master Narrative

There is considerable drama and seduction to descriptions of hyperstimulation, "terror of boredom," "nervous indifference," and homogenization of sensation, from Simmel to more contemporary authors. It is in fact rare to come across analyses of the quotidian rhythms of networked media that do not veer toward cultural pessimism, or even hopelessness. Like most generalizing diagnoses of culture, they hold appeal as "strong theory," namely, that which Tomkins (2008, 519) identified as a "theory of wide generality...capable of accounting for a wide spectrum of phenomena which appear to be very remote, one from the other, and from a common source." As Eve Sedgwick (2003, 134–135) notes, strong theories are strong by virtue of both producing and necessitating unambiguous results. Firm in their premises, they also tend to be totalizing in their outcomes (these being very similar to the premises), even when lacking in evidentiary basis.

As a strong theory, the narrative of modern boredom and flatness does away with nuances and diversities of experience—thus failing to capture or acknowledge their complexity. Jane Bennett (2001) positions Max Weber as the key author of the grand narrative of disenchanted modernity. For Weber, disenchantment was fueled by the enlightenment, advances in science, and the increasing dominance of rational worldviews that resulted in a general flattening of experience and loss of fullness: gone were the wonders of religion, the enchantments of magic, and the captivations of fantasy. Weber's narrative of disenchantment is connected to the overruling principle of calculability (Bennett 2001, 59). The contemporary moment of pervasive computing, massive server farms, data archives, and ubiquitous network connectivity seems to represent an acceleration and overdrive of such principles. The notion of disenchantment at the heart of Weber's narrative of modernity stands for "a kind of subjective malaise, where the romantic longing for an authentic reunification of the meaningfulness of the world is no longer an option" (Johnsen 2011, 487). Bennett (2001, 3, 63–64) forcefully critiques this narrative for discouraging affective attachment with the world while positioning itself against a lost age of magic that, "under the haze of nostalgia," becomes an object of desire.

The story of disenchanted modernity comprises something of a master narrative that postulates a premodern, agrarian, idealized moment of meaningfulness, emotional richness, and sensory fullness that is required as a contrast to later developments—one that the people articulating it, or reading the analysis, can have no firsthand access to. Empty lives only make sense in relation to something much fuller, just as distracted modes of attention presume preceding modes of sustained clarity of focus of the kind that are unlikely to have ever existed. Similar problems are inherent in Goodstein's (2005, 420) broad discussion of "rationalized modern world in which the present has been abbreviated into oblivion—in which experience itself has atrophied."

Counter to the conceptualization of disenchanted modernity entailing accelerating, mechanical speeds and social dispersion and isolation, there must have been a premodern realm of more authentic and communal life (as indicated in Ferdinand Tönnies's division between *Gemeinschaft* and *Gesellschaft*, community and society, made in the 1880s and later developed by Weber). In all this, premodern life operates as something of an unstable object of retrospective nostalgia. Looking at the issue more closely, we know that in premodern Europe, societies were caste based, people's social and physical mobility was highly limited, social hierarchies were drastic, and rights to physical autonomy belonged to very few: many were virtual, or actual, slaves. Wars were common, as was scarcity of nourishment. People died young and rarely saw much of the world beyond their own village. This picture of social life could, just as well, be defined as one of stratified stuckness. In geographical locations such as Finland, winter months allowed for few daylight hours, which, modes of lighting being few, were spent in semi-darkness confined to dwellings shared with extended family and possibly livestock. Since very few could read or had access to books, and as theater and other popular spectacles were largely limited to touring groups and urban centers, this lack of mobility became combined with little stimulation except for that which the immediate environment could provide—as in the stories, anecdotes, and jokes told by one's relatives, day in and day out. Urban life, in contrast, afforded social mobility, as encapsulated in the saying "City air makes you free" (*Stadtluft macht frei*), referring to the medieval Germanic law according to which serfs became free men after dwelling in a city for a year and one day. The premodern enchanted world of magic, religion, community, and fullness of meaning à la Weber can just as well be defined as one where people lived in constant fear of superhuman powers, sickness, and natural conditions alike—all this depends on the kind of past we choose to imagine as a contrast to the current moment.

Meme shared on Facebook, November 2019.

In premodern and early modern societies—should we diagnose the current one as late modern (e.g., Fornäs 1995)—universal human rights were yet to be coined, political rights belonged to a select few, and not many people had the option to pursue a life of their interest separate from familial ties dictated by social caste, class, gender, and normative heterosexuality governed through matrimonial ties connected to land ownership. To argue this is not to advance some neoliberal paean for individualism gone rampant; it is instead to argue for foregrounding equal civil and human rights in how we consider social and cultural transformation. It is also to argue for distinguishing between an assumption, or fantasy, of life as it may have been during previous centuries and decades and the lived realities as these may or may not have been documented. Nostalgic longing for a better time past tends to come at the cost of ignoring social hierarchies, as well as with the

rhetorical necessity of imagining hypothetical, and hence to a degree fictitious, forms of experience. For, as Benjamin (1996, 391) once asked, "With
whom does historicism actually sympathize? The answer is inevitable: with
the victor. And all rulers are the heirs of prior conquerors. ... Whoever has
emerged victorious participates to this day in the triumphal procession in
which current rulers step over those who are lying prostrate." If history is
written from the perspective of the victors, by foregrounding the views and
experiences of the ones in power as Benjamin suggests, it remains crucial
to question any generalization concerning experiences of everyday life in
centuries past.

Modern boredom has been associated with the invention of leisure and
the spread of *ennui* since the nineteenth century with its increase across
social strata. Consequently, Leslie Paul Thiele (1997, 492) argues that ennui,
historically identified as a condition of the ruling classes, has become a
dominant cultural mood as a "product of idleness that has lost its meaning, or rather idleness that has lost its capacity to generate meaning"—an
idea not too distant from Asimov's prediction for life in the year 2014. Following this line of thinking, ennui was once a plague of the powerful with
ample time on their hands while the so-called peasants, tied to the grind of
physical labor, were excluded from its grasp, and nineteenth-century bour-
geoisie was newly suffering from its effects. However, although the English
word for boredom was not in use before the nineteenth century, this does
not necessarily mean that experiences of boredom did not exist before this
point in time, let alone that all other languages in the world would have
lacked similar concepts. I find it questionable to argue that premodern life
was not boring, or that only members of the social elite were familiar with
the numbing effects of boredom, for this is something that we simply cannot know. Arguments can be made of the overall dynamics and realms of
life available to people in a particular historical moment. To build one's
argument critical of contemporary culture on them is another thing. It is
yet another thing to postulate particular kinds of subjects in and for all this.

Subject to Boredom

Let me briefly consider the narrative of boredom and modernity, as nar-
rated in connection with urbanization, industrialization, and the rise of
modern capitalism, from the perspective of gender. The default subject

of narratives of modernity has generally been male so that the male has functioned as neuter representative for people as a whole. For this subject, boredom resulted from alienation caused by capitalist systems of production and conditions of existence where familial and communal ties had been severed or disturbingly altered. It should however equally be asked what role differences between subject positions play in this, as well as how the sites and subjects of boredom may have been differently distributed: Who, in these accounts, gets to become bored, out of what, and why? Who is boring, what is boring, and where is it boring to be? Whose boredom counts, and how?

On the one hand, it is the modern city, with its abundant urban flicker and monotonous life within commodity capitalism, that, for Simmel, distracts people to boredom. "The boredom of everyday city life is the boredom of the assembly line, of one thing after another, of pieces locked in an infinite series that never really progresses: the more it changes, the more it remains the same" (Langbauer 1999, 131). On the other hand, the discourse of modern boredom often either lacks a specific subject—implying that these experiences are of the shared, collective kind, and hence apply to all—or is exemplified through bored white men of the higher social classes. Looking at modern literary fiction on boredom, Laurie Langbauer (1999, 143) notes that it was also the women, and not just the urban city, that were seen as the cause and source of male boredom in gendered "fantasies of confinement and escape." Meanwhile, Allison Pease (2012, vii; also 1–2), writing of boredom as an early-twentieth-century structure of feeling, argues that modernist literature rather foregrounded and explored women's boredom as "emptiness or deadness, a lack, or simply passive dissatisfaction" connected to social realities:

> Open a novel written in England between 1900 and 1940, and the odds are you will encounter a bored woman. Modernist literature is replete with women reclining on sofas, muttering to themselves on trains, moping about country villages, rolling dental papers in offices, pouring out tea and stifling yawns while engaging in small talk.... In its simplest form, boredom is the inability to find interest or meaning. As manifest in British representations and discussions of women in the early twentieth century, boredom can appear as emptiness or deadness, a lack, or simply passive disaffection.

Pease argues that the figure, or trope, of female boredom was inseparable from women's struggle for public participation and equal human rights. In this framework, boredom resulted from difficulties in "accessing authenticity, productivity, and desire—all qualities attributed to one's success as an individual" (Pease 2012, vii). Within the broad narrative of modern boredom, women became objects of particular concern not only in literature but equally in popular journalism, medical, political, and psychoanalytical texts in connection with truncated opportunities for acting in the world, as drawn along the lines of gender (and, I presume, equally along those of social class, age, and race). The trope of female boredom then involved a critical edge, as did the cultural imaginary of postwar suburbia as a site of profound boredom: consider, for example, Betty Friedan's (1963) influential *The Feminine Mystique*, which associated suburbia with deep discontent and meaningless concerning (white, middle-class) women's limited sense of agency (Burns 2011; Johnson and Lloyd 2004; Pease 2012, 120).

The modern city could, then, be boring, just as it could offer alluring alternatives to the utter boredom of suburbia. Men could be bored by leisure, by modernity, or by women. Women could be bored by the limitations set on their lives; commodity capitalism could be a bore, or the root of boredom could be found in sexism and gendered relations of power—and so on, and so forth. In all instances, as Pease (2012, x–xi; also 23) argues, the subjects of boredom have come as particularly construed, valued, and gendered:

> Women...were bored, without viable selves to access truth or meaning. Bored women were put under the care of medical professionals who diagnosed them as neurasthenic, pathologically unfit to pursue their own interests in the world, and prescribed bed rest—more boredom—as a cure. Female discontent was given neither philosophical nor political legitimacy, but rather was pathologized and relegated to the body. Where male ennui is of the cultivated soul, ennoblingly individualized, women's boredom is of the singular, pathologized body.

In the cultural diagnoses that Pease analyzes, the experiences of some (men) were afforded depth and meaning of the kind refused to others (women). A similar division is at play, for example, in Siegfried Kracauer's (1995, 292) discussion of "little shopgirls" going to the movies and "Little Miss Typists" modeling themselves on characters seen on the cinema screen: here, female subjects are not even allowed sufficient internality to be able to experience boredom. In their enjoyment taken in "stupid and unreal film fantasies," little shopgirls are paradigmatic subjects representative of mass culture—indeed, as generic and flat as the films that they so avidly and uncritically consume (Kracauer 1995, 292; see also Kendall 2018, 82–83; Lacey 2000, 283). Such conflation of lack of psychological depth with the category of young urban working women, diminutively character-ized as "little" and "girls," is hardly accidental as the categories of gender, age, and social class all coconstitute a girly figure of homogeneous culture bordering on the inane. The trivialization of women and their boredom—as well as the trivializing of women as boring—speaks loudly of gendered assessment of worth and agency, bringing us to the question of who are the subjects of grand narratives of loss connected to media, technology, and their speeds of communication. Additional variations of this story—and, indeed, *other stories* mindful of diverse subject positions and realms of experience—are sorely needed.

Microevents

Contra the Weberian narrative of loss, Bennett is interested in the capti-vating aspects of modernity fueled by its rhythms, diversions, and envi-ronments. She theorizes enchantment as mundane somatic moments of captivation: as instances of being "struck and shaken by the extraordinary that lives amid the familiar and the everyday" (Bennett 2001, 4). "Enchant-ment includes, then, a condition of exhilaration or acute sensory activ-ity. To be simultaneously transfixed in wonder and transported by sense, to be both caught up and carried away—enchantment is marked by this odd combination of somatic effects" (Bennett 2001, 5). Instead of resent-ing developments in the rhythms and speeds of culture, Bennett (2001, 4–5) opens up affirmative analytical avenues that are premised on horizons of pos-sibility emerging in experiences of everyday marvel, wonder, and "shocked surprise." Her rewriting of the story of modernity produces an alternative entrance to considerations of cultural transformations and their impact on affective capacities. This is also a line of inquiry pursued here, as it affords an alternative telling of what networked culture and its affective formations may entail.

Enchantment, as discussed in this context, need not be a matter of exqui-site rapture: it can just as well come in scales of fascination and interest that serendipitously surface within the everyday. Writing in 1975, Mihaly Csik-szentmihalyi (2000, 142, 184–185), examined mundane "microflow" expe-riences of enjoyable, trivial, unnecessary, and simple behavior practiced for the sake of pleasure. Activities such as coffee breaks during office hours or doodling during meetings facilitate escapes from sensations of boredom and anxiety that, for Csikszentmihalyi, otherwise lace and haunt every-day lives (as already implied in his book title, *Beyond Boredom and Anxiety*). Such microflow experiences increase one's sense of aliveness, vitality, relaxation, interest, and energy (Csikszentmihalyi 2000, 146, 169–170). In *Escape Attempts*, originally published the same year as Csikszentmihalyi's book, Stanley Cohen and Laurie Taylor (1992) sketch out everyday life as a series of minor escapes from boredom and routine. Habit, in particular, emerges as a key feature of existence that yields "boredom, monotony, tedium, despair" connected to the fact that while there are always things to do, these are already familiar, known, and hence short in fascination (Cohen and Taylor 1992, 50–51). The persistent, tedious flow of everyday life is, however, interrupted with "interludes, temporary breaks, skirmishes, glimpses of other realities" in acts such as daydreaming, media use, sex, drugs, or art (Cohen and Taylor 1992, 45). As "momentary slips through the fabric," such micro experiences may well be meaningless, yet they hold value in stressing "*relief, risk* and *movement*" in lives that may otherwise feel stuck, or as going around in a predictable circle (Cohen and Taylor 1992, 171, 197, emphasis in the original).

These accounts of minor enchantments resonate with Tomkins's (2008, 15, 18) view of people as being "equipped with innate affective responses which bias … [us] to want to remain alive and to resist death, to want sexual experiences, to want to experience novelty and to resist boredom. … [We are] biased toward novelty and mastery and against boredom and help-lessness. … [We are] biased toward excitement and joy in communion with others." Understood in this vein, boredom (like anxiety) is antagonistic to what excites us—and, consequently, to what we are. This view is clearly opposed to Heidegger's discussion of anxiety and boredom as that which allows for a reflection of our existence and its nothingness. For both Csik-szentmihalyi and Tomkins—and, indeed, for Spinoza (1992)—people are geared toward that which adds to their overall liveliness and enjoyment taken in life. In more of a new materialist phrasing, microflow experiences then increase and affirm one's life forces and potentials to act.

In his quite distinct discussion of microshocks, Brian Massumi (2015, 53) addresses them as affective encounters with the world as entailing a change in focus: "In every shift of attention, there is an interruption, a momentary cut in the mode of onward employment of life" (Massumi 2015, 54). For Massumi, such instances of sensory commotion modulate and transform our ways of being in the world. While remaining mostly imperceptible in their instantaneity, microshocks may also register as interruptions. In instances of affective intensity, attention clusters and possibly sticks. This is also an issue of temporality: "What we perceive is what unfolds from that interpenetration of moments, as the coming event plays itself out. We perceive the trailing into the situation of the past already tending out that situation towards the future of the event's having happened" (Massumi 2015, 60–61). It is in this way that we, for Massumi (2015, 61), "experience duration, that we feel time to have an extension" beyond the now. Extending this articulation of affect, speed, and time to the context of networked media, it allows for alternatives to totalizing accounts of capture in the present.

Combining these formulations and understandings of microevents helps to foreground engagements with networked media as intentional activity involving searches, quests, and pursuits (*microflow experiences*), on the one hand, and as unpredictable encounters, affectations, and transformations impossible for an individual to control (*microshocks*) on the other. Considered as microevents, new posts, alerts, clicks, and messages involve oscillations in affective intensity—in how things register, grab, linger, resonate, and matter. While being firmly set in the present, user attention extends both back and forth in time, from updates to past posts repackaged as memories that hold the promise of microevents (see also chapter 3). These minor interruptions recircuit some of the habitual flow of everyday life while at the same time giving rise to habitual routines of checking, refreshing, and searching.

Microevents are brief, geared toward diversion, and easily dismissed as meaningless and banal—since this, of course, is what they are, involving "low, often hard-to-register flicker of affect" (Ngai 2015, 18). As in Kracauer's and Benjamin's accounts, the speeds and rhythms of microevents catered through the media have been seen as causes for boredom: "Print, film, television and electronic media have accordingly shortened and accelerated ... [people's] units of stimulation in an effort to plug the ever-reappearing holes from which boredom issues. Sound bites and rapid image projection ensure a fickle attentiveness" (Thiele 1997, 495). Writing on entertainment, Alan McKee (2016, 18–19) points out that ever since the concept was first marked out as distinct from culture in the nineteenth century, it has been singled out as vulgar and offensive to upper and middle-class guardians of good taste. Importantly, vulgar entertainment has, from music hall numbers to pop songs and popular magazines' miscellanea, been short in its lengths and formats (McKee 2016, 22). The ease with which popular literature, music, and film can be consumed has long led to diagnoses of their addictive, drug-like qualities. In fact, "'short attention span' (or perhaps, 'fast information processing ability') has been a feature of entertainment since the nineteenth century" (McKee 2016, 23). It can then be argued that current concerns about the speeds and distractions of the online attention economy hark back to critiques of "common people's" fast, vulgar habits dating to the birth of modern media culture and tainted with gendered implications of feminine frivolousness and banality. Framing them through enchantment, again, helps in outlining their value in and for how lives are lived.

Michel Foucault (1995, 26) identified the seemingly dispersed "microphysics of power" as composing a plane where the powers of social organization meet individual bodies "with their materiality and their force" and produce uniformity of being in practices of everyday life. Micropower entails a cluster of relations and, while facilitating variation and resistance, basically operates from the top down, and through the force of repetition (Foucault 1980, 190, 201). Applied to social media's microevents, such microphysical, habitual operations of power can, following Kracauer, be identified as the mass-scale reordering of focus and attention that serves the ends of neoliberal governance. This view of microevents is in line with how a 2016 *Money* clickbait article, based on David Cheng and Lu Wang's study on the effect of humor on boring work tasks, redeems people's guilt over watching cat videos by highlighting the productivity of such encounters:

> The idea is that, by giving yourself a short mental break, you effectively recharge your batteries and have renewed vigor to tackle whatever dull, frustrating, or challenging task is in front of you at work. Experiment subjects who got the "humor break" worked longer on the task they were given and were more engaged with the material.
>
> The researchers wrote that their findings dispelled the belief that doing a tough job means eradicating all distractions until you're finished. (White 2016)

The study referenced suggests several things, including the affective value of distraction for white- or no-collar desktop laborers. It certainly proposes that such distractions can be literally valuable in an economical sense by ramping up individual productivity. "Humor breaks" feed flickering attention promising micro-instances of affective intensity. Rather than being in conflict with the dictates of desktop labor, such breaks fuel work efficiency. It is telling of the contemporary cultural conjuncture that arguments of this kind, where "humor breaks" translate as increased individual productivity in a work environment otherwise characterized as "dull, frustrating, or challenging," are the ones to justify the mundane quest for pleasurable distraction. Meanwhile, autotelic quests for pleasure—pleasure for its own sake alone—fall outside things to be encouraged or recommended, despite these being key to how people cope with their mundane routines. In her discussion of cute animal videos, Allison Page (2017, 80) frames them as "cruel relief, a much-needed break from new norms of work and productivity that further bolster capitalism and erode anti-work resistance." Their cuteness offers "a disruptive affective excess that provides a tool for coping with not just the drudgery of work and office life, but also the devastations of neoliberalism and its attendant social and political effects" (Page 2017, 76). In doing so, instances of affective excess brought forth by cuteness can "escape the logic of capital even as capital seeks to capture, contain, and use it" (Page 2017, 79). In other words, affect is in excess to the logics of capture involved in contemporary practices of surplus value creation—be it as forms of desktop labor or through the traffic in user data.

For his part, Dominic Pettman (2016, viii, 19) sees social media as tweaking and modulating micro pleasures and micro experiences that result in a disturbing collective shattering of attention in "the homeopathic parceling of tiny and banal moments of recognition, reassurance, ego reinforcement, humblebragging, notoriety, curiosity, shame, and a galaxy of other modest—but collectively significant—affects" (Pettman 2016, 9–10). To Pettman (2016, 132), "Silly memes are not the problem. An economic system that provides silly memes as pellets toward enduring another day of work is the problem." In this Adorno-influenced framing, social media operates as novel opium for the masses: in an ideal or at least noncapitalist world, there simply would be no need for entertainment (Pettman 2016, 133). As Pettman nevertheless points out, Benjamin—Adorno's close friend and pen pal—would not have been in full agreement on the matter. He might have considered social media instead as "the digital arcades of multitude—both promising and camouflaging new democratic possibilities, new interpersonal configurations, and new collective sensibilities" (Pettman 2016, 134). In such a more ambivalent framing, as also fostered in this book, micro experiences involve volatile potential that cannot be categorically known or anticipated, and that do not simply operate from the top down.

For Kendall (2018, 85), networked media target boredom in microtemporal circuits in ways that disable experiences of profound boredom à la Heidegger, "downplaying its value as a mode of critical introspection, and repurposing it instead as an agent of value extraction for capitalist industries." As Thiele (1997, 502, 503) explains, for Heidegger, boredom operates as an "anesthetizing mood" that "inhibits thought and reduces feeling to torpor." In its most profound form, boredom results in nihilism that evaporates the significance of significance as such. In this sense, it closely resembles diagnoses of clinical depression as severe despondency entailing an overall collapse of interest, meaning, and worth: deep in this zone, being dead or alive may not matter all that much, or the option of death may even hold allure as some kind of resolution. As there are obvious limits to what can be learned from deep boredom that threatens meaning, thinking, and the sense of aliveness, I would be cautious about celebrating it as a desirable end in itself.

Furthermore, as suggested above, microtemporal self-management also holds other than strictly financial and economic value—while operating within data capitalism, it also escapes full capture in its logics. As one of my students put it, "When things are frustratingly boring, I open the computer as last resort in order to have the net entertain me. If the net doesn't work, I'm doomed to boredom" (female, b. 1991). In the diverting microevents and pleasurable releases that it caters—here resembling microflow events—networked media simply promises rescue from the very tedium of everyday life.

Such microevents occur in specific social, spatial, and temporal contexts, and among particularly situated subjects. Judy Wajcman (2014, 154), for example, points out that when children playing games or listening to music on their mobile phones aim to mitigate boredom, the device "offers new sites for separation and autonomy, allowing the person to be present but also absent or withdrawn." Larissa Hjorth and Ingrid Richardson's (2009, 31) young female informants similarly, yet also differently, made use of mobile phone games when and for "'waiting', 'boredom', 'time-filling', and 'switching off'—each of which describes a form of delay or 'putting on hold'; that is, a complex variation of telepresent distraction enacted when co-present or co-proximate with unfamiliar others." In other words, networked microevents afford not only affective breaks but also possibilities for social distancing and isolation (see also Light 2014; Mowlabocus 2016). As Hjorth and Richardson (2009, 32) point out, engagement with smartphones allowed some of their study participants "a means of safe seclusion from unwelcome interaction in potentially risky situations of co-present waiting, yet allowed them to remain 'open' or attentive to the proximity of that risk." Looking at a screen makes it possible not to meet the eyes of others or talk with them unless this is something desired, while possibly messaging with those that one wishes to engage with, as was the case with the young women in Hjorth and Richardson's study. Shivers of distraction that may in another instance be sources of displeasure can be enjoyable in the release that they offer from situations that one cannot easily escape—be these ones involving impending boredom or the unpleasant physical proximity of other people.

Connectedness to networked media can allow for a sense of safety from potential harassment or violence, sexual or other, as a sheltering social shell of sorts. As students of mine explain: "The phone is a safety creating device that I'd use to call for help, should something happen" (female, b. 1994), and its breakdown "creates an immediate sense of the lack of safety, especially when walking out in the evenings and at night" (female, b. 1994). "For me, phone's existence signifies first and foremost safety; as long as I can even call 911 while out, that creates safety" (female, b. 1993). Interpreting all this as indicative of sad amputation of sociability brought forth by addictive networked media would clearly be beside the point. Such accounts rather speak of multidirectionality of attention and communication where potential vulnerabilities in urban nocturnal spaces are acutely present for young female subjects. In such contexts, microevents are not engaged in for the purposes of becoming distracted from one's immediate surroundings; rather, they enable a divided attention that does not invite unknown others to interrupt one's activities yet makes it possible to remain alert to possible risks. In addition, the mere potentiality of communication and contact operates as a self-perceived safety measure.

Microevents make lives more livable as tiny instances of potentiality, enchantment, and richness of experiences through that which Bennett identifies as mundane instances of marvel, wonder, and shocked surprise.

As such, they are not only instrumental—as in the accounts just cited above—but equally autotelic. In both increasing one's capacity to act and in transforming available modes of experience, microevents are key to how we take interest in and become excited about the world. It is therefore not just to automatically label them as being void of political potentiality or resonance. A focus on microevents brings us away from master narratives outlining a past that was full and a present that is wrongly full, or just plain empty, just as it helps to zoom in on the experiential in analyses of data capitalism focusing on the macro rather than the micro. The micro and the mundane acutely matter, as this is where the politics of everyday life take shape.

Gradations of Experience

Networked media make it possible to escapes boredom by "killing time" when it seems to be moving too slowly and when time is spent in situations where other stimuli of interest remains scarce. As discussed in chapter 2, in the course of having become habitual as part of bodily schema, the affordances and rhythms of high-speed network connectivity have become ingrained in the textures of everyday life:

> Last week I had to take my computer for maintenance as the battery didn't properly work. I had already previously checked that changing the battery would take a week and cost a lot. I wasn't however shocked about the price but more about how I'd be able to cope without the computer…I felt that I was facing a huge ordeal that I'd just have to bear with in order to get my computer fixed and back to use. So, I had to come up with alternative things to do instead of surfing [*surffailu*], which felt really challenging at first. Occasionally boredom struck as it felt that the only thing for me to do was to browse different sites or to watch Netflix. Realizing this also startled me as you'd imagine there to be many other good things to do instead of sitting down and staring at a screen for hours. But it's become my daily habit. (female, b. 1994)

> The summer of 2016…I lived in Seoul in South Korea.…What made the summer particularly unique was however the week when multiple mundane technologies of mine failed by coincidence…in a few days, I lost the use of my computer, online bank, and phone alike…
>
> Afterwards, I've considered the scenario mainly with amusement, and by belittling it. After all, I was a privileged young adult enjoying the luxury of travel. The anxiety experienced during those days was nevertheless completely real. Although I lived in a city of millions, without a phone I felt very lonely, and

constantly desperate. … The day spent without a phone felt like eternity and I remember going to bed at seven in the evening in order to avoid boredom. This may be the heart of the tragicomedy: I lived in Seoul, and without smart devices I felt bored. (female, b. 1994)

Without the network access that one is habituated to, capacities to act become truncated in ways that can give rise to seemingly excruciating sensations of boredom and frustration, even in settings where alternative sources of diversion are easily available. A sense of blandness or stuckness may equally come about when the access in question is experienced as being too slow. With slow connections, a student describes the overall speed of her experience slowing down:

Sitting on this train … suffering with the Wi-Fi network I began to ponder what it actually feels like again when the net doesn't work. I've had to go through these sensations myself for a range of reasons but I also noticed this state of mind that I become immersed in when using a slow connection. It feels as if the whole reality slows down and everything else around me becomes almost meaningless. You just stare at the screen, or out the train window for example, but nothing else gets done until you manage opening just that specific website. It's actually quite a distressing state, not only when being in a hurry but also in regular uses [of networked media]. It's distressing when you're nevertheless constantly aware that you could already be on that page and move from this moment to the next, forward in life. But due to slow connectivity you just have to wait. (female, b. 1993)

Here, the unbearably slow tempos of web browsing broaden into a diminished form of existence. This state of mind is intimately akin to boredom where the present moment "seems to be dragging itself along unbearably, it is as if nothing leads up to it and nothing will come of it" (Johnsen 2011, 485). For the bored, the here and the now spread ahead as void of variety or intensity that would somehow transform it or make it richer: things do not move or stick, catch attention, intrigue, or tickle. Goodstein (2005), after all, defines it as "an experience without qualities." When nothing moves, time may seem to slow down, or even to be standing still, and things basically lack meaning and purpose.

Following Goodstein, boredom, as an encounter with nothingness, allows for no "distinguishing in here from out there, for the world in its failure to engage collapses into an extension of the boredom subject who empties out in the vain search for an interest, a pleasure, a meaning. Self and world collapse in a nihilistic affirmation that nothing means, nothing pleases, nothing matters" (Goodstein 2005, 1; also 99). As discussed in chapter 3, affective intensity, in contrast, makes things matter, or may make a difference: it is a connection that happens, an encounter as impact that somehow moves bodies from one state to another. This makes it possible to conceptualize boredom as being in dynamic relation with interest and excitement—boredom representing lack of intensity and excitement an abundance thereof. Rather than considering boredom as the opposite of fascination, interest, or excitement, they can, like distraction and attention addressed above, be understood as modulation in forms, intensities, and rhythms of experience, from the flat to the heightened and all things in between—as "subtle gradation with many nuances" (Veel 2011, 313). In such a framing, boredom and excitement point to intermeshing affective intensities.

Writing in the framework of literary analysis, Sianne Ngai (2000) discusses the paradoxical unison of astonishment and boredom—of excessive excitation and extreme desensitization or fatigue—through the notion of *stuplimity*. Based on repetition and refrain, stuplimity is an aesthetic strategy bordering on the obtuse that dulls, irritates, and agitates. For Ngai, it characterizes certain examples of modernist and contemporary literature and hence her classification can be adapted to a discussion of social media only with considerable liberties. A similarly tension-ridden combination of wonder and dullness, excitement and boredom, nevertheless comes about in encounters with platforms as users refresh and recheck in a search for fascinating posts, links, and comments. Microevents may be simultaneously captivating and tiresome, simultaneously reinforcing and atrophying one's life forces. In this sense, their dynamic bares resemblance to Ngai's (2015) later analysis of the interesting as an aesthetic of circulation specific to contemporary capitalism. For Ngai (2015, 1), the interesting is "about difference in the form of information and the pathways of its movement and exchange." Involving constant evaluations of interestingness, this is an elusive aesthetic experience often defined through its absence, one that oscillates between interest and boredom (Ngai 2015, 45–46).

Some of this dynamic is evident in an excerpt from a class assignment submitted to Michael Petit's class on Emotions and the Internet, where a Canadian student describes the circular rhythm of web browsing experienced when searching for novelties that would grab attention and provide momentary breaks from the ever-looming threat of boredom:

So if I'm bored, I go on the internet and surf. And if I find something fun, then I won't be bored anymore. … Like, let's say 9gag. It's never ending, but when you see the same pictures from the one you just visited earlier, then you get bored again, since you already saw that. Then the fun ends. Now you go on to a different website, let's say Reddit. You see a new picture, sure fun, then you see the same pictures again, and like the ones you visited earlier, boredom again. Now you go to YouTube. You see the cycle, right. So it's bored, not bored, bored, not bored, bored. (Petit 2015, 180)

Boredom can be evoked by the repetition of motions—as when incessantly checking and refreshing the same site without there being much novel content of interest—or by the sheer difficulty of deciding *what* exactly to browse. Boredom is both that which is being escaped in and that which results from clicks and swipes from one application and screen to another. There is a certain magnetism and optimism to quests for entertaining distraction—even if, following Lauren Berlant (2011), this optimism might turn out to be cruel indeed as aspirations and investments that, while promising to make our everyday lives richer and fuller, are in practice making them less manageable. Social media's microevents can involve such cruelty, or at least the hollowness of promise, in that quests to break away from boredom via TikTok or Imgur may just as well result in experiences of boredom when the content browsed fails to be distracting enough or when these quests start to feel routine.

For Petit (2015, 180), this involves a hypnotic kind of engaged disengagement, or distracted attention: "This rhythm, both hot and cool, and which operates on a continuum from lull to intense affective attention, resonates with the pattern of an errant electrocardiagram: the flatline of disaffective lull punctuated by pulses of affectivity." The qualities of boredom, detachment, ennui, and flatness connected to networked media can, following Petit, be collectively thought of as "digital disaffect," a state characterized by tenacious blandness. Martin Hand (2017, 115) similarly refers to the phenomenon of "digital boredom" in describing contemporary life as "technologically mediated, repetitive, rushed and denying solitude" within which "multiple practices of presencing, tracking and connecting are at once efforts to alleviate boredom, contributing to experiences of boredom, and occluding the possibility of a more profound boredom." Berlant (2015), in a different context, conceptualizes the sensation of "flat affect." As Robbie Duschinsky and Emma Wilson (2015, 185) note, the concept of flat affect draws from psychiatric discourse, where it signifies expressionless presentation: "Whereas a depressed patient might look sad, flat affect is a kind of emotional opacity in which affective display, in the face in particular, has little range, intensity and mobility, and subjectively, it is not clear to the patient what the feelings they experience mean or what bearing they may have for them."

In Berlant's account, flatness is akin to an affective formation in that "it has particular appeal at a historical moment in which subjects and collective movements feel a sustained crisis in their ability to make effective and consistent claims on the world, particularly in relation to politics but also in terms of intimate relations—this leaves things rather apprehensively suspended" (Duschinsky and Wilson 2015, 185). Understood in this vein, flat affect accompanies a sense of uncertainty, or that of precarity, in a cultural moment where all things solid melt into air or have never been available in a solid form to begin with (see also Coleman 2016). In a more Heideggerian phrasing, the issue might be described as lack of attunement toward that which one is surrounded by (Ahmed 2014, 16)—as a sense of being out of sync with the world. Seen as moods, boredom and blandness of experience can be understood as affective lenses that orient ways in which we are affected (Ahmed 2014, 14). They are social, are relational, and color our engagements with the world.

If intensity is "more than," then digital disaffect is "less than." The disaffected have seen the same thing before—been there, done that, with nothing new left to see. This sense of blandness or the blasé is coupled simultaneously to longing for the promise of intensity. Digital disaffect then describes a sensation of always being about to attain the thing that will bring satisfaction yet finding that it lies just beyond reach. When one has discovered a particularly gratifying nugget of data—a witty meme, a skillful deepfake video, a virtuoso oral sex clip, a winning meme, or a truly vitriolic Twitter exchange—the trick is not necessarily easy to repeat. Since the issue is one of serendipitous encounters, the objects of one's future interest and fasciation are not necessarily all too evident. The sharp edge of microevents builds on the affective dynamics of surprise–startle and interest–excitement, as outlined by Tomkins (2008), the routes of which are unpredictable just as they are transient. There is dullness to waiting for further pleasurable data nuggets, just as the experience of trolling through posts and updates that fail to catch one's interest is easily steeped in frustration.

Much of this dynamic is encapsulated in the routines of search connected to online pornography. In a fundamental paradox, porn is a genre intended and planned to sexually arouse and excite and hence to facilitate escapes from mundane boredom by moving the user's body from one state to another (see Paasonen 2011). Online porn is currently on free offer in massive volumes and in endless subcategories, yet the experience of watching it is regularly identified as boring, and its content as being boring in its mere repetitiveness (Schaschek 2013, 39, 54, 65). In her discussion of online porn of the early 2000s, Zabet Patterson (2004, 109) describes its use as being rife in lags, frustrations, and waiting. Despite the promise of immediate gratification, users were faced with constant delays in finding and accessing content of their interest. In a variation of cruel optimism, users set out on a quest for a perfect image and scene, only to discover inadequate variations thereof: hence the search continued, frustrating and titillating, boring and exciting, at once (on the pleasures of searching for porn, see also Keilty 2012, 2016). A similar dynamic wherein boredom is intermeshed with, and inseparable from, excitement characterizes exchanges in networked media well beyond the genre of pornography. The abundance of available content holds constant promise yet also increases awareness of repetition and sameness in that which one encounters.

Toxic Presentism?

In the discussions addressed above, boredom involves the sense of time standing still, empty moments extending in time, and time slowing down. The rhythms of social media, again, have been connected to attention hovering on the immediately and the imminently present. All this leads to questions concerning temporality, from a sense of immediacy to that of perceived acceleration of time. Simmel associated intense feelings catered by otherwise affectively flat and blasé modernity as involving an "absolute presentness" cut off from both the remembrance of things past and the anticipation of the future (see Aho 2007, 456). Writing in the 1950s and 1906s, Henri Lefebvre (1995, 165) argued that, within modernity, the lived "sinks down into history and is swallowed up" and that "everything comes to an end virtually as soon as it begins, and vanishes as soon as it appears." In alignment with Postman's later line of argumentation, Lefebvre (1995,

166) saw the demand for news, and especially news of a sensational nature, as emerging within this dynamic of acceleration as a fetish of sorts, resulting in repetition:

> The all-too well known problem of saturation, of boredom, of lightning transitions from interest to tedium, produce techniques aimed at overcoming those very reactions; techniques of *presentation*. ... Facts, ideas—what ideas there are—and subjects come back again and again. No one recognizes them. Non-recognition is organized technically to combat memory and previously acquired information. The confusion of triviality which no longer appears trivial and sensationalism which is made to appear ordinary is cleverly organized: News shrinks to the size of the socially instantaneous, and the immediate instant tends to disappear in an instant which has already passed.

Lefebvre was particularly concerned with how speedy media dynamics manipulate young people and the effects that this is likely to have on culture and society in the years to come (see also Gardiner 2012). The dynamic of saturation, boredom, amnesia, and the manipulation of attention, as laid out by Lefebvre, echoes debates connected to media technology both before the 1960s and within the current moment. Douglas Rushkoff (2013, 14), known for his 1990s cyberpunk writings, characterizes the contemporary as one of presentism entailing an exclusive focus on the fleeting here and now: "As a result, our culture becomes an entropic, static hum of everybody trying to capture the slipping moment. Narrativity and goals are surrendered to a skewed notion of the real and the immediate; the tweet; the status update." This pessimistic account, the tone and logic of which are most likely familiar at this point into this book as a variation of the grand narrative of loss, sees the temporalities of social media as revolving around the perpetual present in ways that erode memory and future orientation and ultimately result in effacement of meaning and purpose.

Reiterating the argument, Evgeny Morozov (2013), a fellow tech writer (partly inspired by Lefebvre), suggests that "One reason that mediated boredom is so hard to notice is that it cloaks itself in the rhetoric of nowness and newness. ... When one is living only in the present ... it's easy to mistake a constant invasion by the new—status updates or tweets or e-mails—for a radical break with everything that has come before." In this articulation, updates, despite their promises of novelty, translate as sameness and boredom under a different name. It nevertheless seems that both Rushkoff and Morozov, in their notably unhappy accounts, remain somehow resistant to such a biased sense of temporality and novelty themselves. Unlike other people trapped in the forced, flat sense of immediacy, these authors appear to have a sense of both the past and the future, novelty and familiarity, and are certainly able to hold on to a narrative.

Critically addressing diagnoses of digital dementia, Marcel O'Gorman (2015) points out that, despite there being "no conclusive empirical evidence that the Internet and other media technologies undermine cognitive skills such as memory and attention…arguments based on anecdotal evidence and technological determinism continue to persuade readers, many of whom, such as best-selling author Nicholas Carr, have a vague sense that they are not thinking like they used to think, and that technology is to blame." This rhetorical move, of course, is at the heart of Coupland's I MISS MY PRE-INTERNET BRAIN project addressed in chapter 1. In *The Shallows*, Carr (2010, 55) points out that already Plato, in his critique of the written word, saw it as eroding the capacity to think and remember. In *Phaedrus*, Plato (1952, 157), using Socrates as his mouthpiece, saw writing as not preserving as much as destroying memory functions:

> If men learn this, it will implant forgetfulness in their souls. They will cease to exercise memory because they rely on that which is written, calling things to remembrance no longer from within themselves, but by means of external marks; what you have discovered is a recipe not for memory, but for reminder. And it is no true wisdom that you offer your disciples, but only its semblance, for by telling them of many things without teaching them you will make them seem to know much, while for the most part they know nothing; and as men filled, not with wisdom, but with the conceit of wisdom, they will be a burden to their fellows.

While Carr's decision to discuss Plato may seem surprising in the context of networked culture, it is far from a novel move within media studies. Although this field does not, in general, extensively engage with the classics of Greek philosophy (with the obvious exception of rhetorical inquiry building on Aristotle), *Phaedrus* has been something of a staple point of reference at least since Walter Ong's 1982 *Orality and Literature* addressing Plato's take on writing as an inhuman, manufactured product that threatens memory and weakens the mind. Ong (1982, 78) connected the consideration with more recent technological developments:

> Today, parents and others fear that pocket calculators provide an external resource for what ought to be the internal resource of memorized multiplication tables. Calculators weaken the mind, relieve it of the work that keeps it strong.…a

written text is basically unresponsive. If you ask a person to explain his or her statement, you can get an explanation; if you ask a text, you get back nothing except the same, often stupid, words which called for your question in the first place. In the modern critique of the computer, the same objection is put, "Garbage in, garbage out."

As Jacques Derrida (1981, 70) points out, in *Phaedrus*, Socrates compares written text to pharmakon, a drug or philter. While promising to help to preserve live, finite memory as a mnemonic, prosthetic device—to function as a supportive repair of sorts—writing in fact aids forgetting by bringing forth a dull repetition and by substituting the "the passive, mechanical 'by-heart' for the active reanimation of knowledge" (Derrida 1981, 108). In something of a reverb of Freud's (1957) discussion of ambivalence as simultaneously loving and hostile attachments toward objects, this kind of "bad pharmakon" is, for Derrida, a default parasite of "good pharmakon," there not being one without the other. "There is no such thing as a harmless remedy. The *pharmakon* can never be simply beneficial... [it] partakes of both good and ill, of the agreeable and the disagreeable" (Derrida 1981, 99, emphasis in the original). Both good and bad, and hence ambiguous, the pharmakon disturbs or even undoes the kinds of clear-cut divisions through which it is defined: that which is presented as a poison may, after all, turn out to be the cure, and vice versa (Derrida 1981, 125).

In separating internal processes of knowledge creation from learning through written texts indicative of shallowness (and as opposed to acts of live speech and memory), Plato argued for distinguishing between the different qualities, or intensities, of memory and wisdom as these are mapped onto speech and writing. This is also a delineation that interests Derrida, and one on which Bernard Stiegler (2012a, 2013) later built his theorization of pharmakon in the context of networked society and its different technics of memory and attention. While cultural commentators like Rushkoff and Morozov emphasize the detrimental effects of networked media, the analytical framework of the pharmakon equally focuses attention toward their apparent flip side. It can also be argued that writing does not just erode the functions of human memory but allows for them to be put to different use, and that all kinds of prosthetic memory techniques transform, extend, erode, as well as support ways of remembering, connecting, and making sense.

In a cultural moment characterized by vast flows of data and the tenacious accumulation of data—*Phaedrus* alone being only a Google search

the scale of externalized and datafied memory—both within our reach, as social media data that we can access and delete, and as massive archives of user data that we have no access to—makes forgetting hard, if not impossible (Mayer-Schönberger 2011). The data nuggets that social media feeds back to users of their past actions, current connections, and all kinds of links to the world spark involuntary memory (Chun 2016, 88) while these same data archives equally allow for personal reminiscence and reflection.

The plenitude of available stimulation does not automatically signify poverty of life, for *more can also be more*. Arguing against diagnoses of digital dementia, Kristin Veel (2011, 310) identifies the contemporary preference for abundance of information as instrumental means for avoiding boredom but also as connected to the predominance of the archive, and specifically to that of the database, as a cultural metaphor and practice. Opening up multiple possible connections, the database foregrounds simultaneity over selection. This is a "multichannel" form of engagement—one of simultaneous attention and distraction—premised on the copious accessibility of content and the imminent availability of upcoming attractions. In considering abundance less as oversaturation than as richness, Hartmut Rosa (2013, 13) further argues that diagnoses of acceleration based on economic factors, or on capitalist speeds of production only, fail to grasp the cultural underpinnings of the dominant modern ideal of a *"fulfilled life*, i.e., a life that is rich in experiences and developed capacities."* Here, the acceleration of the speeds of life translates as an increase in both realized and realizable options and hence as a general increase in the potential richness of life. All this results in an overload of choices, both realizable and not, both pleasurable ones and those heavily laced with anxiety (see also Adam 2003, 49). Rosa, Veel, and Bennett all evoke the notion of richness, rather than that of flatness or blandness, to describe transformations in ways of sensing and making sense of the world brought forth by networked media. Microevents, from microflow experiences to microshocks, contribute to a plenitude where "shocked surprise" is promised to be only a click away.

I argue that a focus on enchantment and the richness of experience does not efface or dull the critical edge of cultural inquiry but rather affords it depth and nuance—for, if we approach the affective formations examined in this book through the concept of the pharmakon, addressing them solely in terms of their toxicity is a partial, dissatisfactory solution at best. Microevents and minor enchantments amplify life forces and make lives more livable. If cultural inquiry is to be life-affirming, then pessimistic and nihilistic critiques do not suffice. With this in mind, the final part of this chapter takes a little detour by considering boredom and networked media in the framework of university pedagogy and by teasing out some of the more positive dimensions connected to this.

Learning through Boredom?

Boredom is perpetually present in the university classroom where performative aids are readily at hand in the plethora of how-tos and suggestions for teachers to be more engaging. In classes on university pedagogy, it is suggested that we tell jokes, show clips, and make students discuss in small groups, stand up, and stretch at regular intervals so as to avoid getting bored. Seen as a risk and an impediment for learning, boredom then ultimately indicates shortcomings in a teacher's pedagogical skill. In their study of university lectures in the United Kingdom, Sandi Mann and Andrew Robinson (2009) found boredom to run rife, to correlate with lower scores, and hence to pose a problem to be solved.

To escape boredom, students would "play games on phone, text people, write shopping list, talk to neighbour, calculate finances, leave mid-session, stare into space, switch off, doodle, write notes to neighbour, colour in letters on handout and decide not to attend the next lecture" (Mann and Robinson 2009, 248). Most popularly, 75 percent would daydream, 66 percent doodle, and 62 percent just switch off, as if illustrating the mundane practices of resistance that Cohen and Taylor (1992) once examined. Should this study be repeated today, over a decade later, the role of smart devices in microflow practices would most likely be much more pronounced, even if they are banned from many classrooms because of their distracting qualities that are seen to work against the goals and aims of pedagogical practice premised on extended focus. Meanwhile, scholars are not in agreement over the productivity of such bans, some promoting the integration of smart devices in interactive, engaged learning through multitasking instead (see Grinols and Rajesh 2014).

In Mann and Robinson's (2009, 246, 255) study, the use of PowerPoint slides came across as a key contributor to boredom: while intended to aid student engagement, the slides led to disengagement instead. In contrast, seminars, practical sessions, and group discussions were experienced as the least boring. A lecture, similarly to a research monograph, generally involves a singular authorial voice and offers a linear representation on a (more or less) fixed theme. In *The Gutenberg Galaxy*, McLuhan (2011/1962) outlined a shift to the electronic age that is, in contrast with the typographic and mechanical ages, characterized by the accumulation of information, media content, and possibilities for communication. If the printing press gave rise to a form of narration that is linear and largely reliant on one perspective, the electronic age entailed an expansion of voices and points of view without relying on linearity as its organizing principle. If we consider such simultaneity and a multitude of perspectives as characteristic of contemporary media, it can be asked whether banning smartphones in the classroom is the optimal solution—especially when teaching media studies. There are reasons to question the productivity of university pedagogy resorting to the conceptual template of digital detox, just as to advice against extensive use of smart devices independent of pedagogical context and nuance. The use of pen and paper, and the structure of an exam where several books are read in order to memorize them and to then exhibit learning results by summarizing their content forces students to operate within a pedagogical format that has been in use for centuries. There is clear attraction to such a linear model among educators as, for some, it speaks of the very capacity to focus, to remember, and to process information. It may not, however, be fully productive from the perspective of students for whom word processing is integral to thinking:

> I sometimes miss the time…when you could still write essays on paper without anyone giving you a weird look. Although I probably could still hand in essays as hand-written paper copies, I honestly wouldn't know how to write long essays of quality by hand anymore, as I'm too used to using word-processing software where you can remove entire paragraphs with one click and move words around in a fully arbitrary way. This is why it's grown more difficult to write essays in exams, as the computer is no longer there to help. So, although on the one hand I miss a return back to a time before the "dominance" of technology and media, on the other hand I've grown so dependent on them that I wouldn't be able to operate without them. This also partly evokes irritation and fear. What if e.g. power was cut off for a long time, or if my computer broke and I didn't have the money to immediately buy a new one? How would I be able to do schoolwork? Would I be able to manage at all … ? (female, born 1990)

In a context of prosthetic dependency on technologies to think with, relevant—and, in pedagogical discourse, transferable—skills include the ability to combine information from multiple sources and to compose essays in a processual vein allowing for edits, changes, and novel associations to come about. Analogue learning media necessitate a different cognitive framework—one that can be useful to experiment with but one for which students may not have much use in their future working practices. A digital detox connected to learning may be motivated by claims for authenticity, as in paper-based reading and writing practices being deeper, richer, and more meaningful than digital ones based on glancing, yet, as the excerpt above suggests, there may not be much authenticity to go around for students who have learned to read and think with digital devices.

Meanwhile, much remains to be done with digital media in the classroom beyond watching video clips to alleviate boredom or to just spice things up (although I am by no means opposed to such uses, either). As the boundaries between media producers and consumers have grown porous, pedagogical practice, even when not focused on media production as such, benefits from hands-on approaches instead of being confined to content analysis. This positions smartphones very differently from devices offering microflow escapes from the boring grind of the classroom, as they become pedagogical actors instead, facilitating learning through various exercises— from analyzing apps through a "walkthrough method" exploring interface design and terms of use in order to understand their rationale, models of operation, and modes of governance (Light, Burgess, and Duguay 2018); to experiments of social curation and visual communication using the camera phone (e.g., Victoria 2018); to GIF building as a means of considering remix culture, copyright, and virality; to the creation of word clouds allowing for insight into repetitions and trends; or to mapping the flows of user data to third parties through tracking apps in order to gain firsthand insight into the operating principles of the social media economy. In more advanced uses, editing and visual analysis tools can extend aesthetic analysis to non-human, algorithmic forms of seeing, contrasting, and measuring (Rantala 2016) while web-based, "born digital" analysis tools afford facile insight into the circulation of social media content (Pilipets 2018). The options are multiple and hardly covered in this short listing. There is no reason to delimit contemporary methodological experimentation within media studies to templates building on literary studies via film analysis, or from studies of journalism, broadcast culture, and political communication, not least since digital tools allow for the kinds of insight that we otherwise have no access to. This also means that instructors need to remain open toward apps and approaches that they were not previously familiar with, yet which the undergraduate students in the classroom may well master.

All this does not mean that boredom is simply to be done away with in practices of teaching and study through the magical addition of digital tools—just that smart devices should be understood more expansively than as tools of boredom and distraction. Reading oneself into any singular body of scholarly literature, let alone a larger field, is bound to be a boring exercise due to both the singularity of the effort and the expanse of work to be covered: I can guarantee that immersion in scholarship on boredom alone eats away at one's affective capacities. Boredom is largely unavoidable when becoming acquainted with disciplinary histories and methodological approaches, and as such it is a necessary part of curricula in most academic disciplines and majors/programs. And if this is so, and there is no effacing boredom as a fact of life, could something be learned from it? Many suggest so.

In one very practical application, Sandi Mann and Rebekah Cadman (2014) engaged students in boring tasks, such as mechanically copying telephone numbers, and then compared their performance in creative problem-solving exercises. The rationale of the study builds on previous research, according to which boredom, as disinterest toward the situation that one is facing, and possibly trapped in, involves the shifting of attention "from an external focus on the task, to a more internal focus on inner thoughts, feelings, and experiences" allowing for stimulation (Mann and Cadman 2014, 166). Such attention shifting may involve daydreaming, understood here as a by-product of boredom. According to Mann and Cadman's (2016, 171) findings, creative solutions increased when preceded by boring tasks while especially boring writing tasks facilitated daydreaming and resulted in increased creativity. In other words, the study points to boredom as involving oscillations of affective intensity and interest where attention turns both inward and outward and extends toward novel objects in situations where the current ones fail to stimulate. As it alters in intensities of attention and focus, boredom ceases to be a dead-end of nothingness and meaninglessness. While Mann and Roberts draw on psychological inquiry, David Lewkowich (2010, 132), also writing in the context of university pedagogy, builds on cultural theory to explore radical boredom as a "variable mode of being and a way of standing in and towards the world, which carries within it different and distinct transformative possibilities for emancipation, recognition, and creativity." But what does this mean?

Blissful Inactivity

In order to counter what he perceived of as the profound flatness caused by mass culture, Kracauer promoted surrendering to boredom of the thorough and radical kind—a call both similar and dissimilar to Heidegger's embrace of profound boredom. The task of finding oneself through boredom was, for Kracauer (1995, 332–333), nevertheless made difficult by the distractions on offer, from the film palace catering illusions of life to noisy cafés and radio stations feeding a "state of permanent receptivity…instead of fostering cultivated conversation (which certainly can be a bore), one becomes a playground for worldwide noises that, regardless of their own potentially objective boredom, do not even grant one's modest right to personal boredom." In contrast to such unfortunate "antennal fate," Kracauer (1995, 334) saw boredom as a guarantee of being in control of one's own existence. For "if one were never bored, one would presumably not really be present at all?"

Boredom achieved by doing nothing in accordance with Kracauer's guidelines would, however, not be a state of disaffected flatness but rather one of patience and focus—a sense of heightened presence eerily likening to the much later techniques on mindfulness. It is, in fact, a state of heightened affective intensity, a "great *passion*": for if one has the "patience specific to legitimate boredom, then one experiences a kind of bliss that is almost unearthly" (Kracauer 1995, 334, emphasis in the original). For Kracauer, a thoughtful kind of boredom becomes a form of contemplation, or focused attention resulting in discovering unprecedented richness in one's immediate environment—and hence something of an opposite to Benjamin's "reception in a state of distraction" addressed in chapter 3. Understood as a heightened sense of presence, boredom is meditative and is a far cry from nothingness and meaninglessness bordering on depression in the vein proposed by Heidegger. Already bordering on enchantment, it then fails to meet most other scholarly accounts and definitions of boredom on offer. Commenting on Kracauer's essay, Morozov (2013) nevertheless complains how

these days, "the state of permanent receptivity" has become the birthright of anyone with a smartphone. We are under constant assault by "interestingness," as new-media aficionados—"curators," they call themselves—prowl for bizarre factoids and quaint cartoons. The anti-boredom lobby has all but established its headquarters in Silicon Valley: cue Facebook's celebration of a "more connected" world, or Apple's reassurances that its latest gadget could do everything "twice as fast." Google is so boredom-averse that it seems to change its logo every day....

Information overload can bore us as easily as information underload. But this form of boredom, mediated boredom, doesn't provide time to think; it just produces a craving for more information in order to suppress it.

Morozov's proposed solution is predictable: that of disconnection. Identifying as a recovering distraction addict, he describes enclosing his smartphone and internet cable in a safe with a built-in timer, to force temporary disconnection, and watching DVDs instead of streaming video, thus no longer being slave to the machine. Similarly to the work-efficiency apps and digital detox retreats discussed in the previous chapter, such disconnect strategies aim at balancing the stress of networked life and bringing it into better focus. Morozov is hardly alone in trying to achieve this. Via Heidegger, Thiele (1997, 512) offers boredom as antidote to the compulsory quest for novelty: "Just as one may embrace technological distractions to alleviate boredom, so one may embrace boredom for its analgesic powers in the face of incessant technological change." Here, the embrace of boredom becomes a passive strategy for countering the relentless loops of novelty—a turning away, or inward, of sorts (see also Gibbs 2011; Mansikka 2009).

Lewkowich sees similar potentiality in Benjamin's (2002, 881) discussion of boredom as "a warm gray fabric lined on the inside with the most lustrous and colorful of silks. In this fabric we wrap ourselves when we dream." For Lewkowich (2010, 133), Benjamin's bored subject is externally still yet internally "experiences of boredom can be dazzling and luminous, a sort of ineffable disengagement from a disenchanting world. A brilliance, too, that can only be experienced in a slumber disconnected from the world, and which remains inarticulable." Boredom, understood in this vein, involves enchanting potential that cannot be perceived from the outside—and this sounds promising indeed. My somewhat pragmatic concern connected to pedagogy nevertheless is that authors thus writing on the dazzling, brilliant, and contemplative aspects of boredom are notably often abstract, failing to addressing concrete situations of learning. Their focus tends toward the virtual, rather than the actual, and without necessarily considering how the virtual might be actualized.

Boredom is likely to be the bleakest of the affective formations examined in this book in that it truncates the body's very capacities to act. For the bored, nothing is exciting, and if, following Tomkins, I am, above all, what excites me, then boredom entails a literal shrinking of the self. At the same time, boredom in academic accounts operates as an evasive, expansive referent encompassing seemingly anything from the lack of external stimuli—as in having nothing specific to do, vacantly staring out the window, letting one's mind wander from one daydream and association to another—to states of existential flatness bordering on, or indicative of clinical depression. *Not doing anything*, one of my very favorite preoccupations, does not equal being bored. Just as being alone does not necessitate loneliness, the lack of activity does not translate as boredom. It is entirely possible to look at the waves on a lake or the people passing by without really paying attention, to play the same numbingly repetitive casual video game over and over again for extended stretches of time, or to merely contemplate the shadows on a wall without thinking much or focusing on anything in particular—and not feel bored. With the further addition of daydreaming, such a state of inaction may even come close to bliss. If one is, in contrast, deeply and utterly bored to the point of lethargy, then creative innovations, engrossing daydreams, and dazzling insights are unlikely to emerge. For this is a state where nothing—whether inner or outer—manages to interest, excite, or matter. Having been there, I am wary of celebrating the possibilities of boredom without attending to the diversity of registers that it involves. I argue that the issue is better framed as one of affective intensities and oscillations within, between, and across them.

Building on Michèle Huguet's theorization of boredom, Ara Osterweil (2004, 452) argues that it is not an issue of lack of desire as much as indetermination: when not finding anything quite interesting enough to focus on and to turn toward, subjects wander without a clear goal, unable to choose a direction or orientation. Boredom, then, comprises something of a temporal limbo and a deeply bodily experience of inertia:

> Boredom renders the thickness of the body and the density of the mind excruciatingly palpable. It is precisely when we find ourselves bored that we are most aware of our own "carnal density"—of the turgidity of our thighs, the heaviness of our eyelids, and the dull but unbearable pulsating of genitals.... [Boring things return] us to our bodies, impregnating us with apprehension, imagination, and desire. When we are bored, our minds are saturated with thought: we *feel* ourselves thinking. (Osterweil 2004, 452–453, emphasis in the original)

Boredom, conceptualized in this vein, is less about bodies being helplessly paralyzed than about them being set in motion. Here, boredom breeds imagination, desire, and thought alike as a process of turning inward where one feels one's body in acutely intense ways. A book one is reading, a porn clip one is watching, or a Facebook news feed one is browsing may be void of interest and excitement and, hence, boring as such. One can equally be dulled into boredom by virtue of the abundance of options on offer. Lingering boredom can nevertheless also open up affective, cognitive, and sensory connections that make it possible to approach and relate to the world differently. Following this line of thought, my proposal is, simply, to reframe boredom as an affective formation encompassing fascination, enchantment, interest, and excitement—and, in doing so, to refuse a diametrical opposition between that which paralyzes (boredom) and that which animates (excitement).

Microevents cut through boredom and interest by carving out enchantments, shocks, and surprises, the fascination of which may well be premised on the ever-looming mundane presence, or fact, of flat disaffection, making evident the dynamic relationship of boredom, interest, and attention (see also Kendall 2019, 216). Boredom can be fleeting, it can linger, or it can weigh us down in an incapacitating manner. It can set things in motion by entailing a desire to move to another affective state, other objects of focus and interest. Boredom can be something to fight through in minutely painstaking academic inquiry or something to overcome when watching an overtly long art house film meandering on with intolerably low tempo. It can equally yield surprising outcomes that add to one's overall liveliness. But none of this is set or predetermined, as boredom is not one thing.

5 Nostalgia: A Toxic Pursuit

This book builds on the premise that the intensities of anxiety and frustration connected to networked media speak of their infrastructural role extending from instrumental functions to ways of being, thinking, and relating. In the student essays that I have been working with, the frustrating lack of network access seems to detach people from the world, bringing forth an almost existentialist revelation connected to the inability to act. Being cut off from one's diverse social connections, entertainment, and information resources results in a perceived crisis of agency—and even in one of meaning. This book proposes taking such dependencies seriously in rendering evident our fundamental embeddedness in networks composed of human and nonhuman actors. This makes it possible to question, as well as to resist, the premise of authenticity at the heart of nostalgic critiques of the current moment clustering around the trope of loss.

The specter of authenticity haunts discussions of media-saturated lives in persistent ways. For Trine Syvertsen and Gunn Enli (2019, 6), the quest for authenticity is connected to "a longing for a less complicated time, when people lived authentically in the moment." Digital detoxes, purges, and fasts are offered as means for reconnecting with one's authentic self, as well as for crafting more meaningful relations with other people and the world at large (see chapter 3). The same premise can be discovered with little effort in diagnoses of internet addiction, as addressed in chapter 2. The notion of authenticity is tightly wound up with that of nostalgia in that a return to a much less media-saturated and networked way of being is also seen as a return to a better, more real and substantial way of existence. Contra to such organic understandings of the self that see technologies as external, and as potentially harmful to people's ways of being and relating, this book argues for individual agency as more of a contingent enterprise reliant on technological actors (and hence as something always already technological). In this perspective, broadly inspired by ANT, people are parts of continually transforming networks on which they are dependent, and which define them. Instances of being cut off from these networks make evident less the particularity of one's inner being than the gravity and width of one's multiple connections, attachments, and dependencies (see also Escudero 2014, 12).

Off the Grid, Back in Time?

Writing on instances of technological failure, the students cited in this book voice fundamental ambiguities connected to the devices and services that they daily use. On the one hand, smart devices make life easier, they have grown indispensable in the management of everyday lives, and they yield all kinds of pleasures. On the other hand, there is an uneasy edge to such dependency, given that technological failure is always possible and one's capacity to act is therefore to a degree precarious to begin with. There can nevertheless be surprising joy to temporary lack of access as a passing adventure of sorts:

> On one level, I criticize contemporary technology but I'm still quite happy about how easy everything is. Although it feels that contemporary technology has made people lazier and helpless, I wouldn't want to go back in time to when everything had to be pre-agreed many days ahead...
>
> A couple of years ago there was a winter storm. ... My grandma's house is ... in the middle of the forest and trees falling on power lines caused blackouts that lasted for days. The army evacuated people from their homes but our granny refused to go anywhere. She said that she wouldn't leave her home and she'd manage just fine ... but my mom and I went to keep her company for a couple of days.
>
> We arrived midday at my grandma's house, which was the time of day when there was momentary daylight. My grandma warned already beforehand that the TV didn't work and you couldn't charge phones either. It was fun to notice all the things you came up with when not being able to use any electronic devices. There was so much to do! We went to a wood-heated sauna and read magazines by candlelight and spent more time outdoors than in a long while. ...
>
> Power came back after four days of darkness. Although we'd managed the blackout together with the help of humor, we did cheer aloud a little when the digital clock started to blink with four red zeroes at eight in the morning. My

grandma immediately dashed to put on the morning TV, and my mom and I started to make coffee. After that I did appreciate contemporary technology in a completely different way, and how easy everything ultimately is. As is typical of people these days, I've almost forgotten this four-day experience and I'm so used to so-called easy life again that I complain about even the smallest of adversities. (female, b. 1987)

While warmly remembered, the experience of a longer power outage made evident the ease of life that diverse technologies, from electric lights to coffee makers and TV, afford. In the following excerpt, another student reminisces about a blackout in a similarly positive vein, yet without any desire to experience one again:

I wouldn't want to be a stupid contemporary person who misses the computer's artificial life to brighten up her everyday life. But this is what I've grown into and very much stuck in this role.

So, I've grown into a person whose life is very dependent on electronic devices. … It's lousy, actually even hard, to be without a cell phone or a computer. And it would be hard to do much of the schoolwork without the internet. Yet I always feel like an idiot when losing my nerves over something like the net not working. I recall an incident from my childhood when we had a blackout for four days. My father was away on business so my mother had to spend those days at home with me and my brother. We did fine there although it was almost impossible to prepare food and there really weren't any activities. You could oddly come up with things to do just by using your imagination and it wasn't until towards the end that my mother started to lose her nerves over the situation. Now that I think of many days without electricity, it feels absolutely impossible. I get my nerves into tatters already when a net connection plays tricks, what if there wasn't any net, no television, and not even lights? (female, b. 1991)

Both students cited above note that a couple of days without electricity were possible, even fine, yet undesirable. The idea of a simpler life unencumbered by network connectivity, let alone void of any electronic devices at all, did not hold promises of mindfulness or authenticity but simply came across as unappealing. At the same time, the essays equally point to glimpses of pleasure. Describing smartphones breaking down and the need to momentarily resort to their older devices, the following two excerpts describe enjoyment in having the routines of communication transformed:

As a smartphone user, I'm used to browsing the web even several times an hour but the shell [shaped phone] made it only possible to call, send SMS, and play Snake. Against all expectation, using a device several years old felt very liberating rather than frustrating as it was completely unnecessary to constantly fiddle with the phone. Especially during the second breakdown, I enjoyed net-free life very much as I happened to spend the week alone at the summer cottage: I wandered in the woods, had sauna, and read a lot. During this time, contact with my close ones also felt considerably more meaningful and satisfying as, rather than chatting uselessly, so to say, on Facebook, I sent messages with actual content or called people that I hadn't spoken with for a long time. During the first days, it really felt like I'd missed out on important info and discussion by being unreachable to WhatsApp groups but the feeling was quickly surpassed by the joys of swimming in the sea and heating up the fireplace. (female, b. 1993)

It was fascinating to notice that during those two days I actually felt quite liberated. Instead of WhatsApp I needed to call or send traditional text messages, I didn't check Facebook every 15 minutes and when I wanted to know what the weather was like, I had to look out the window instead of just staring at the forecasts on the phone's weather app. (female, b. 1993)

These students describe instances of technological failure as facilitating a reflexive reverting to earlier communication habits dictated by the concrete limitations of older generation devices. While describing their FOMO, the students equally write of shifting from phatic social media communication—that is, communication for communication's sake (Miller 2008)—to more substantial forms of personal messaging. Such transformations are described as liberating for the period of time that it took to get the cell phones back from repair: a week and two days, respectively. The enjoyment taken in breaks from habitual smartphone use was nevertheless dependent on the situation being temporary rather than one involving more sustained rupture. For, as they continue,

These days I still occasionally dream that my technical gadgets broke down and I could focus on the really essential things in life. A very ascetic setting like the summer cottage where information is available only and just by listening to radio works well for such relaxation but in the city relaxing out of internet's reach could be more difficult, or at least less pleasant. (female, b. 1993)

When one doesn't for example check the phone all the time while at the summer cottage or on a trip abroad, or even have it with you, it's relieving and liberating to momentarily let go of "the imperative of constant presence." Of course, it's a different thing to give it up voluntarily than because a phone for example breaks. ... If and when the problem is then solved and technology starts to work again, one doesn't necessarily feel relieved. For a while one can of course be relived but it's scary how quickly one starts to take the device for granted again. When a phone brought back from repair has been in use for a day, one doesn't even remember the problems—until they sooner or later come back again. That's when the whole emotional cycle starts all over again, and every time technology failing feels at least like the end of the world. (female, b. 1993)

Lack of connectivity can then be enjoyable on a nonpermanent, chosen basis, and in spaces and times of leisure (such as the Finnish institution of a summer cottage that is often off the power grid), yet when it comes to studies, work, and the maintenance of social ties, connectivity is a necessity. A few days' getaway from the habitual uses of gadgets and apps can be something of a relief, yet anxiety builds up if such disconnections drag on against one's volition. Consider, for example, these two accounts of music festivals where cell phone coverage failed. For one student, this involved pleasure—for another, not so much:

I thought probably for the first time how dependent we are on technology and how much technology, and its malfunctions, affect our lives. Scary. On the other hand, the whole weekend without a cell phone was a very refreshing experience. The best memory of the summer is probably connected to [the festival] and how we just lay in the sun and nobody knew what time it was as nobody had any cell phone battery life. (male, b. 1990)

Sure, such action is nostalgic, that you can return back to some ancient age and to the experiences of your parents' age group of how everything used to be better or worse, but I don't necessarily see that as being purposeful. The more important it is to reach someone, the more infuriating it is when networks don't work. (female, b. 1987)

The latter student, for whom lack of connectivity was insupportable, points out that while the discourse of nostalgia—as articulated in the joy of returning back to a simpler, disconnected life—comes across as recognizable, it fails to hold any allure for her on a personal level. For yet others, this discourse can be appealing as a fantasy: "I sometimes wish that I'd been a 1960s youth for whom radio and TV were the only technologies," a student born in 1984 writes, obviously without having the possibility to know first-hand whether she would indeed have enjoyed such a context of life.

Media Nostalgia: Please Don't

Nostalgia, derived from the Greek terms *nostos*, return home, and *algos*, pain, literally signifies acute homesickness but is generally used to communicate a longing for things past, otherwise missed, or out of reach. According to the OED, nostalgia stands for "a sentimental longing or wistful affection for a period in the past" and "something done or presented in order to evoke feelings of nostalgia." Nostalgia's temporary orientation and focus can be ephemeral, geared toward not only the past but equally the present, or an imagined future. As Katharina Niemeyer (2014, 2) points out, nostalgia "is related to a way of living, imagining and sometimes exploiting or (re)inventing the past, present and future." As such, it operates as a mood and a mode—as both a feeling and a style involving negative and positive associations (Grainge 2000, 29; Niemeyer 2014, 6). Understood in this vein, nostalgia entails affective management that coins distances and proximities between the past and the present moment, the objects lost and those now present, the person feeling the loss, and the world as it is and as it (presumably) previously was.

The persistent trope of loss and crisis connected to networked media, as examined throughout this book, more or less explicitly frames the preceding moment—be it one of premodernity or a time preceding the era of personal smart devices—as somehow simpler, better, fuller, and more authentic or human than the present one or future ones (see also Sundén 2015b, 135). Syvertsen and Enli (2019) note how "authenticity is often used as a synonym of originality, and nostalgia for a historic past before commercialization and mass-production culture." Yet, as the culture critic Mary McNamara (2019) sharply argues, times were never, simply, simpler: "Unless you were a member of the white, male, Christian, heterosexual, able-bodied, culturally conforming, nonaddicted, mentally well, moneyed elite, there was literally no time in history that was simpler, better, easier, or greater. For most people, history is the story of original oppression gradually lessened through a series of struggles and setbacks."

A similar antinostalgic punch is evident in the online meme "I wish America could go back to the 50s when things were simpler," which, illustrated with a full-blown retro rendition of happy white American midcentury family life, outlines some of the social limitations and relations of power involved. "I can't get through my day without a shit ton of drugs," reads a caption attached to a smiling young woman. "I'm secretly gay," goes the identification for a merry young man. "I'm not allowed to wear pants or go to college," is the caption for a girl holding a bottle of Coke. "I have polio," exclaims the caption for a boy leaning on a baseball bat. Finally, the caption for a grinning older man states, "I beat the shit out of my son and molested my daughter and no one will ever do a goddamn thing about it."

Antinostalgia meme, https://me.me/i/i-wish-america-could-go-back-to-the-50s-when-f 02e85bd6d7249488ace5f899d4fd47d.

Operating through the juxtaposition between a lushly nostalgic retro image and sarcastic captions, the meme more than readily reads as an exposé of heterosexual nuclear family life, equating the ideal of a simpler life with stifling gendered and sexual norms—as well as with deadly infectious diseases that have since been virtually eliminated.

As some of the sources cited in this book have made evident, the dominant voices articulating narratives of deterioration connected to media technology—and, more broadly, to modernity—have notably often been those of older white men belonging to the established cultural elite within the Global North, contributing to what is in popular parlance unfavorably referred to as a "sausage fest" (defined by the Urban Dictionary as referring to "a surplus and disproportionate ratio of males to females at a social gathering"). Although a sausage-rife gender imbalance is not unusual in cultural theory as such, it necessarily speaks of an imbalance of voice in diagnoses of both the past and the present—a point already raised in chapter 4 in the context of gendered boredom. Racialized, feminist, and queer scholars have

seldom contributed to narratives of loss looking back to an assumedly better past. Most feminist authors, for example, have not articulated nostalgia
for the arguably enchanted premodern days preceding women's social suf-
frage, possibilities for financial independence, rights to bodily autonomy,
education, political participation, or profession, any more than racialized
subjects living in North America or Europe—with the possible exception of
indigenous people—have recalled most past decades as eras of better life.
LGBTQ+ communities are similarly unlikely to consider the good old days
preceding the 1960s counterculture as a really great time, given that these
involved the imminent threat of incarceration and state violence, diagnoses
of mental disorder allowing for medical inquiry, the social enforcement of a
closeted life, and the corresponding devastation of social isolation. Indeed,
it can be asked to what degree the strain of nostalgia cutting through discourses of loss spanning from the mid-nineteenth century to the current
day implies longing for days past when the social roles and positions were
more clear and fixed, where high culture was marked apart from the femi-
nized trivia of commercial entertainment, and when the public sphere was
an arena for white upper class men to be heard in.

Modernization, urbanization, and the rise of media culture have all played
a role in the democratization of society from one built on caste distinctions
to one allowing for social diversity and acknowledging, even if not necessarily respecting, equal human, civil, and political rights. These same
developments have contributed to late (or, depending on the perspective
taken, advanced) capitalism that is actively destroying the planet through
climate change and the mass extinction of species—a fact worthy of vocal
lament if ever there was one. Anthropocentric analyses of media and technology offering general accounts of the fate and state of humankind tend
not to account for the broader worldly contexts or impacts of these developments (these are foregrounded in discussions on media and the Anthropocene instead; see Parikka 2015a, 2015b; Zylinska 2014). Meanwhile, despite
human-centric narratives decrying the impact of media technology on the
fate and state of humankind, society, and culture, such losses have not been
equally distributed or registered.

I argue that critiques of the contemporary, for which there is certainly
much need, should build on something other than wistful nostalgia if they
are to hold a critical edge. Moreover, these critiques need to be careful
and nuanced in terms of the contexts and the subjects that they presume

and build on. This point is connected to how social positions of privilege map onto ways of registering and articulating losses and gains connected to modernity and networked media, as well as to how a fuller and more meaningful past, as postulated in so many critiques of the contemporary moment, may be little else than a figure of fantasy (albeit, as discussed in chapter 4, a discursively compelling one). As Dominic Pettman (2016, 127) argues in his critique of nostalgic romanticization of a pre-internet world, "as if people were organically more considerate or intelligent or empathetic. One casual glance at the twentieth century will put a lie to that little fantasy."

The overall shift from a media culture of relative scarcity to one of abundance, which John Ellis (2000) addressed in the context of transforming television culture, extends to all forms of media. Consider, for example, the media landscape of early 1980s Finland, which consisted of newspapers and magazines available for subscribers; an expansive public library system; two national television channels with limited commercial airtime and approximately six hours of daily programming; two public service radio stations and no commercial ventures till 1985; cinemas and video rentals mainly available in towns; and LPs, audiocassette tapes, and videotapes available in shops and via mail order nationwide. An entire week's television programming could fit on one magazine spread whereas the current mass of freely available daily televisual content well exceeds such spatial confines. Looking at the programming schedules of the 1980s with a class mainly born in the 1990s is an efficient means of visualizing transformations in both the volume and content of televisual entertainment—if, indeed, entertainment is an apt term to be used for the programming once on offer. In classroom discussions, these schedules, and the broader media landscape they speak of, generally fail to be seen as representative of any golden era of deeper and more meaningful media consumption; rather, they speak of scarcity, centralized distribution, and inevitable boredom connected to the shortage of alternatives.

In this landscape preceding the accumulation of archival content on online platforms, media objects could grow fascinating and gain cult value merely by virtue of their inaccessibility: just having access to a rare film— such Todd Haynes's endlessly bootlegged 1988 short film *Superstar*, enacting the career and demise of Karen Carpenter with Barbie dolls, or David Lynch's equally elusive *Eraserhead* of 1977—was an event in itself, independent of what one made of it. As once rare movies can be viewed as streaming video, or downloaded as torrents from specialist sites, their value and criteria of interest and relevance is differently drawn, this being less a loss than an option for people to construe their own hierarchies of interest and preference as detached from degrees of unavailability. Furthermore, in spite of the invasive governance and surveillance practiced by data giants through which much of social media traffic circulates, or the data and filter bubbles that polarize public debate and fuel aggressive antagonisms, the multiplicity of perspectives and voices available in contemporary media is unparalleled. Affective publics emerge and wither on; collective action becomes organized through; and intimate ties are founded, maintained, and severed via platforms affording access to diverse stories told, opinions debated, and archives opened up for use. This list could go on, and on—as could a listing of the things arguably being lost.

Despite the anxieties connected to the dictates of ubiquitous connectivity, something is obviously gained from them beyond filling a social obligation—a point cutting through this book. Networked media are frequently experienced as pleasurable, and it is central to understand the serendipitous intensities that they cater as not merely being synonymous with fun but equally as connected to that which is interesting, exciting, distressing, infuriating, distracting, and important (Sicart 2014, 3). Without degrees of interest and excitement, things simply fail to attract and hold attention. Returning to Silvan Tomkins's notion, "I am, above all, what excites me," it is crucial for cultural inquiry to focus on minor instances of richness and excitement, and to take them seriously, if we are to explain the appeal of networked media, or even that of popular culture more broadly, in terms other than those of false consciousness and dementing powers that are assumedly eating away at our powers of rational thought and meaningful sociability.

Ambiguity does not exactly thrive in the recurrent, broad diagnoses of networked culture examined in this book. In their diverse applications as "strong theory," diagnoses of addiction, acceleration, shallowness, unhappiness, distraction, and boredom tend toward both the generalized and the bleak by highlighting things lost over that which may be coming about or transforming in less unequivocal ways. Reading these more or less pessimistic diagnoses connected to modernity, media, urbanization, technology, and social media in some depth and range makes evident the degree to which semidystopian writing becomes conflated with, or mistaken for, critical work (such a collapse being, of course, inherent in how the notion of critical theory refers to the legacy of the Frankfurt school at the expense of other critical forms of theorizing).

By asking what forms of experience may appear as others are bound to undergo change, it is possible to eschew totalizing narratives while remaining open to ambiguity and the possibilities of multiple knowledges. There is no way for us to construe with any certainty the degrees and qualities of focus that people held only a decade ago, even if considering ourselves and our experiences within the confines that these can be retrospectively recalled and reconstructed. We surely cannot know what the future may bring, yet we do know that focusing on macrolevel diagnoses alone will leave us blind to the complexity that makes culture in the first place. For, as Kylie Jarrett (2015a, 102) points out, "Binaries are fundamentally unhelpful in understanding the complexity of economically significant but socially important labour such as…digitally mediated communication." Keeping this in mind, and being equally mindful of unsteady, spasmodic, and convoluted affective attachments between devices, platforms, and people, it is central to break away from binary framings of optimism versus despair, and to center critical investigation on ambiguity instead.

Through my use of student essays, I have proposed making use of the university classroom as a reflective space for tackling the current sociotechnical conjuncture and the affective formations that it entails. In describing dependence as giving rise to frustration, attention as blending into distraction, and fascination, interest, and excitement as vacillating with boredom, these accounts cut across the personal and the social, the singular and the structural, affording resonant connections between different levels of critical analysis. When extending to historical investigation, it becomes evident that similar affective formations have been identified and described at different points of modernity in connection with transformations in media technology. The persistent recurrence of distraction and boredom in particular helps to see how contemporaneous concerns are not merely specific to this particular moment. Historical and contextual inquiry also makes evident the clustering of the persistent concern of loss on younger people. Marcel O'Gorman (2015) suggests that the seduction of narratives of loss connected to networked media, as presented in diagnoses of digital dementia, for example, is built on "a desire to find relief from the digital devices to which we are constantly tethered." Furthermore, especially for those who have not been co-evolving with digital media since their birth, a diagnosis of digital dementia would be a great excuse to take a vacation from the tyranny of e-mail, texting, Facebook, and so on. The existence of such a *disease* also provides the baby boomer generation, which is facing the very real prospect of age-related dementia, with evidence that the digital natives who follow them are possibly less intelligent than their elders. Digital dementia, then, will be viewed by many as a pseudoscience fuelled by curmudgeonly jealousy and fear. (O'Gorman 2015, emphasis in the original)

Framing the issue as one of generational friction and envy, O'Gorman explains the compelling qualities of pessimistic accounts as stemming from incompatibilities between how different subjects—"the boomers" and "the kids"—live out in the world and conceptualize their agency within it. Although this explanation may cut some corners short, it points to an imbalance of voice, and the ensuing imbalance of perspectives covered in diagnoses of connectivity. It is also one foregrounded in analyses of moral panics as "a remarkably common phenomenon in our culture, arising repeatedly in our history seemingly whenever a new generation asserts its values (which are often at odds with the previous generation's) on society" (Tarantola 2018). In many of the diagnoses examined in this book, media technology, and networked media in particular, is positioned as a threatening, nefarious force (or pharmakos) overriding individual and collective agency. In other diagnoses, it is the logic and rhythms of capitalism that are at stake, networked media representing the symptom rather than the cause. All in all, networked media and smart devices feature rhetorically as both poison and scapegoat—but much more rarely as any kind of a cure (see also Pettman 2016, 4–5). When applied as a conceptual framework in studies of networked media, the pharmakon, in encompassing all these dimensions, works against interpretations focusing solely on either good or bad effects, while also allowing for critiques of scapegoating where devices, apps, specific companies, or infrastructural connections are to blame for broad and complex social, political, and economic developments.

Causes, Effects, and Unhappy Affect

In a 2014 study published in *Science*, Timothy D. Wilson and his research group conducted eleven studies in which people were left alone in an unadorned room, stripped of their belongings such as smartphones for six to fifteen minutes, with nothing else to do than to think "happy thoughts." The first test group consisted of college students who, on average, found it difficult to concentrate: their mind wandered, and they did not much enjoy the experience (Wilson et al. 2014, 75). The experiment continued in domestic environments, without a significant difference in the findings. In one experiment, participants were given the option to engage in activities such as web browsing, reading, or listening to music, which they found more enjoyable than just thinking. Another test group, ages 18 to 77, was recruited, and the results were similar, leading the researchers to conclude that there "was no evidence that enjoyment of the thinking period was related to participants' age, education, income, or the frequency with which they used smart phones or social media" (Wilson et al. 2014, 76). In other words, the findings did not support the assumption that younger people are more easily bored or more unable to concentrate or think than older ones, or that the uses of networked media have much of an impact on the whole matter.

The part of the study to attract media attention was nevertheless the feature of its research design wherein participants could choose between just being alone in the room with no external stimulus, trying to think their happy thoughts, and experiencing negative stimulation in the form of an electric shock. Two thirds of the male and one quarter of the female study participants opted for the shock, inspiring news headlines such as "Why Students Chose to Shock Themselves Rather Than Sit Alone with Their Thoughts" (Ghomogu 2014) and "Shocking but True: Students Prefer Jolt of Pain to Being Made to Sit and Think" (Sample 2014). In such clickbait-worthy titles, contrary to actual findings, the study seemed to confirm the worst of fears concerning young adults and their alarmingly dysfunctional cognitive capacities. Commenting on the study for *The Guardian*, cognitive scientist Jessica Andrews-Hanna however argued that "many students would probably zap themselves to cheer up a tedious lecture." She further questioned the overall research setup: "A person is told to sit in a chair with wires attached to their skin, and a button that will deliver a harmless but uncomfortable shock, and they are told to just sit there and entertain themselves with their thoughts.... As they sit there, strapped to this machine, their mind starts to wander, and it naturally goes to that shock" (in Sample 2014). Writing for *The New Yorker*, Ferris Jabr (2014) similarly pointed out,

On average, participants rated their fifteen minutes of contemplation slightly below the midpoint of "somewhat enjoyable," and those who zapped themselves did not rate being alone with their thoughts as significantly less agreeable than those who refrained. Some participants likely regarded the contraptions—to which, after all, they were attached—as a mild temptation or a moment's amusement. And who's to say someone can't enjoy a little daydreaming punctuated by an electric thrill or two? Perhaps, rather than offering a respite from thought, the shocks stimulated new ideas or steered thinking in new directions.

As these commentators suggest, the study cannot be used to argue for people's inability to think, or their aversion toward doing so. In any instance, it cannot be used to argue for the exceptionality of students over the rest of the population in terms of their capacity to endure isolation from external stimuli or to think happy thoughts on request without having self-driven motivation to do so. Would the people in question have considered zapping themselves without the option being offered? No, probably not. Can they enjoy being alone with their thoughts outside a controlled test environment? Perhaps, yes. The study involving forced disconnection and mandatory happy thoughts was simply not experienced as enjoyable. This is unsurprising, and, unlike the researchers propose, it does not quite follow that the participants suffer from a "disengaged mind" that would benefit from meditation and other techniques for its better control (Wilson et al. 2014, 77). No evidence pointed to correlations (let alone causalities) between failing to enjoy the experiment and being used to constant networked media use, nor was there any evidence of students being more unhappy about being alone with their thoughts than people in their seventies. This, of course, did not stop media coverage from singling out the millennials as suffering from worrisome cognitive crisis.

The 2019 *World Happiness Report*, published by the United Nations Sustainable Development Solutions Network, offers yet another investigation into the causes and effects of unhappy affects and contemporary networked media—one focusing on adolescents rather than young adults (Helliwell et al. 2019). Happiness and life satisfaction among U.S. adolescents has, according to the report, been on the decrease since 2012. This is associated with an increase in "screen activities (especially digital media such as gaming, social media, texting, and time online)" via smartphones: "By 2017, the average 12th grader (17–18 years old) spent more than 6 hours a day of leisure time on just three digital media activities (internet, social media, and texting …).

By 2018, 95% of United States adolescents had access to a smartphone, and 45% said they were online 'almost constantly'" (Twenge 2019, 89).

Connected to a decrease in face-to-face communication, in attending religious services, and in reading printed matter, screen time is identified as bringing forth unhappiness among the young (Twenge 2019). This diagnosis is disconnected from qualitative studies on the myriad roles that networked media play in the lives of young people and families, which argue that it replaces face-to-face communication since American parents, vigilant about their children's safety, do not let them run around independently so as to have physical space and time alone with their friends (e.g., boyd 2014; Clark 2013). Perhaps even more crucially, the report eschews contextual factors, simply arguing that "adolescents who spend more time on electronic devices are less happy, and adolescents who spend more time on most other activities are happier" (Twenge 2019, 92). The study then suggests that it does not matter what adolescents do with their devices: in a reverberation of Marshall McLuhan's (1964) slogan, "The medium is the message," networked media comes across as a killer of happiness.

A young person handling a smart device may nevertheless grow distressed when coming across news items on the spread of COVID-19 in their own cities, climate change, rainforests being burned down, species dying out virtually on camera, documentations of school shootings, gun violence, and their aftermath, continuous incidents of sexual, racial, and gendered violence, the level of college tuition fees and student debt, the threat and fact of global and domestic terrorism, or the striking precarity of available career paths where financial stability is seldom promised. The millennials have, for some years now, been identified as a generation that will never reach their parents' standard of living, and there is little reason to expect that things will grow any better for those even younger. The younger generations are not, in short, promised a particularly sweet deal in terms of future careers, income, or even an inhabitable planet. To paraphrase a Finnish proverb, knowledge adds to agony—or, as Pettman (2016, x) puts it, "The more we notice about how the world works, the more we are likely to feel a crippling combination of fury, resentment, depression, shame, and helplessness." The message, and not just the medium, may also matter in the equation.

The narrative positioning of digital technologies, and networked media in particular, as "bad objects" responsible for young people's unhappiness is ironically critiqued in a 2017 tweet by the U.K.-based writer Parker, which has, in the time of this writing, had some 150,000 retweets and had been liked close to 350,000 times. The tweet, also broadly appropriated and recirculated as a meme on other social media outlets, presents a fictional exchange between parents and children:

Parents: Kids are more depressed these days, I wonder why?

Kids: You destroyed the economy for us, the earth is literally dying, we are going to work until we die and on top of that the Nazis are back.

Parents: It's those pesky iPhones. (November 28, 2017)

The scapegoating connected to networked media as agents of unhappiness may involve specific devices (as in "those pesky iPhones"), the addictive qualities of apps and sites, the consuming pressure of FOMO, or the envy experienced toward Instagram posts depicting aspirational influencer lives well beyond one's own reach. There may certainly be uneasiness and displeasure to all this, yet unease and displeasure concerning life, and the world at large, is hardly confined to the realm of networked media.

As an attempt to measure, quantify, and compare experiences of happiness, World Happiness Rankings builds on self-reporting measuring positive affect as "the average frequency of happiness, laughter and enjoyment on

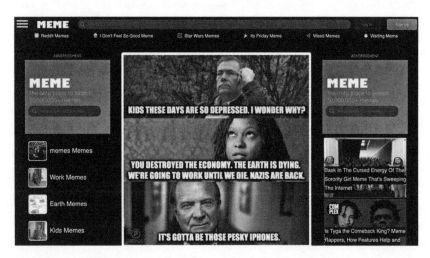

"Pesky iPhone" meme variation framed as a conflict between baby boomers and young people, https://me.me/i/kids-these-days-are-so-depressed-i-wonder-why-you-destroyed -19652836.

the previous day" and negative affect as "the average frequency of worry, sadness and anger on the previous day." In addition, it considers a range of societal parameters, from social support to healthy life expectancy, gross domestic product, and indexes of freedom to make life choices (Helliwell, Huang, and Wang 2019, 12). The United States was ranked nineteenth in 2019, with low scores in life choices in particular. Meanwhile, Finland, a country with even higher network connectivity and particularly high mobile data use among young people, came in first, implying that screen time may not directly correlate with happiness as it can be measured. All the top-rated countries in the study were wealthy, North European countries combining high internet use with some welfare state infrastructure still in place, suggesting that the quality of life is higher in countries where social equality is infrastructurally supported through free educational opportunities and universal health care, for example. Without going further into a discussion of the study in question, the point I want to make is that here, as elsewhere, screen time and smart devices operate as facile scapegoats attracting attention away from more complex economic and societal explanations that hold much more analytical leverage.

Examining a 2011 survey on attitudes toward the economic and social climate in the United Kingdom, which also aimed to chart levels of happiness, Rebecca Coleman (2016) argues that it speaks of a conjuncture wherein austerity politics and indebtedness feed a particular pessimistic mood concerning the kinds of futures there can be. In other words, pessimism about the future comes about as a mood, or "enveloping atmosphere," of austerity (Coleman 2016, 84). In Coleman's analysis, austerity politics leading to extensive cuts in public spending and increased disparities in levels of income, in combination with awareness of both national and personal debt, weigh heavily on people who cannot imagine the future as being a better place and who experience stress, anxiety, and anger about surviving in the present. The survey studied framed the mood of pessimism as particularly concerning "today's youth," positioning the young as prone to "fears about the diminished future" (Coleman 2016, 96). Even though pessimism was equally registered among female and low-income respondents, young people were seen to have especially lost touch with their own future (see also Hakim 2019, 15). Since young people symbolically stand for futurity, the British society at large was effectively seen as losing its grip on the future.

Pessimism, for Coleman (2016, 96), ranges from the flatness of depression to the sharpness of alertness and anxiety: "It is not (only) that the future cannot be imagined as better … but it is (also) that the financial situations that austerity induces 'traps' attention in and on the present." The difference from contemporary analyses focused on the ill effects of smart technology is nothing short of striking here. The issue, for Coleman, does not concern the habits and speeds of networked media but rather the overall horizon of expectation over one's possibilities to live, let alone prosper. Anxiety, depression, and sense of perpetual presentness surface from the overall mood of austerity where the future keeps on changing and where planning is impossible, enveloping the subjects in question, and rendering the affective formations of networked media an adjacent (rather than a determining) issue. It is not, however, simply the issue that presentness evacuates a sense of the future, as "the future does not become irrelevant or wiped out" (Coleman 2016, 99). Applying Lauren Berlant's (2011) notion of "cruel optimism," Coleman argues that pessimism and optimism need not be seen as mutually conflicting or opposing states. Rather, both can be flattening and enlivening, and experienced through a range of affects. Pessimism may also entail hopefulness—albeit hardly that of an unreserved kind—toward the future: "Hopeful pessimism can be understood as a mood that involves being worn out by debt and austerity and a resistance to this wearing out" (Coleman 2016, 100).

Coleman's analysis is important here in (at least) three ways. *First*, it points to the centrality of contextual nuance in considerations of the affective formations of contemporary culture by highlighting how social and economic inequalities impact bodies in different ways, giving rise to different senses of precarity, insecurity, and anxiety. Rather than addressing the operations of late capitalism, neoliberal capitalism, or data capitalism on a general, undifferentiated plane of experience (that of "us all"), it is necessary to consider which subjects become figures of concern, as well has how subjects themselves make sense of the present and future alike. *Second*, this contextual insistence inevitably means that smart devices, networked connections, or screen time can offer only partial explanations of the ambiguities involved in our ways of feeling out the world and our agency within it. Focusing on networked media alone is likely to result in analytical myopia. *Third*, and in connection with the previous point, the seeming oxymoron of "hopeful pessimism" and the different figures of the future that it helps to coin speak of affective ambiguity, wherein contradicting forces pull bodies into different states that can simultaneously exhaust and exhilarate them. Coleman's mood of hopeful pessimism is closely akin to the kind of hybrid affective formations mapped out in this book, from distracted attention and attentive distraction to bored (or boring) enchantment and enchanting boredom, in that it refuses to be pinned down into the singularly negative registers and takes seriously the enlivening forces that live amid the apparently flat.

A Persistent Topos

While the studies addressed above—the experiment measuring the displeasure of solitary happy thoughts and the national happiness rankings—are drastically different, and their findings differently ambiguous, in public debate they have both been used as proof of the pernicious impact of networked media on young people in particular. The power of this recurring narrative formula, or topos, is such that it seems resistant to alternative interpretations even when these are more than readily on offer. Whether the young people evoked are children, teenagers, young adults, or combinations thereof—these so-called "digital generations" (Buckingham and Willett 2006)—they are associated with loss, or even degeneration, affected by prosthetic dependency on networked devices and apps.

This leads to a caricature of young people as duped by the attractions of smartphones and the gloss of social media, haunted by FOMO, and unable to either think or focus. This caricature figure is passive and lacking in both critical and analytical capacity and, as such, is clearly incompatible with the parallel figure characterizing the millennials as a "woke generation" attuned to social justice and injustice (in terms of race, sexuality, gender, and ability alike). Activists even younger, such as Emma González and David Hogg, survivors of the Parkland high school shooting advocating for gun control since 2018, or Greta Thunberg, the Swedish climate activist who, at the age of fifteen, launched the international school strike for climate the same year, have similarly little room in this topos of concern. By 2019, the climate strike had spread to 125 countries and involved over a million participants: without social media, none of this would have happened.

The categorical, dismissive characterization of young people as helpless pawns of data capitalism is connected to long-standing rhetorical figures used in cultural theory for addressing cultural and technological transformations taking place. In addition to often being young, these figures have regularly been female—as in Siegfried Kracauer's "little shopgirls" symbolizing shallow, flat cultural homogeneity lacking the capacity for critical thought—even when the developments discussed assumedly encompass the society at large. On the one hand, the broad zeitgeist diagnoses addressed in this book are largely disinterested in, and hence fail to acknowledge, diversity in how different subjects experience the world and operate in it: there is selective blindness at play. On the other hand, the figure of unhappy young people evoked to address and embody a cognitive crisis remains very much connected to, and sticks to, particular subjects.

Scholarship addressing the impact of media technology is, especially in its more historical incarnations, rife with not only ageism but also sexism, racism, and classism: here, a cursory reading of Marshall McLuhan's discussion of gender and technology in *The Mechanical Bride* (1951) or his characterizations of racial differences in *Understanding Media* (1964) suffice as illustration. Meanwhile, Martin Heidegger, key philosopher of technology, boredom, and mood alike, was famously a member of the National Socialist German Worker's Party (vernacularly known as the Nazi Party) since 1933 and consequently not my first personal pick for thinking issues of social equality with. There is obvious tension involved in drawing on such bodies of literature in feminist cultural studies inquiry. My starting point has not, however, been to launch a critique of any specific bodies of work but instead to think alongside them from a reflective distance and to outline alternative narrative trajectories to the ones amply on offer. Rather than adopting any singular theoretical framework, I have drawn on multiple ones with the general aim of challenging singular and deterministic readings of the current conjuncture.

My solution to work with student accounts, as micronarratives of sorts, has been motivated by a desire for an interpretative framework detached from totalizing zeitgeist diagnoses involving both generalized and specific model subjects (which, generalized as they are, fail to be identified in their specificity). As the essay excerpts cited in this book show, students, as young adults, have considerable analytical skill in making sense of their own lives, the meanings and roles of different media, and the commercial frameworks that they are embedded in and feed to—from the traffic of user data to the planned obsolescence of the devices they can barely afford to purchase. Their accounts are resistant to overarching narratives of either truncated attention spans or sovereign multitaskers, offering fine-spun reflections instead. In doing so, they help us to think beyond stories of loss and lament—as well as beyond those of optimistic, peppy celebration. These are not "happy stories" but ambivalent and contradictory ones. Within them, the pleasures and, hence, the affective value of social media come haunted by blandness and disaffection, and the very access to platforms may well be laced with regular bouts of participatory reluctance.

Following Jacques Derrida (1981, 125), who argues that the "essence" of the pharmakon lies in its lack of stable essence or characteristics, the effects or experiences of networked media are never singular and thus remain open to multiple, mutually contradicting interpretations. As a pharmakon, networked media feed the affective formation of dependence that grants a sense of sustained connection to people, media content, and information resources that matter. Networked media function as an infrastructure of intimacy that we depend on for living, even when such dependencies yield sensations of helplessness, frustration, and anxiety—both in instances when such networks are unavailable and when the toll of connectivity seems to eat away at our very capacity to act. Networked media equally fuel the affective formation of distraction, which is generally seen to impede and damage the capacity to focus. Digital distractions abound, and focus is fickle but also grows acute, moving from one object to another, and possibly back again, in accordance with one's levels of interest. When distraction and attention are, in their speedy rhythms, understood as two sides of the same coin, or even as possibly the very same side, gradations within them become connected to perceived importance and affective investment. Attention becomes recalibrated as matters of interest are weeded out from the mass of inconsequential stuff.

Finally, these distractions are seen to bore us through acceleration and oversaturation of stimulation. The affective formation of boredom is connected to the more toxic aspects of networked-media-as-pharmakon as persistent flatness and dullness of experience where things do not matter or stick. As I have argued above, boredom is in dynamic relation with enchantment, fascination, interest, and excitement, entailing affective intensity, and hence never constant. Occurring as fleeting microevents that may be barely registered, or as more sustained affective attachments, enchantments yield meaning and sense of worth to our mundane engagements and make things matter.

The pharmakon constitutes an ambiguous "medium in which opposites are opposed" (Derrida 1981, 126), and this malleability of function undoes the oppositions through which the concept itself is being defined. As Bernard Stiegler (2012a, 2013) argues in his take on the concept, networked media both fuel cognitive capitalism and generate alternative modes of social existence and exchange. A similar tension is inherent in the notion of captivation connected to devices and apps: a captive is held hostage, yet captivation also equals being attracted by, enchanted by, or interested in the things that enchant and catch one's attention. Focusing solely on the direness of developments connected to networked media blocks from view the complexities and rifts that exist and that allow for imagining different kinds of futures (see also Lemmens 2011). Hence the importance of considering dependence in connection with agency, distraction as tied in with attention, and boredom as breeding instances of richness and enchantment.

For Coleman, the mood of pessimism may swiftly slide to optimism and the two can share the same qualities. I have similarly argued for understanding distraction as a form of attention, and vice versa, the differences between the two being ones of rhythm and intensity—and, consequently, investments of time and affect. Boredom, interest, and excitement can similarly be seen as patterns in the same fabric, as oscillations of affective intensity that endow experience with particular qualities. Here, smart devices are made sense of as prosthetic extensions evoking equivocal sensations of dependence, yet also as that which make it possible for individuals to operate in the world and for their everyday lives to work.

The appeal of networked media owes to such infrastructural qualities, just as it does to microevents where jolts of disgust, amusement, sentimentality, rage, and lust intermesh and layer into an ambivalent, mutable, and possibly sticky tapestry of affective value resistant to clear-cut categorization. Within it, user attention travels and halts, and shivers of interest stand out from lingering boredom, while excitement and offence bleed into one another. These variations, in their both rhythmic and erratic movements, increase and diminish our capacities to act, feel, and think, changing from one moment to the next, never quite standing still. Our engagements with networked media are captivating just as they are dull, arresting as well as immobilizing, and absolutely routine-like yet extraordinary in the unexpected pleasures that they cater. This ambiguity matters.

References

ACC Art Association. 2017. Facebook post, February 14. https://www.facebook.com /ACCArtAssociation/photos/the-idea-is-to-occupy-facebook-with-art-breaking-up-all -the-political-posts-whoe/719051411595075.

Adam, Barbara. 2003. "Comment on 'Social Acceleration' by Hartmut Rosa." *Constellations* 10 (1): 49–52.

Ahmed, Sara. 2004. *The Cultural Politics of Emotion*. Edinburgh: Edinburgh University Press.

Ahmed, Sara. 2010. *The Promise of Happiness*. Durham: Duke University Press.

Ahmed, Sara. 2014. "Not in the Mood." *New Formations* 82: 13–28.

Aho, Kevin. 2007. "Simmel on Acceleration, Boredom, and Extreme Aesthesia." *Journal for the Theory of Social Behaviour* 37 (4): 447–462.

Anderson, Ben. 2004. "Time-Stilled Space-Slowed: How Boredom Matters." *Geoforum* 35: 739–754.

Anderson, Sam. 2009. "In Defense of Distraction." *The New Yorker*, May 17. http:// nymag.com/news/features/56793/.

Andreassen, Cecilie Schou, Torbjørn Torsheim, Geir Scott Brunborg, and Ståle Pallesen. 2012. "Development of Facebook Addiction Scale." *Psychological Reports* 110 (2): 501–517.

Andrejevic, Mark. 2011. "Surveillance and Alienation in the Online Economy." *Surveillance & Society* 8: 278–287.

Andrejevic, Mark. 2013. *Infoglut: How Too Much Information Is Changing the Way We Think and Know*. New York: Routledge.

Arcand, Rob. 2019. "David Byrne Launches *Reasons to be Cheerful* Online Magazine." *Spin*, August 24. https://www.spin.com/2019/08/david-byrne-launches-reasons-to-be -cheerful-online-magazine/.

Arcy, Jacquelyn. 2016. "Emotion Work: Considering Gender in Digital Labor." *Feminist Media Studies* 16 (2): 365–368.

Asimov, Isaac. 1965. "Visit to the World's Fair of 2014." *New York Times*, August 16. https://timesmachine.nytimes.com/timesmachine/1964/08/16/issue.html.

Bem, Caroline. 2019. "Cinema | Diptych: *Grindhouse | Deathproof.*" *JCMS: Journal of Cinema and Media Studies* 58 (2): 1–22.

Benjamin, Walter. 2007/1968. *Illuminations.* Edited by Hannah Arendt, translated by Harry Zohn. New York: Shocken Books.

Benjamin, Walter. 1996. *Selected Writings: 1938–1940. Vol. 4.* Translated by Howard Eiland and Michael W. Jennings. Cambridge, MA: Harvard University Press.

Benjamin, Walter. 2002. *The Arcades Project.* Translated by Howard Eiland and Kevin McLaughlin. Cambridge, MA: Harvard University Press.

Bennett, Jane. 2001. *The Enchantment of Modern Life: Attachments, Crossings, and Ethics.* Princeton: Princeton University Press.

Bennett, Sue, Karl Maton, and Lisa Kervin. 2008. "The 'Digital Natives' Debate: A Critical Review of the Evidence." *British Journal of Educational Technology* 39 (5): 775–786.

Bergson, Henri. 2007/1896. *Matter and Memory,* translated by Nancy Margaret Paul and W. Scott Palmer. New York: Cosimo.

Berlant, Lauren. 2000. "Intimacy: A Special Issue." In *Intimacy,* edited by Lauren Berlant, 1–8. Chicago: University of Chicago Press.

Berlant, Lauren. 2006. "Cruel Optimism." *Differences: A Journal of Feminist Cultural Studies* 17 (3): 20–36.

Berlant, Lauren. 2011. *Cruel Optimism.* Durham, NC: Duke University Press.

Berlant, Lauren. 2015. "Structures of Unfeeling: *Mysterious Skin.*" *International Journal of Politics, Culture and Society* 28: 191–213.

Billington, James. 2017. "Facebook Wants to Secretly Watch You through Your Smartphone Camera." *IB Times*, 9 June. http://www.ibtimes.co.uk/facebook-wants-secretly -watch-you-through-your-smartphone-camera-1625061.

Bjerg, Ole. 2008. "Drug Addiction and Capitalism: Too Close to the Body." *Body & Society* 14 (2): 1–22.

Bogard, William. 2000. "Distraction and Digital Culture." *Ctheory.* http://www.ctheory .net/articles.aspx?id=131.

Bourdieu, Pierre. 1984. *Distinction: A Social Critique of the Judgement of Taste.* Translated by Richard Nice. London: Routledge.

boyd, danah. 2014. *It's Complicated: The Social Lives of Networked Teens*. New Haven: Yale University Press.

Bratton, Benjamin H. 2015. *The Stack: On Software and Sovereignty*. Cambridge, MA: MIT Press.

Brennan, Theresa. 2004. *The Transmission of Affect*. Ithaca, NY: Cornell University Press.

Bucher, Taina. 2018. *If ... Then: Algorithmic Power and Politics*. Oxford: Oxford University Press.

Buckingham, David, and Rebekah Willett, eds. 2006. *Digital Generations: Children, Young People, and the New Media*. London: Routledge.

Bulow, Jeremy. 1986. "An Economic Theory of Planned Obsolescence." *The Quarterly Journal of Economics* 101 (4): 729–749.

Burns, Belinda. 2011. "Untold Tales of the Intra-Suburban Female." *M/C Journal* 14 (4). http://www.journal.media-culture.org.au/index.php/mcjournal/article/view/398.

Caliman, Luciana. 2006. "The Concept of Attention in William James–'Make Matrix.'" In *Introspective Self-Rapports: Shaping Ethical and Aesthetic Concepts 1850–2006*, edited by Katrin Solhdju, 21–38. Berlin: Max Planck Institute for the History of Science.

Carr, Nicholas. 2010. *The Shallows: What the Internet Is Doing to Our Brains*. New York: Norton.

Cassidy, Elija. 2016. "Social Networking Sites and Participatory Reluctance: A Case Study of Gaydar, User Resistance and Interface Rejection." *New Media & Society* 18 (11): 2613–2628.

Ceaparu, Irina, Jonathan Lazar, Katie Bessiere, John Robinson, and Ben Shneiderman. 2004. "Determining Causes and Severity of End-User Frustration." *International Journal of Human-Computer Interaction* 17 (3): 333–356.

Chan, Anita Say. 2008. "Slashdot.org." In *The Inner History of Devices*, edited by Sherry Turkle, 125–137. Cambridge, MA: MIT Press.

Choi, Jenn. 2015. "The 2015 Gift Guide for Raising Your Family's EQ." *Forbes*, November 7. https://www.forbes.com/sites/jennchoi/2015/11/07/the-2015-gift-guide-for-raising-your-familys-eq/#694108951a58.

Chun, Wendy Hui Kyong. 2016. *Updating to Remain the Same: Habitual New Media*. Cambridge, MA: MIT Press.

Chun, Wendy Hui Kyong. 2018. "Queering Homophily." In *Pattern Discrimination* by Clemens Apprich, Wendy Hui Kyong Chun, Florian Cramer, and Hito Steyerl, 59–97. Minneapolis: Meson Press.

Clark, Schofield Lynn. 2013. *The Parent App: Understanding Families in the Digital Age.* Oxford: Oxford University Press.

Clark, Lynn Schofield, and Lynn Sywyj. 2012. "Mobile Intimacies in the USA among Refugee and Recent Immigrant Teens and Their Parents." *Feminist Media Studies* 12 (4): 485–495.

Clarke, Roger. 2014. "Persona Missing, Feared Drowned: The Digital Persona Concept, Two Decades Later." *Information Technology & People* 27: 182–207.

Cohen, Stanley, and Laurie Taylor. 1992. *Escape Attempts: The Theory and Practice of Resistance to Everyday Life.* 2nd ed. London: Routledge.

Coleman, Rebecca. 2012. *Transforming Images: Screens, Affect, Futures.* London: Routledge.

Coleman, Rebecca. 2016. "Austerity Futures: Debt, Temporality and (Hopeful) Pessimism as an Austerity Mood." *New Formations* (87): 83–101.

Coleman, Rebecca. 2018. "Theorizing the Present: Digital Media, Pre-Emergence and Infra-Structures of Feeling." *Cultural Studies* 32 (4): 600–622.

Collins, Keith. 2017. "Google Collects Android Users' Locations Even When Location Services Are Disabled." *Quartz,* November 21. https://qz.com/1131515/google -collects-android-users-locations-even-when-location-services-are-disabled/.

Coté, Mark, and Jennifer Pybus. 2007. "Learning to Immaterial Labour 2.0: MySpace and Social Networks." *Ephemera: Theory and Politics in Organization* 7 (1): 88–106.

Couldry, Nick, and Ulises A. Mejias. 2019. "Data Colonialism: Rethinking Big Data's Relation to the Contemporary Subject." *Television & New Media* 20 (4): 336–349.

Coupland, Douglas. 2014. "I Miss My Pre-Internet Brain." *The Telegraph,* September 14. https://www.telegraph.co.uk/culture/books/11089597/Douglas-Coupland-I-miss -my-pre-internet-brain.html.

Coyne, Richard. 2016. *Mood and Mobility: Navigating the Emotional Spaces of Digital Social Networks.* Cambridge, MA: MIT Press.

Crary, Jonathan. 1999. *Suspensions of Perception: Attention, Spectacle, and Modern Culture.* Cambridge, MA: MIT Press.

Crary, Jonathan. 2014. *24/7: Late Capitalism and the Ends of Sleep.* London: Verso.

Crogan, Patrick, and Kinsley, Samuel. 2012. "Paying Attention: Towards a Critique of the Attention Economy." *Culture Machine* 13. http://svr91.edns1.com/~culturem /index.php/cm/article/view/463/500.

Csikszentmihalyi, Mihaly. 2000. *Beyond Boredom and Anxiety: Experiencing Flow in Work and Play. 25th Anniversary Edition.* San Francisco: Jossey-Bass.

Dean, Jodi. 2005. "Communicative Capitalism: Circulation and the Foreclosure of Politics." *Cultural Politics* 1: 51–74.

Dean, Jodi. 2010. *Blog Theory: Feedback and Capture in the Circuits of the Drive*. Oxford: Polity.

Deleuze, Gilles. 1988. *Spinoza: Practical Philosophy*. Translated by Robert Hurley. San Francisco: City Lights Books.

Deleuze, Gilles. 2002. "The Actual and the Virtual." In *Dialogues II*, edited by Claire Parnet, translated by Eliot Ross Albert, 148–152. New York: Columbia University Press.

Derrida, Jacques. 1981. *Dissemination*. Translated by Barbara Johnson. London: Athlone Press.

Derrida, Jacques. 1993. "The Rhetoric of Drugs: An Interview." Translated by Michael Israel. *Differences* 5 (1): 1–25.

Dickey, Megan Rose. 2013. "This 20-Year-Old Is the Mastermind Behind Distractify, a Fast-Growing Media Startup." *Business Insider*, November 22. http://www.businessinsider.com/distractify-media-startup-2013-11.

Duschinsky, Robbie, and Emma Wilson. 2015. "Flat Affect, Joyful Politics and Enthralled Attachments: Engaging with the Work of Lauren Berlant." *International Journal of Politics, Culture, and Society* 28 (3): 179–190.

Duttlinger, Carolin. 2007. "Between Contemplation and Distraction: Configurations of Attention in Walter Banjamin." *German Studies Review* 30 (1): 33–54.

Ellis, John. 2000. *Seeing Things: Television in the Age of Uncertainty*. London: I.B. Tauris.

Ellison, Nicole B., and danah boyd. 2013. "Sociality through Social Network Sites." In *The Oxford Handbook of Internet Studies*, edited by William H. Dutton, 151–172. Oxford: Oxford University Press.

Escudero, Jesús Adrián. 2014. "Heidegger on Selfhood." *American International Journal of Contemporary Research* 4 (2): 6–17.

Farman, Jason. 2015. "Infrastructures of Mobile Social Media." *Social Media + Society* (April–June): 1–2.

Featherstone, Mike. 2010. "Body, Image and Affect in Consumer Culture." *Body & Society* 16 (1): 193–221.

Fischer, Claude S. 1994. *America Calling: A Social History of the Telephone to 1940*. Berkeley: University of California Press.

Fisher, Dana. R. 2019. "The Broader Importance of #FridaysForFuture." *Nature Climate Change* 9 (6): 430.

Foddy, Bennett, and Julian Savulescu. 2007. "Addiction Is Not an Affliction: Addictive Desires Are Merely Pleasure-Oriented Desires." *American Journal of Bioethics* 7 (1): 29–32.

Fornäs, Johan. 1995. *Cultural Theory and Late Modernity*. London: Sage.

Foucault, Michel. 1980. *Power/Knowledge: Selected Interviews and Other Writings 1972–1977*, edited by Colin Gordon, translated by Colin Gordon, Leo Marshall, John Mepham, and Kate Soper. New York: Pantheon Books.

Foucault, Michel. 1982. *The Archeology of Knowledge & The Discourse of Language*, translated by Robert Swyer. New York: Vintage.

Foucault, Michel. 1995/1977. *Discipline and Punish: The Birth of the Prison*, translated by Alan Sheridan. New York: Vintage.

Fox, Jesse, and Jennifer J. Moreland. 2015. "The Dark Side of Social Networking Sites: An Exploration of the Relational and Psychological Stressors Associated with Facebook Use and Affordances." *Computers in Human Behavior* 45: 168–176.

Freud, Sigmund. 1957. "Mourning and Melancholia" (1917). In *The Standard Edition of the Complete Psychological Works of Sigmund Freud, Vol. XIV (1914–1916): On the History of the Psycho Analytic Movement, Papers on Metapsychology and Other Works*, translated by James Strachey, with Anna Freud, Alix Strachey, and Alan Tyson, 237–258. London: Hogarth Press.

Friedan, Betty. 1963. *The Feminine Mystique*. New York: W.W. Norton.

Fuchs, Christian. 2011. "Web 2.0, Prosumption, and Surveillance." *Surveillance & Society* 8: 288–309.

Fuchs, Christian, and David Chandler. 2019. "Introduction: Big Data Capitalism-Politics, Activism, and Theory." In *Digital Objects, Digital Subjects*, edited by David Chandler and Christian Fuchs, 1–20. London: University of Westminster Press.
Gardiner, Michael E. 2012. "Henri Lefebvre and the 'Sociology of Boredom.'" *Theory, Culture & Society* 29 (2): 37–62.

Gardner, Howard, and Katie Davis. 2013. *The App Generation: How Today's Youth Navigate Identity, Intimacy, and Imagination in a Digital World*. New Haven: Yale University Press.

Garfield, Bob. 2013. "Banning the Negative Book Review." *New York Times*, November 29. http://www.nytimes.com/2013/11/30/opinion/banning-the-negative-book-review.html?_r=0.

Garza, Alicia. 2014. "A Herstory of the #BlackLivesMatter Movement." In *Are All the Women Still White? Rethinking Race, Expanding Feminisms*, edited by Janell Hobson, 23–28. Albany: SUNY Press.

Gehl, Robert W. 2011. "The Archive and Processor: The Internal Logic of Web 2.0." *New Media & Society* 13 (8): 1228–1244.

Gell, Alfred. 1992. "The Technology of Enchantment and the Enchantment of Technology." In *Anthropology, Art and Aesthetics*, edited by Jeremy Coote and Anthony Shelton, 40–63. Oxford: Oxford University Press.

Ghomogu, Mbiyimoh. 2014. "Why Students Chose to Shock Themselves Rather Than Sit Alone with Their Thoughts." *The Higher Learning*, July 10, http://thehigherlearning .com/2014/07/10/why-students-chose-to-shock-themselves-rather-than-sit-alone-with -their-thoughts.

Gibbs, Paul. 2011. "The Concept of Profound Boredom: Learning from Moments of Vision." *Studies in Philosophy and Education* 30: 601–613.

Gillespie, Tarleton. 2018. *Custodians of the Internet: Platforms, Content Moderation, and the Hidden Decisions That Shape Social Media*. New Haven: Yale University Press.

Gleick, James. 1999. *Faster: The Acceleration of Just About Everything*. New York: Vintage.

Goddard, Michael. 2015. "Opening Up the Black Boxes: Media Archaeology, 'Anarchaeology' and Media Materiality." *New Media & Society* 17 (11): 1761–1776.

Goldhaber, Michael H. 1997. "The Attention Economy of the Net." *First Monday* 2 (4). http://firstmonday.org/article/view/519/440.

Gomart, Emilie, and Antoine Hennion. 1999. "A Sociology of Attachment: Music Amateurs, Drug Users." In *Actor-Network Theory and After*, edited by John Law and John Hassard, 220–248. Oxford: Blackwell.

Goodstein, Elizabeth S. 2005. *Experience without Qualities: Boredom and Modernity*. Stanford: Stanford University Press.

Gosling, Francis D. 1987. *Before Freud: Neurasthenia and the American Medical Community 1870–1910*. Urbana: University of Illinois Press.

Grainge, Paul. 2000. "Nostalgia and Style in Retro America: Moods, Modes, and Media Recycling." *Journal of American and Comparative Cultures* 23(1): 27–34.

Gregg, Melissa. 2011. *Work's Intimacy*. Cambridge: Polity Press.

Gregg, Melissa. 2015. "Getting Things Done: Productivity, Self-Management, and the Order of Things." In *Networked Affect*, edited by Ken Hillis, Susanna Paasonen, and Michael Petit, 187–202. Cambridge, MA: MIT Press.

Gregg, Melissa. 2018. *Counterproductive: Time Management in the Knowledge Economy*. Durham, NC: Duke University Press.

Grevet, Catherine. 2013. "Combating Homophily Through Design." *Proceedings of the 2013 Conference on Computer Supported Cooperative Work Companion*, 57–60, https://dl .acm.org/doi/abs/10.1145/2441955.2441971.

Griffiths, Mark D. 2012. "Facebook Addiction: Concerns, Criticism, and Recommendations—A Response to Andreassen and Colleagues." *Psychological Reports* 110 (2): 518–520.

Grinols, Anne Bradstreet, and Rishi Rajesh. 2014. "Multitasking with Smartphones in the College Classroom." *Business and Professional Communication Quarterly* 77 (1): 89–95.

Grusin, Richard. 2010. *Premediation: Affect and Materiality after 9/11*. New York: Palgrave.

Guiltinan, Joseph. 2008. "Creative Destruction and Destructive Creation: Environmental Ethics and Planned Obsolescence." *Journal of Business Ethics* 89 (1): 19–28.

Hakim, Jamie. 2019. *Work That Body: Male Bodies in Digital Culture*. Lanham: Rowman and Littlefield.

Han, Byung-Chul. 2017. *Psychopolitics: Neoliberalism and New Technologies of Power*. Translated by Erik Butler. London: Verso Books.

Hand, Michael. 2017. "#boredom: Technology, Acceleration, and Connected Presence in the Social Media Age." In *Boredom Studies Reader: Frameworks and Perspectives*, edited by Michael E. Gardiner and Julian Jason Haladyn, 115–129. London: Routledge.

Hardt, Michael, and Antonio Negri. 2001. *Empire*. Cambridge, MA: Harvard University Press.

Hassan, Robert. 2012. *The Age of Distraction: Reading, Writing, and Politics in a High-Speed Networked Economy*. New Brunswick: Transaction Publishers.

Hassan, Robert. 2014. "A Temporalized Internet." *The Political Economy of Communication* 2 (1). http://polecom.org/index.php/polecom/article/view/27/204.

Hayles, N. Katherine. 2007. "Hyper and Deep Attention: The Generational Divide in Cognitive Modes," *Profession*: 187–199.

Hayles, N. Katherine. 2012. *How We Think: Digital Media and Contemporary Technogenesis*. Chicago: University of Chicago Press.

Heidegger, Martin. 1995. *The Fundamental Concepts of Metaphysics: World, Finitude, Solitude*. Translated by William McNeill and Nicholas Walker. Indianapolis: Indiana University Press.

Heidegger, Martin. 1997. *Basic Writings: Nine Key Essays, Plus the Introduction to Being and Time*, edited by David Farrell Krell. New York: Harper & Row.

Helliwell, John F., Haifang Huang, and Shun Wang. 2019. "Changing World Happiness." In *World Happiness Report*, edited by John F. Helliwell, Richard Layard, Jeffrey D. Sachs, and Jan-Emmannuel De Neve. https://worldhappiness.report/ed/2019/changing-world-happiness.

Helliwell, John F., Richard Layard, Jeffrey D. Sachs, and Jan-Emmannuel De Neve, eds. 2019. *World Happiness Report 2019*. https://worldhappiness.report.

Hellman, Matilda. 2009. "Designation Practices and Perceptions of Addiction—A Diachronic Analysis of Finnish Press Material from 1968–2006." *Nordic Studies on Alcohol and Drugs* 26 (4): 355–372.

Hepp, Andreas, Stig Hjarvard, and Knut Lundby. 2015. "Mediatization: Theorizing the Interplay between Media, Culture and Society." *Media, Culture & Society* 37 (2): 314–324.

Hesmondhalgh, David. 2010. "User-Generated Content, Free Labour and the Cultural Industries." *Ephemera* 10: 267–284.

Hjorth, Larissa, and Sun Sun Lim. 2012. "Mobile Intimacy in the Age of Affective Mobile Media." *Feminist Media Studies* 12 (4): 477–484.

Hjorth, Larissa, and Ingrid Richardson. 2009. "The Waiting Game: Complicating Notions of (Tele) Presence and Gendered Distraction in Casual Mobile Gaming." *Australian Journal of Communication* 36 (1): 23–35.

Houpt, Simon. 2018. "Trump's Acts of Distraction: Don't Take the Bait." *Globe and Mail,* November 8. https://www.theglobeandmail.com/arts/article-trumps-acts-of-distraction-dont-take-the-bait/.

Howe, Neil, and William Strauss. 2000. *Millennials Rising: The Next Great Generation.* New York: Vintage.

Illouz, Eva. 2014. *Hard-Core Romance: "Fifty Shades of Grey," Best-Sellers, and Society.* Chicago: University of Chicago Press.

Ito, Mizuke, and Daisuke Okabe. 2005. Intimate Connections: Contextualizing Japanese Youth and Mobile Messaging. In *Inside the Text: Social Perspectives on SMS in the Mobile Age,* edited by Richard H.R. Harper, Leysia Palen, and Alex S. Taylor, 127–145. Dordrecht: Springer.

Jabr, Ferris. 2014. Actually, People Still Like to Think. *The New Yorker,* October 9. https://www.newyorker.com/tech/annals-of-technology/thinking-alone.

James, William. 2012/1890. *Principles of Psychology, Vol. 1.* Adelaide: The University of Adelaide Library. http://infomotions.com/sandbox/great-books-redux/corpus/html/principles.html.

Jameson, Fredric. 1981. *The Political Unconscious: Narrative as a Socially Symbolic Act.* Ithaca, NY: Cornell University Press.

Jarrett, Kylie. 2003. "Labour of Love: An Archaelogy of Affect as Power in E-Commerce." *Journal of Sociology* 29 (4): 335–351.

Jarrett, Kylie. 2014. "A Database of Intention?" In *Society of the Query Reader: Reflections on Web Search,* edited by René König and Miriam Rasch, 16–29. Amsterdam: Institute of Network Cultures.

Jarrett, Kylie. 2015a. *Feminism, Labour and Digital Media: The Digital Housewife.* London: Routledge.

Jarrett, Kylie. 2015b. "'Let's Express Our Friendship by Sending Each Other Funny Links instead of Actually Talking': Gifts, Commodities, and Social Reproduction in Facebook." In *Networked Affect,* edited by Ken Hillis, Susanna Paasonen, and Michael Petit, 203–220. Cambridge, MA: MIT Press.

Jenkins, Henry. 2006. *Fans, Bloggers and Gamers: Exploring Participatory Culture*. New York: New York University Press.

Jenkins, Henry, Sam Ford, and Joshua Green. 2013. *Spreadable Media: Creating Value and Meaning in a Networked Culture*. New York: New York University Press.

Johansson, Agneta, and K. Gunnar Götestam. 2004. "Internet Addiction: Characteristics of a Questionnaire and Prevalence in Norwegian Youth (12–18 Years)." *Scandinavian Journal of Psychology* 45: 223–229.

Johnsen, Rasmus. 2011. "On Boredom." *Ephemera* 11 (4): 482–489.

Johnson, Cat. 2015. "15 Apps to Boost Your Happiness." *Shareable*. http://www.share able.net/blog/15-apps-to-boost-your-happiness.

Johnson, Lesley, and Justine Lloyd. 2004. *Sentenced to Everyday Life: Feminism and the Housewife*. Oxford: Berg.

Karaiskos, Dimitris, Elias Odusseas Tzavellas, Goergia Balta, and Thomas Paparrigopoulos. 2010. "Social Network Addiction: A New Clinical Disorder?" *European Psychiatry* 25: 855.

Karppi, Tero. 2014. *Disconnect.Me: User Engagement and Facebook*. Turku: University of Turku.

Karppi, Tero. 2015. "Happy Accidents: Facebook and the Value of Affect." In *Networked Affect*, edited by Ken Hillis, Susanna Paasonen, and Michael Petit, 221–234. Cambridge, MA: MIT Press.

Karppi, Tero. 2018. *Disconnect: Facebook's Affective Bonds*. Minneapolis: University of Minnesota Press.

Keilty, Patrick. 2012. "Embodiment and Desire in Browsing Online Pornography." *Proceedings of the 2012 iConference*, 41–47.

Keilty, Patrick. 2016. "Embodied Engagements with Online Pornography." *The Information Society* 32 (1): 64–73.

Kember, Sarah, and Joanna Zylinska. 2012. *Life after Media: Mediation as a Vital Process*. Cambridge, MA: MIT Press.

Kendall, Tina. 2018. "'#BOREDWITHMEG': Gendered Boredom and Networked Media." *New Formations* 93: 80–100.

Kendall, Tina. 2019. "(Not) Doing It for the Vine: #Boredom Vine Videos and the Biopolitics of Gesture." *NECSUS. European Journal of Media Studies* 8 (2): 213–233.

Kirschenbaum, Matthew G. 2016. *Track Changes: A Literary History of Word Processing*. Cambridge, MA: Harvard University Press.

Korkeila, J., S. Kaarlas, M. Jääskeläinen, Tero Vahlberg, and Tero Taiminen. 2010. "Attached to the Web—Harmful Use of the Internet and Its Correlates." *European Psychiatry* 25 (4): 236–241.

Kracauer, Siegfried. 1995/1963. *The Mass Ornament: Weimar Essays*, translated and edited by Thomas Y. Levin. Cambridge, MA: Harvard University Press.

Kracauer, Siegfried. 1998/1930. *The Salaried Masses: Duty and Distraction in Weimar Germany*, translated by Quintin Hoare. London: Verso.

Kramer, Adam D. I., Jamie E. Guillory, and Jeffrey T. Hancock. 2014. "Experimental Evidence of Massive-Scale Emotional Contagion through Social Networks." *Proceedings of the National Academy of Sciences of the United States of America* 111 (24): 8788–8790.

Kristensen, Dorthe Brogård, and Minna Ruckenstein. 2018. "Co-Evolving with Self-Tracking Technologies." *New Media & Society* 20 (10): 3624–3640.

Krug, Sammi. 2016. "New Feed FYI: What the Reactions Launch Means for News Feed." Facebook Newsroom. http://newsroom.fb.com/news/2016/02/news-feed-fyi-what-the -reactions-launch-means-for-news-feed/.

Lacey, Kate. 2000. "Towards a Periodization of Listening." *International Journal of Cultural Studies* 3 (2): 279–288.

Langbauer, Laurie. 1999. *Novels of Everyday Life: The Series in English Fiction, 1850– 1930*. Ithaca, NY: Cornell University Press.

Lasén, Amparo, and Elena Casado. 2012. "Mobile Telephony and the Remediation of Couple Intimacy." *Feminist Media Studies* 12 (4): 550–559.

Latour, Bruno. 1999a. "On Recalling ANT." In *Actor-Network Theory and After*, edited by John Law and John Hassard, 15–25. Oxford: Blackwell.

Latour, Bruno. 1999b. *Pandora's Hope: Essays on the Reality of Science Studies*. Cambridge, MA: Harvard University Press.

Latour, Bruno. 2011. "Reflections of an Actor-Network Theorist." *International Journal of Communication* 5: 796–810.

Leeker, Martina. 2017. "Intervening in Habits and Homophily: Make a Difference! An Interview with Wendy Hui Kyong Chun by Martina Leeker." In *Interventions in Digital Cultures: Technology, the Political, Methods*, edited by Howard Caygill, Martina Leeker, and Tobias Schulze, 75–85. Lüneburg: Meson Press.

Lefebvre, Henri. 1995. *Introduction to Modernity: Twelve Preludes September 1959–May 1961*. Translated by John Moore. London: Verso.

Lemmens, Pieter. 2011. "'This System Does Not Produce Pleasure Anymore': An Interview with Bernard Stiegler." *Krisis: Journal of Contemporary Philosophy* 1: 33–41.

Levine, Caroline. 2017. *Forms: Whole, Rhythm, Hierarchy, Network.* Princeton, NJ: Princeton University Press.

Levy, David. 2016. *Mindful Tech: How to Bring Balance to Our Digital Lives.* New Haven: CT: Yale University Press.

Lewkowich, David. 2010. "The Possibilities for a Pedagogy of Boredom: Rethinking the Opportunities of Elusive Learning." *Journal of Curriculum Theorizing* 26 (1): 129–143.

Light, Ben. 2014. *Disconnecting with Social Networking Sites.* London: Palgrave.

Light, Ben, Jean Burgess, and Stefanie Duguay. 2018. "The Walkthrough Method: An Approach to the Study of Apps." *New Media & Society* 20 (3): 881–900.

Lindgaard, Gitte, and Cathy Dudek. 2003. "What Is This Evasive Beast We Call User Satisfaction?" *Interacting with Computers* 15: 429–452.

Lorenz, Taylor. 2018. "Generation Z Is Already Bored by the Internet." *The Daily Beast,* April 3. https://www.thedailybeast.com/generation-z-is-already-bored-by-the -internet.

Lovink, Geert. 2019. *Sad by Design: On Platform Nihilism.* London: Pluto Press.

Lundby, Knut, ed. 2009. *Mediatization: Concept, Changes, Consequences.* New York: Peter Lang.

Lundemo, Trond. 2003. "Why Things Don't Work: Imagining New Technologies from *The Electric Life* to the Digital." In *Mediaa Kokemassa: Koosteita ja Ylityksiä/Experiencing the Media: Assemblages and Cross-overs,* edited by Tanja Sihvonen and Pasi Väliaho, 13–28. Tampere: University of Turku.

Lupton, Deborah. 1995. "The Embodied Computer/User." *Body & Society* 1 (3–4): 97–112.

Lupton, Deborah, and Greg Noble. 1997. "Just a Machine? Dehumanizing Strategies in Personal Computer Use." *Body & Society* 3 (2): 83–101.

Mäenpää, Pasi. 2005. *Narkissos Kaupungissa: Ttutkimus Kuluttaja-Kaupunkilaisesta ja Julkisesta Tilasta* (Narcissus in the City: Study on the Consumer-Citizen and Public Space). Helsinki: Tammi.

Mann, Sandi, and Rebekah Cadman. 2014. "Does Being Bored Make Us More Creative?" *Creativity Research Journal* 26 (2): 165–173.

Mann, Sandi, and Andrew Robinson. 2009. "Boredom in the Lecture Theatre: An Investigation into the Contributors, Moderators and Outcomes of Boredom amongst University Students." *British Educational Research Journal* 35 (2): 243–258.

Mansikka, Jan-Erik. 2009. "Can Boredom Educate Us? Tracing a Mood in Heidegger's Fundamental Ontology from an Educational Point of View." *Studies in Philosophy and Education* 28 (3): 255–268.

Marinova, Polina. 2019. "What Tumblr's 2013 Billion-Dollar Valuation Tells Us about How We Value Startups Today: Term Sheet." *Forbes*, August 13. https://fortune.com /2019/08/13/term-sheet-tuesday-august-13/.

Massumi, Brian. 2002. *Parables of the Virtual: Movement, Affect, Sensation.* Durham, NC: Duke University Press.

Massumi, Brian. 2015. *The Politics of Affect.* Cambridge: Polity.

Maybin, Simon. 2017. "Busting the Attention Span Myth." *BBC*, March 10. https:// www.bbc.com/news/health-38896790.

Mayer-Schönberger, Viktor. 2011. *Delete: The Virtue of Forgetting in the Digital Age.* Princeton, NJ: Princeton University Press.

McCullough, Malcolm. 2013. *Ambient Commons: Attention in the Age of Embodied Information.* Cambridge, MA: MIT Press.

McGee, Micki. 2005. *Self-Help, Inc.: Makeover Culture in American Life.* Oxford: Oxford University Press.

McKee, Alan. 2016. *FUN! What Entertainment Tells Us about Living a Good Life.* London: Palgrave.

McLuhan, Marshall. 1951. *The Mechanical Bride: Folklore of Industrial Man.* New York: Vanguard Press.

McLuhan, Marshall. 1964. *Understanding Media: The Extensions of Man.* New York: McGraw-Hill.

McLuhan, Marshall. 2011/1962. *The Gutenberg Galaxy: The Making of Typographic Man*, with W. Terrence Gordon, Elena Lamberti, and Dominique Scheffel-Dunand. Toronto: University of Toronto Press.

McLuhan, Marshall, and Quentin Fiore. 1967. *The Medium Is the Massage: An Inventory of Effects.* Corte Madera, CA: Gingko Press.

McNamara, Mary. 2019. "'Once Upon a Time … in Hollywood' Is Quentin Tarantino's 'Make America Great Again.'" *LA Times*, July 31. https://www.latimes.com/entertain-ment-arts/movies/story/2019-07-31/once-upon-a-time-in-hollywood-nostalgia-make -america-great-again.

McPherson, Miller, Lynn Smith-Lovin, and James M. Cook. 2001. "Birds of a Feather: Homophily in Social Networks." *Annual Review of Sociology* 27 (1): 415–444.

McSpadden, Kevin. 2015. "You Now Have a Shorter Attention Span Than a Goldfish." *Time*, May 14. http://time.com/3858309/attention-spans-goldfish/.

Microsoft Canada, 2015. *Consumer Insights: Attention Spans.* https://advertising.microsoft .com/en/WWDocs/User/display/cl/researchreport/31966/en/microsoft-attention -spans-research-report.pdf.

Miller, Daniel. 2011. *Tales from Facebook*. Cambridge: Polity.

Miller, Jason. 2016. "The Great Goldfish Attention Span Myth—and Why It's Killing Content Marketing." *LinkedIn*, October 4. https://business.linkedin.com/en-uk/marketing-solutions/blog/posts/B2B-Marketing/2016/The-great-goldfish-attention-span-myth-and-why-its-killing-content-marketing.

Miller, Vincent. 2008. "New Media, Networking and Phatic Culture." *Convergence* 14 (4): 387–400.

Milner, Ryan M. 2016. *The World Made Meme: Public Conversations and Participatory Media*. Cambridge, MA: MIT Press.

Mittell, Jason. 2004 *Genre and Television. From Cop Shows to Cartoons in American Television*. New York: Routledge.

Morozov, Evgeny. 2013. "Only Disconnect." *The New Yorker*, October 28. http://www.newyorker.com/magazine/2013/10/28/only-disconnect-2.Mowlabocus, Sharif. 2016 "The 'Mastery' of the Swipe: Smartphones, Transitional Objects and Interstitial Time." *First Monday* 21 (10): https://firstmonday.org/ojs/index.php/fm/article/view/6950.

Ngai, Sianne. 2000. "Stuplimity: Shock and Boredom in Twentieth-Century Aesthetics." *Postmodern Culture* 10 (2): 1–20.

Ngai, Sianne. 2015. *Our Aesthetic Categories: Zany, Cute, Interesting*. Cambridge, MA: Harvard University Press.

Niemeyer, Katharina. 2014. "Introduction: Media and Nostalgia." In *Media and Nostalgia: Yearning for the Past, Present and Future*, edited by Katharina Niemeyer, 1–23. London: Palgrave.

Nordau, Max. 1898. *Degeneration*. London: William Heinemann. http://www.gutenberg.org/files/51161/51161-h/51161-h.htm.

North, Paul. 2011. *The Problem of Distraction*. Stanford: Stanford University Press.

OECD Data. 2018. "Mobile Broadband Subscriptions." https://data.oecd.org/broadband/mobile-broadband-subscriptions.htm.

O'Gorman, Marcel. 2011. "Bernard Stiegler's *Pharmacy*: A Conversation." *Configurations* 18 (3): 459–476.

O'Gorman, Marcel. 2015. "Taking Care of Digital Dementia." *C-Theory*. http://www.ctheory.net/articles.aspx?id=740.

Oksman, Virpi, and Pirjo Rautiainen. 2003. "'Perhaps It Is a Body Part': How the Mobile Phone Became an Organic Part of the Everyday Lives of Finnish Children and Teenagers." In *Machines That Become Us: The Social Context of Personal Communication Technology*, edited by James E. Katz, 293–308. New Brunswick, NJ: Transaction Publishers.

Ong, Walter. 1982. *Orality and Literature: The Technologizing of the Word*. London: Methuen.

Osterweil, Ara. 2004. "Andy Warhol's *Blow Job*: Toward the Recognition of a Pornographic Avant-garde." In *Porn Studies*, edited by Linda Williams, 431–460. Durham, NC: Duke University Press.

Paasonen, Susanna. 2009. "What Cyberspace? Traveling Concepts in Internet Research." In *Internationalizing Internet Studies: Beyond Anglophone Paradigms*, edited by Gerard Goggin and Mark McLelland, 18–31. New York: Routledge.

Paasonen, Susanna. 2011. *Carnal Resonance: Affect and Online Pornography*. Cambridge, MA: MIT Press.

Paasonen, Susanna. 2015a. "As Networks Fail: Affect, Technology, and the Notion of the User." *Television & New Media* 16 (8): 701–716.

Paasonen, Susanna. 2015b. "A Midsummer's Bonfire: Affective Intensities in Online Debate." In *Networked Affect*, edited by Ken Hillis, Susanna Paasonen, and Michael Petit, 27–42. Cambridge, MA: MIT Press.

Paasonen, Susanna. 2016. "Fickle Focus: Distraction, Affect and the Production of Value in Social Media." *First Monday* 21 (1). https://firstmonday.org/article/view/6949/5629.

Paasonen, Susanna. 2018a. "Affect, Data, Manipulation and Price in Social Media." *Distinktion: Journal of Social Theory* 19 (2): 214–229.

Paasonen, Susanna. 2018b. "Infrastructures of Intimacy." In *Mediated Intimacies: Connectivities, Relationalities and Proximities*, edited by Rikke Andreassen, Michael Nebeling Petersen, Katherine Harrison, and Tobias Raun, 103–116. London: Routledge.

Paasonen, Susanna. 2018c. *Many Splendored Things: Thinking Sex and Play*. London: Goldsmiths Press.Paasonen, Susanna, Ken Hillis, and Michael Petit. 2015. "Networks of Transmission: Intensity, Sensation, Value." In *Networked Affect*, edited by Ken Hillis, Susanna Paasonen, and Michael Petit, 1–26. Cambridge, MA: MIT Press.

Paasonen, Susanna, Kylie Jarrett, and Ben Light. 2019. *NSFW: Sex, Humor, and Risk in Social Media*. Cambridge, MA: MIT Press.

Page, Allison. 2017. "'This Baby Sloth Will Inspire You to Keep Going': Capital, Labor, and the Affective Power of Cute Animal Videos." In *The Aesthetics and Affects of Cuteness*, edited by Joshua Paul Dale, Joyce Goggin, Julia Leyda, Anthony P McIntyre, and Diane Negra, 75–94. New York: Routledge.

Papacharissi, Zizi. 2015. *Affective Publics: Sentiment, Technology, and Politics*. New York: Oxford University Press.

Parikka, Jussi. 2014. "Cultural Techniques of Cognitive Capitalism: Metaprogramming and the Labour of Code." *Cultural Studies Review* 20 (1): 30–42.

Parikka, Jussi. 2015a. *The Anthrobscene*. Minneapolis: University of Minnesota Press.

Parikka, Jussi. 2015b. *A Geology of Media*. Minneapolis: University of Minnesota Press.

Patterson, Zabet. 2004. "Going On-line: Consuming Pornography in the Digital Era." In *Porn Studies*, edited by Linda Williams, 104–123. Durham, NC: Duke University Press.

Payne, Robert. 2014. *The Promiscuity of Network Culture: Queer Theory and Digital Media*. New York: Routledge.

Pease, Allison. 2012. *Modernism, Feminism and the Culture of Boredom*. Cambridge: Cambridge University Press.

Pelan, Chanda, Cliff Lampe, and Paul Resnick. 2016. "It's Creepy, but It Doesn't Bother Me." *Proceedings of the 34th Annual ACM Conference on Human Factors in Computing Systems*: 5240–5251.

Perrin, Andrew. 2018. "Americans Are Changing Their Relationship with Facebook." *Pew Research Center*, September 5. https://www.pewresearch.org/fact-tank/2018/09/05/americans-are-changing-their-relationship-with-facebook/.

Petit, Michael. 2015. "Digital Disaffect: Teaching through Screens." In *Networked Affect*, edited by Ken Hillis, Susanna Paasonen, and Michael Petit, 169–183. Cambridge, MA: MIT Press.

Pettman, Dominic. 2016. *Infinite Distraction*. Cambridge: Polity.

Phillips, Whitney. 2015. *This Is Why We Can't Have Nice Things: Mapping the Relationship between Online Trolling and Mainstream Culture*. Cambridge, MA: MIT Press.

Pilipets, Elena. 2018. *POP:MEDIATIONS. (Dis)connecting Affect and Meaning in Digital Popular Culture*. PhD Dissertation. Klagenfurt: Alpen-Adria Universität.

Pilipets, Elena. 2019. "From Netflix Streaming to Netflix and Chill: The (Dis)Connected Body of Serial Binge-Viewer and the Branded Value of Attachment." *Social Media + Society* October–December. https://journals.sagepub.com/doi/pdf/10.1177/2056305119883426.

Poster, Mark. 2002. "The Aesthetics of Distracting Media." *Culture Machine* 4. http://svr91.edns1.com/~culturem/index.php/cm/article/view/277/262.

Postman, Neil. 1985. *Amusing Ourselves to Death: Public Discourse in the Age of Show Business*. New York: Penguin.

Prensky, Marc. 2001. "Digital Natives, Digital Immigrants, Part 1." *On the Horizon* 9 (5): 1–6.

Przybylski, Andrew K., Kou Murayama, Cody R. DeHaan, and Valerie Gladwell. 2013. "Motivational, Emotional, and Behavioral Correlates of Fear of Missing Out." *Computers in Human Behavior* 29 (4): 1841–1848.

Pybus, Jennifer. 2015. "Accumulating Affect: Social Networks and Their Archives of Feelings." In *Networked Affect*, edited by Ken Hillis, Susanna Paasonen, and Michael Petit, 235–249. Cambridge, MA: MIT Press.

Race, Kane. 2015a. "'Party and Play': Online Hook-Up Devices and the Emergence of PNP Practices among Gay Men." *Sexualities* 18 (3): 253–275.

Race, Kane. 2015b. "Speculative Pragmatism and Intimate Arrangements: Online Hook-Up Devices in Gay Life." *Culture, Health & Sexuality* 17 (4): 496–511.

Rantala, Varpu. 2016. *Secular Possession: Cinematic Iconography of Addiction*. Turku: University of Turku. PhD dissertation. http://urn.fi/URN:ISBN:978-951-29-6494-9.

Reginster, Bernard. 2007. "Nietzsche's New Happiness: Longing, Boredom, and the Elusiveness of Fulfillment." *Philosophic Exchange* 37 (1): 2–25.

Reith, Gerda. 2019. *Addictive Consumption: Capitalism, Modernity and Excess*. London: Routledge.

Revell, Timothy. 2018. "How Facebook Let a Friend Pass My Data to Cambridge Analytica." *New Scientist*, April 16. https://www.newscientist.com/article/2166435-how-facebook-let-a-friend-pass-my-data-to-cambridge-analytica/.

Richardson, Ingrid. 2010. "Faces, Interfaces, Screens: Relational Ontologies of Framing, Attention and Distraction." *Transformations* 18. http://www.transformationsjournal.org/issues/18/article_05.shtml.

Rickford, Russell. 2016. "Black Lives Matter: Toward a Modern Practice of Mass Struggle." *New Labor Forum* 25 (1): 34–42.

Rosa, Hartmut. 2003. "Social Acceleration: Ethical and Political Consequences of a Desynchronized High-Speed Society." *Constellations* 10 (1): 3–33.

Rosa, Hartmut. 2013. *Social Acceleration: A New Theory of Modernity*. New York: Columbia University Press.

Ruckenstein, Minna. 2013. "Temporalities of Addiction." In *Making Sense of Consumption: Selections from the 2nd Nordic Conference on Consumer Research*, edited by Lena Hansson, Ulrika Holmberg, and Helene Brembeck, 107–118. Gothenburg: University of Gothenburg.

Ruckenstein, Minna. 2014. "Visualized and Interacted Life: Personal Analytics and Engagements with Data Doubles." *Societies* 4 (1): 68–84.

Rushe, Dominic. 2011. "Myspace Sold for $35m in Spectacular Fall from $12bn Heyday." *The Guardian*, June 30. https://www.theguardian.com/technology/2011/jun/30/myspace-sold-35-million-news.

Rushkoff, Douglas. 2013. *Present Shock: When Everything Happens Now*. New York: Penguin.

Russell, James A. 2009. "Emotion, Core Affect, and Psychological Construction." *Cognition and Emotion* 23 (7): 1259–1283.

Sample, Richard. 2014. "Shocking but True: Students Prefer Jolt of Pain to Being Made to Sit and Think." *The Guardian*, July 3. https://www.theguardian.com/science /2014/jul/03/electric-shock-preferable-to-thinking-says-study.

Sampson, Tony D. 2012. *Virality: Contagion Theory in the Age of Networks.* Minneapolis: University of Minnesota Press.

Sampson, Tony D., Darren Ellis, and Stephen Maddison. 2018. "Introduction: On Affect, Social Media and Criticality." In *Affect and Social Media*, edited by Tony D. Sampson, Stephen Maddison, and Darren Ellis, 1–10. Lanham: Rowman and Littlefield.

Schaschek, Sarah. 2013. *Pornography and Seriality: The Culture of Producing Pleasure.* New York: Palgrave.

Scheuerman, William E. 2003. "Speed, States, and Social Theory: A Response to Hartmut Rosa." *Constellations* 10 (1): 42–48.

Schüll, Natasha Dow. 2008. "Video Poker." In *The Inner History of Devices*, edited by Sherry Turkle, 153–170. Cambridge, MA: MIT Press.

Schüll, Natasha Dow. 2012. *Addiction by Design: Machine Gambling in Vegas.* Princeton, NJ: Princeton University Press.

Sedgwick, Eve Kosofsky. 1993. *Tendencies.* Durham, NC: Duke University Press.

Sedgwick, Eve Kosofsky. 2003. *Touching Feeling: Affect, Pedagogy, Performativity.* Durham, NC: Duke University Press.

Seigworth, Gregory J., and Melissa Gregg. 2010. "An Inventory of Shimmers." In *The Affect Theory Reader*, edited by Melissa Gregg and Gregory J. Seigworth, 1–28. Durham, NC: Duke University Press.

Senft, Theresa M. 2008. *CamGirls: Celebrity & Community in the Age of Social Networks.* New York: Peter Lang.

Seymour, Richard. 2019. "The Machine Always Wins: What Drives Our Addiction to Social Media." *The Guardian*, August 23. https://www.theguardian.com/technology /2019/aug/23/social-media-addiction-gambling.

Shenk, David. 1997. *Data Smog: Surviving the Information Glut.* New York: HarperCollins.

Shifman, Limor. 2013. *Memes in Digital Culture.* Cambridge, MA: MIT Press.

Shklovski, Irina, Scott Mainwaring, Halla Hrund Skúladóttir, and Höskuldur Borgthorsson. 2014. "Leakiness and Creepiness in App Space: Perceptions of Privacy and Mobile App Use Mobile." *Proceedings of the 32nd Annual ACM Conference on Human Factors in Computing Systems*: 2347–2356.

Sicart, Miguel. 2014. *Play Matters*. Cambridge, MA: MIT Press.

Simmel, Georg. 2002. "The Metropolis and Mental Life" (1903). In *The Blackwell City Reader*, edited by Gary Bridge and Sophie Watson, 103–110. Oxford: Wiley-Blackwell.

Slaby, Jan. 2010. "The Other Side of Existence: Heidegger on Boredom." In *Habitus in Habitat II—Other Sides of Cognition*, edited by Daniel Margulies Flach and Jan Söffner, 101–120. New York: Peter Lang.

Smith, Jack IV. 2016. "Facebook Is Using Those New 'Like' Emojis to Keep Tabs on Your Emotions." *Tech.Mic*, February 24. http://mic.com/articles/136111/facebook-is -using-those-new-like-emojis-to-learn-a-whole-lot-more-about-you#.acsQ1UdLP.

Spigel, Lynn. 1992. *Make Room for TV: Television and the Family Ideal in Postwar America*. Chicago: University of Chicago Press.

Spinoza, Baruch. 1992/1677. *The Ethics, Treatise on the Emendation of the Intellect and Selected Letters*. Edited by Seymour Feldman, translated by Samuel Shirley. Indianapolis, IN: Hackett.

Spitzer, Manfred. 2012. *Digitale Demenz*. Munich: Droemer Knaur.

Srnicek, Nick. 2017. *Platform Capitalism*. Cambridge: Polity.

Standage, Tom. 1998. *The Victorian Internet: The Remarkable Story of the Telegraph and the Nineteenth Century's Online Pioneers*. London: Bloomsbury.

Statistics Finland. 2018. "The Internet Is Used Ever More Commonly with Mobile Phone—Even for Shopping." December 4. http://tilastokeskus.fi/til/sutivi/2018/sutivi _2018_2018-12-04_tie_001_en.html.

Stewart, Kathleen. 2007. *Ordinary Affects*. Durham, NC: Duke University Press.

Stiegler, Bernard. 2009. *Technics and Time, 2: Disorientation*, translated by Stephen Barker. Stanford, CA: Stanford University Press.

Stiegler, Bernard. 2012a. "Relational Ecology and the Digital *Pharmakon*." *Culture Machine* 13. http://svr91.edns1.com/~culturem/index.php/cm/article/view/464/501.

Stiegler, Bernard. 2012b. *Uncontrollable Societies and Disaffected Individuals*. Cambridge: Polity.

Stiegler, Bernard. 2013. *What Makes Life Worth Living: On Pharmacology*, translated by Daniel Ross. Cambridge: Polity.

Stjernfelt, Frederik, and Anne Mette Lauritzen. 2019. *Your Post Has Been Removed: Tech Giants and Freedom of Speech*. Springer Open, https://link.springer.com/book/10.1007 /978-3-030-25968-6.

Sundén, Jenny. 2015a. "On Trans-, Glitch, and Gender as Machinery of Failure." *First Monday* 20 (4). https://firstmonday.org/ojs/index.php/fm/article/view/5895/4416.

Sundén, Jenny. 2015b. "Technologies of Feeling: Affect between the Analog and the Digital." In *Networked Affect*, edited by Ken Hillis, Susanna Paasonen, and Michael Petit, 135–150. Cambridge, MA: MIT Press.

Sundén, Jenny. 2018. "Queer Disconnections: Affect, Break, and Delay in Digital Connectivity." *Transformations* 31. http://www.transformationsjournal.org/wp-content /uploads/2018/06/Trans31_04_sunden.pdf.

Sundén, Jenny, and Susanna Paasonen. 2020. *Who's Laughing Now? Feminist Tactics in Social Media*. Cambridge, MA: MIT Press.

Suominen, Jaakko. 2006. "Verkon Käytön Rajoilla—Eli Miten Tulimme Riippuvaisiksi Netistä" (At the Edges of Net Use: Or, How We Became Dependent on the Net). In *Raja—Kohtaamisia ja Ylityksiä* (Border: Encounters and Cross-Overs), edited by Petri Saarikoski, Riikka Turtiainen, and Päivi Granö, 37–60. Pori: University of Turku.

Suominen, Jaakko. 2011. "Hurma, Himo, Häpeä ja Hylkääminen: Kaarroksia Konesuhteissa" (Bliss, Lust, Shame, and Abandonment: Turns in Relationships with Machines). In *Digirakkaus II* (Digital Love II), edited by Petri Saarikoski, Ulla Heinonen, and Riikka Turtiainen, 17–32. Pori: University of Turku.

Syvertsen, Trine, and Gunn Enli. 2019. "Digital Detox: Media Resistance and the Promise of Authenticity." *Convergence*, online before print. https://journals.sagepub .com/doi/abs/10.1177/1354856519847325.

Tarantola, Andrew. 2018. "New Tech 'Addictions' Are Mostly Just Old Moral Panic." *Endgadget*, February 9. https://www.engadget.com/2018/02/09/new-tech-addictions -are-mostly-just-old-moral-panic.

Terranova, Tiziana. 2000. "Free Labor: Producing Culture for the Digital Economy." *Social Text* 18: 33–58.

Terranova, Tiziana. 2004. *Network Culture: Politics of the Information Age*. London: Pluto Press.

Terranova, Tiziana. 2012. "Attention, Economy and the Brain." *Culture Machine* 13. http://svr91.edns1.com/~culturem/index.php/cm/article/download/465/484.

Thiele, Leslie Paul. 1997. "Postmodernity and the Routinization of Novelty: Heidegger on Boredom and Technology." *Polity* 29 (4): 489–517.

Thoreau, H. D. 1854. *Walden; or Life in the Woods*. http://www.gutenberg.org/files /205/205-h/205-h.htm.

Tichi, Cecelia. 1991, *Electronic Hearth: Creating an American Television Culture*. Oxford: Oxford University Press.

Tomkins, Silvan S. 2008. *Affect Imagery Consciousness: The Complete Edition*. New York: Springer.

Track Your Happiness. 2019. https://www.trackyourhappiness.org/about.

Tractinsky, Noam, and Dror Zmiri. 2006. "Exploring Attributes of Skins as Potential Antecedents of Emotion in HCI." In *Aesthetic Computing*, edited by Paul Fishwick, 405–422. Cambridge, MA: MIT Press.

Turkle, Sherry. 2007. *Evocative Objects: Things We Think With.* Cambridge, MA: MIT Press.

Turkle, Sherry. 2012. *Alone Together: Why We Expect More from Technology and Less from Each Other.* New York: Basic Books.

Turow, Joseph. 2005. "Audience Construction and Culture Production: Marketing Surveillance in the Digital Age." *The ANNALS of the American Academy of Political and Social Science* 597 (1): 103–121.

Tuuva-Hongisto, Sari. 2007. *Tilattuja Tarinoita: Etnografinen Tutkimus Pohjoiskarjalaisesta Tietoyhteiskunnasta* (Requested Stories: An Ethnographic Study of the North Karelian Information Society). PhD dissertation. Joensuu: University of Joensuu.

Twenge, Jean M. 2019. "The Sad State of Happiness in the United States and the Role of Digital Media." In *World Happiness Report*, edited by John F. Helliwell, Richard Layard, Jeffrey D. Sachs, and Jan-Emmannuel De Neve. https://worldhappiness.report/ed/2019/the-sad-state-of-happiness-in-the-united-states-and-the-role-of-digital-media.

Uotinen, Johanna. 2010. "Digital Television and the Machine That Goes 'PING!': Autoethnography as a Method for Cultural Studies of Technology." *Journal for Cultural Research* 11 (2): 161–175.

Van Alphen, Ernst. 2007. "Configurations of Self: Modernism and Distraction." In *Modernism*, edited by Astradur Eysteinsson and Vivian Liska, 339–346. Amsterdam: John Benjamins.

Van Dijck, José. 2009. "Users Like You? Theorizing Agency in User-Generated Content." *Media, Culture & Society* 31 (3): 41–58.

Van Dijck, José. 2013. *The Culture of Connectivity: A Critical History of Social Media.* Oxford: Oxford University Press.

Veel, Kristin. 2011. "Information Overload and Database Aesthetics." *Contemporary Critical Studies* 8 (2–3): 307–319.

Vickery, Jacqueline Ryan. 2014. "The Curious Case of Confession Bear: The Reappropriation of Online Macro-Image Memes." *Information, Communication & Society* 17 (3): 301–325.

Victoria, Mabel. 2018. "The Verbal and the Visual in Language Learning and Teaching: Insights from the 'Selfie Project.'" *The Language Learning Journal.* Published online before print, June 24. https://www.tandfonline.com/doi/abs/10.1080/09571736.2018.1484797.

Vincent, Jane. 2006. "Emotional Attachment and Mobile Phones." *Knowledge, Technology & Policy* 19 (1): 39–44.

Virilio, Paul. 1995. "Speed and information: Cyberspace alarm!" *CTheory* 8–27. http://www.ctheory.net/printer.asp?id=72.

Vogel-Walcutt, Jennifer J., Logan Fiorella, Teresa Carper, and Sae Schatz. 2012. "The Definition, Assessment, and Mitigation of State Boredom within Educational Settings: A Comprehensive Review." *Educational Psychology Review* 24 (1): 89–111.

Wajcman, Judy. 2014. *Pressed for Time: The Acceleration of Life in Digital Capitalism.* Chicago: University of Chicago Press.

Wallis, Cara. 2015. *Technomobility in China: Young Migrant Women and Mobile Phones.* New York: New York University Press.

Weaver, Warren, and Claude Shannon. 1963. *The Mathematical Model of Communication.* Chicago: University of Illinois Press.

Webster, James G. 2014. *The Marketplace of Attention: How Audiences Take Shape in a Digital Age.* Cambridge, MA: MIT Press.

Weinberg, Darin. 2002. "On the Embodiment of Addiction." *Body & Society* 8 (4): 1–19.

West, Sarah Myers. 2019. "Data Capitalism: Redefining the Logics of Surveillance and Privacy." *Business & Society* 58 (1): 20–41.

White, Martha C. 2016. "Watching Cat Videos at Work Could Make You More Productive." *Money*, 15 March. https://money.com/humor-helps-productivity/.

Wiener, Norbert. 1999. *Cybernetics: Or Control and Communication in the Animal and the Machine.* 2nd ed. Cambridge, MA: MIT Press.

Williams, Oscar. 2015. "Upworthy's Co-Founder Said the Most Amazing Thing about Clickbait." *The Guardian*, February 26. https://www.theguardian.com/media-network/2015/feb/26/upworthy-peter-koechley-clickbait-charity.

Williams, Raymond. 1977. *Marxism and Literature.* Oxford: Oxford University Press.

Wilson, Ara. 2016. "The Infrastructure of Intimacy." *Signs: Journal of Women in Culture and Society* 41 (2): 247–280.

Wilson, Timothy D., David A. Reinhard, Erin C. Westgate, Daniel T. Gilbert, Nicole Ellerbeck, Cheryl Hahn, Casey L. Brown, and Adi Shaked. 2014. "Just Think: The Challenges of the Disengaged Mind." *Science* 345 (6192): 75–77.

Wise, J. MacGregor. 2015. "A Hole in the Hand: Assemblages of Attention and Mobile Screens." In *Theories of the Mobile Internet*, edited by Andrew Herman, John Hadlaw, and Thom Swiss, 224–243. New York: Routledge.

Zhao, Xuan, Niloufar Salehi, Sasha Naranjit, Sara Alwaalan, Stephen Voida, and Dan Cosley. 2013. "The Many Faces of Facebook: Experiencing Social Media as Performance, Exhibition, and Personal Archive." *Proceedings of the SIGCHI Conference on Human Factors in Computing Systems*: 1–10.

Zuboff, Shoshana. 2015. "Big Other: Surveillance Capitalism and the Prospects of an Information Civilization." *Journal of Information Technology* 30 (1): 75–89.

Zuboff, Shoshana. 2019a. *The Age of Surveillance Capitalism: The Fight for the Future at the New Frontier of Power*. London: Profile Books.

Zuboff, Shoshana. 2019b. "Surveillance Capitalism and the Challenge of Collective Action." *New Labor Forum*. Online before print January 24. https://journals.sagepub .com/doi/abs/10.1177/1095796018819461.

Zylinska, Joanna. 2014. *Minimal Ethics for the Anthropocene*. London: Open Humanities Press.

Index